S P R I N G S

A faith-development programme by
Brentwood Religious Education Service

Illustrated by Jim Bray

GEOFFREY
CHAPMAN

A Geoffrey Chapman book published by
Cassell Publishers Limited
Artillery House, Artillery Row
London SW1P 1RT

First published 1989

ISBN 0 225 66535 2
British Library Cataloguing in Publication Data
SPRINGS.
  1. Catholic Church. Christian doctrine.
Catechetics
  I. Brentwood Religious Education Service
268'.6

Typeset by Selectmove Ltd., London.
Printed and bound in Great Britain
by Hollen Street Press Ltd., Slough.

Contents

Acknowledgements

This book has taken several years to reach its present shape. Many people have been involved in the various stages of its development and the authors, members of Brentwood Religious Education Service, are truly grateful for all the contributions made, whatever form they took. As a team, we are conscious that all our present efforts are a maturing of the work of previous members of BRES, without whose 'spade-work' we would not be able to accomplish the work we do today.

Members of the BRES team who, over the years, have been directly involved in the development of this book include Brian O'Higgins, Agnes Roche, George Stokes, Helen McMahon, Frank Campbell, Josephine Payne, Bernadette Helvin, Bernard Westcott, Clare Grimes and Lynn Walker.

Apart from the BRES team, the following people, in particular, have been involved in the production of this book and to them we would like to express our gratitude:

Sheila Conrad and Val Ronan—who typed and re-typed the many working documents uncomplainingly.

James Bray—for his inspiring illustrations and his reflections on Christian symbolism.

Jill Bray—for her insights into spirituality and relationships, drawn from her experience as a mother and her work in therapeutic centres.

Damian Lundy, Charles Reutemann and others at St Cassian's, Kintbury, Berkshire and Sangre de Christo, New Mexico—for sharing their years of pastoral experience.

Joe Laishley—who explored with us the essential theological implications arising from our project.

Arthur Keegan, Herman Lombarts and Marie Strong—for sharing their expertise in planning, evaluation and management.

The people of La Salette Parish, in Rainham, Essex—for sharing with us their struggles, hopes and fears as they courageously sought a way forward.

The people of dozens of parishes in the diocese of Brentwood who worked and re-worked the material we produced.

Dr Sophie Tomlinson—for the *challah* recipe.

Anne Boyd—for helping us sharpen our focus and give some shape to the mountain of material we had.

Robert Kelly—for his help in the final stages of publishing.

Finally, we gratefully acknowledge the various publishers who have granted permission for us to reprint copyright material:

to Darton, Longman & Todd Ltd and to Doubleday, a division of Bantam, Doubleday, Dell Publishing Group Inc, for the use of the *Jerusalem Bible* texts;

to ICEL (International Committee on English in the Liturgy) for the use of liturgical texts from the English translation of *The Roman Missal*;

to William Collins Sons & Co Ltd for the use of the extract from *Mister God, this is Anna*;

to Servant Publications, for the extract from *The Life of the Spirit*;

to Celebration (administered by Thankyou Music) for the use of Jonathan Asprey's *The Potter's Song*,

to Lexicon (administered by Cherry Lane Music) for the use of Jimmy Owens' *In Love for me*;

to Word of God Music for the use of Donald Fishel's *The light of Christ*;

and to *New REview* for the teenagers' 'Letters to God'.

Introduction

This is a book of practical suggestions and ideas for anyone working with groups of adults and young people who want to grow and develop in faith. Its purpose is to provide a RESOURCE from which ideas may be SELECTED and ADAPTED to suit the particular needs of the group concerned.

The ideas contained in the book have all been tried and tested. They proved to be particularly successful when groups included people from as many walks of life as possible. Men and women of every social, racial and cultural background, and of every age group, found that they were greatly enriched by sharing the stories of people whose lifestyle and age were somewhat different from their own. Some groups found further enrichment in sharing the stories of husbands, wives and neighbours of other denominations and faiths.

The Realities Underpinning the Contents of the Book

are:

God is present, always and everywhere, to each and every person.

For **every** human being, life is a journey of faith involving many changes—changes through which God draws near.

By sharing our faith we help others find purpose and meaning in their lives while **at the same time** deepening our understanding of our own faith.

What is faith?
How does it develop?

'Faith' is part and parcel of being human. It is the person-to-person relationship with a loving God—and, through God, with other people. It is life-giving; a relationship of LOVE which gives meaning and purpose to life. God's loving activity is gradually revealed to us in and through our human relationships, the ordinary ups and downs of daily living and the changes brought about by circumstances and events. Not everyone, however, recognises the presence of God in their lives. Not everyone is aware of the specifically religious dimension of their faith. It is as we grow in awareness of God at work in our lives—and respond to that awareness—that our faith is deepened, extended and transformed.

Gradually, we come to recognise that God's loving activity remains constant—in good times and bad, through thick and thin. Such knowledge deepens our relationship with God and with each other. It is part of the lifelong process of conversion through which we become fully alive, fully human—'completely filled with the very nature of God' (Eph 3:19b).

Initially many people hesitate to share their faith with others. They feel shy, unsure, afraid that they 'won't know the right answers', that they have little faith or that they are 'not really religious'. Once they begin to share their stories of life, however, they find that the stories of others resonate with their own and they begin to recognise the work of God in their lives. They discover that each person is at a different stage of the journey—and that THAT IS QUITE ALL RIGHT! Those who find it difficult to respond in faith to their own life's journey often find that they are helped by others who have already travelled a similar path and are willing to share their experience.

Stages of development in faith

Our Christian tradition is deeply rooted in an understanding of human life as a journey from womb to tomb. Throughout that journey we grow, develop and change. Our ability to respond and cope with life is quite different at each stage of our journey.

The stories handed on to us, especially those in the Scriptures, are vital in our search for meaning in the ordinary ups and downs of daily living. They tell of the human experiences of fear and hurt, security and love, joy and hardship, death and pain. The truths they embody are for every man, woman and child of every 'tribe, tongue, people and nation' (Rev 5:9).

There are many aspects of the human journey that are common to all of us, although each person's journey is unique. Every stage of the journey has a landscape, colour and form of its own. We become familiar with these and feel at home, so that moving from one stage to another may cause a painful sense of insecurity and upheaval. There may be other times, however, when moving from one particular stage to another results in an exuberant feeling of liberation!

This book focusses on eight aspects or stages of the faith journey that are common to all of us. They are landmarks to which we return repeatedly during the course of our lives, but our experience and understanding of them is continually changing as we grow and develop in faith. The pattern they provide is similar to that of the development of faith described by St Luke in both his Gospel and the Acts of the Apostles, as well as to that of the prayer cycle of the Church's liturgical year.

The stages of faith upon which we focus are:

1 • Starting to Journey Together
2 • Becoming Aware of God in my Life
3 • Called to be Christians
4 • Empowered by the Spirit
5 • Gifted to Serve
6 • Remembering
7 • Alive!
8 • Watching . . . Waiting . . .

We could go on at great length on each of these stages of faith. We have found, however, that it is in the actual SHARING and CELEBRATING of them with others that our own understanding and appreciation have grown and developed—and are continuing to do so! The whole experience has been so enriching for us that we would like to share some of the ideas with you so that you, too, may enjoy similar growth and development in your Christian Community.

Some of the ways in which growth in faith is stimulated

Over the past few years members of the BRES team have been working with groups of people who wanted to grow in faith and share their faith with others. Hundreds of adults from widely differing walks of life were involved, including rich and poor, employed and unemployed, young and old, Asians and Europeans, Americans and Africans. Together we discovered that our faith is stimulated into growth in many different ways. We would like to share with you some of the insights we have had of the nature of the process—as we have come to understand it.

This pictorial presentation gives an overview of some of the ways in which growth in faith is stimulated. Each ray of colour is important to the formation of the rainbow.

As we examine the content of each ray it will become evident that they all focus on ordinary everyday life. Whatever the backgrounds of the group members—be they of different races or cultures, employed or unemployed, rich or poor—they will find something here which resonates with their own experience and invites them to grow both in life and in faith. And of course there are some rays of the rainbow we cannot see. So too with faith.

Stories

Stories illustrate and express the meaning of life. They may challenge or threaten, encourage or excite, motivate or entertain. They need not carry facts, but they always carry experiences and truths. As such, they come from the depths of a person and meet the listener in the same place, thus enabling people to meet at other than an intellectual level. We must never presume, however, that everyone hears the same message! People will identify with those truths within the story that are relevant to their own life and faith.

Three types of stories are particularly important in our moulding and shaping as we progress on our Christian journey:

1 • *Our own stories* are very important. In each person's story there are truths that are real for all people at all times. In telling parts of that story we

discover new depths of meaning in our lives. Some of us find it nerve-wracking, initially, to share our story with others, but it is not long before we discover that other people feel the same way! Once we actually have the courage to begin, we find we are encouraged by the attentive and supportive listening of others.

2 • *Other people's stories* resonate with our own. As we listen, we find we are comforted, inspired or challenged by them. We also find tremendous support in our own struggle to understand our life and our faith.

3 • *The Christian story* embraces all these stories and many, many more. It contains stories in which the meaning of life is richly expressed for all time. They are particularly powerful in that they encapsulate the great truths of what life is about. Although we may hear them over and over again, we will always be discovering new meaning in them in the light of lived experience. The people who told these stories were very close to God and in them they reveal deep truths to us about God—and about ourselves.

Prayer

Every person has the gift of prayer—it is as essential to life as breathing. 'Prayer' is simply another word for God's constant relationship with us. In a certain sense, each one of us IS a prayer, a word of God, expressing God's love and goodness to the rest of the world.

Unfortunately many people tend to think of prayer simply as being a conversation with God. It does, of course, involve talking and listening to God—but it is so much more than that! God communicates so much to us: is with us, touches us, and speaks to us in all we do, say, think and feel. Sometimes we respond to God, but sometimes we do not—either because we are unable to do so, or because we are not even aware of the presence of God at that moment.

As with all our relationships, our response to God is erratic, constantly changing as we journey through life. We reach out to God, as we do to others, when we feel insecure or in need. We sing and shout songs of praise when joyfulness is bubbling up inside us. We may be very aware of God's presence at such times, whereas at other times we take him for granted or even forget he is there at all.

Many of us find there are times when, for all sorts of reasons, it is really difficult to pray. At such times we are often helped either by praying with other people or simply by allowing other people to pray for us, around us or over us, as happens when babies are baptised or when people are very ill. The power of such prayer can be very valuable to us, especially if we approach it with a spirit of stillness, openness and trust in God.

We learn HOW to pray in many different ways, often from and through the example of others. Praying with, for, over and around others and sharing with others our experience of God in the ordinary, everyday events of our lives enables us to become more aware of the movements occurring within us – and helps us to respond to them in a positive manner. In the process we grow in our relationship with God and with each other.

Reflection

We need time to stop and think, to be alone with our thoughts and our feelings. In silence and stillness we grow in our ability to be in touch with ourselves: to 'listen' to ourselves. In such moments we come to know and understand ourselves better.

Listening to our own inner truth can be both challenging and disturbing. To be alone with oneself in this way takes courage—but there are moments when that courage rewards us with glimpses of the source of our strength, the source of our very being.

It is not easy to be reflective in the midst of the clamour of life, but we need to remember the psalmist's call to 'be still, and know that I am God'. Reflection is an essential means of our growth in faith. It enables us to be open to the action of God in our lives—and to respond to that action.

Input

Responding to the need 'to know' is an essential part of our human journey. Most of our knowledge comes from outside ourselves. The help and guidance of others enables us to acquire it in a way that makes sense to us. Knowledge which enlightens our understanding of the meaning of life can open up for us new perspectives, inviting us to advance further on our journey of faith. The truths to be found in the word of God, for example, are often obscurely perceived in the muddle of daily living—but suddenly they spring to life, full of new meaning, when presented to us in an atmosphere of faith-sharing.

Now

God is with us **here and now**, present **always** and **everywhere**. In all the activities of life through which we grow, change and develop, God is there. People who are leading the sessions described in this book need to be particularly sensitive to this. They need to be ready to respond to whatever is happening in the group HERE and NOW. This demands a certain amount of flexibility. It is so much easier to stop up our ears and continue with our meticulously planned schedule than to respond to the word of God spoken in our midst! (Responding in this way also means that we have to be sensitive and sensible. For example, recognise the garrulous man for what he is and do not allow him to dominate the sessions!)

Most of our learning occurs when we are **actively involved** in something. In other words, we learn much more through **doing** than we do through reading, observing or listening (a fact to bear in mind when planning liturgies). Activity involves the **whole** person: it is a form of self-expression. The food cooked, the kiss, the letter, the visit to a friend, the game with the children, the designing of the kitchen, the turning of the garden soil—all are part and parcel of our growing relationship with God and with others, the here and now that we bring to our sessions to share with one another.

We celebrate the here and now of our lives when we come together for such things as birthdays, anniversaries, jubilees, baptisms and weddings. The sacraments are all celebrations of whatever is happening in our lives and of our relationship with God. They are special occasions when we consciously meet with the Risen Lord—and in meeting him we are changed; our lives take on a new dimension.

Groups

As we grow up, our understanding of other people—and of life—changes. We do not always find it easy to enter into relationships with other people because that means we have to risk both sharing ourselves and being open to points of view that differ from our own. It means we have to be sensitive to others, and able, at times, to stand in another's shoes.

In the sessions people will be invited to enter into relationships with others. This will sometimes be in groups of three or four, while at other times everyone will join together to form one large group. The relationships formed are an essential aspect of the development of faith. Through them we are involved in the very nature of people and helped to discover ourselves—often at a very profound level.

Socialising

We are social beings; but all too often we feel we have to 'get on with the job' rather than 'waste time' over a cup of tea. Yet, simply being with others— eating and drinking, sharing and listening—is an essential feature of our journey through life, the kind of human encounter which begins the day we are born and without which there can be no growth in relationships. It is the good soil in which we grow and flourish as individuals who are part of the living body of the Church.

In many ways the time set aside for a social break in each session has proved to be one of the most important periods of the meeting. People feel 'free', true dialogue occurs, genuine questions and fears are aired and relationships develop. It is often the time when 'shy' people quietly voice their thoughts. Those who are leading the session should be alert to whatever is happening and ready to respond, if necessary, after the break.

S · P · R · I · N · G · S

(A memory aid to help you in your planning.)

Stories

Prayer

Reflection

Input

Now

Groups

Socialising

You may find the mnemonic 'S • P • R • I • N • G • S' helps you to remember the different ways in which people learn—and thus plan your sessions to include something of each one of the experiences.

The aim of the project

The aim of this project is to invite people to form or join groups so that together they may grow and develop in faith. They will explore some or all of the following stages of the faith journey:

1 • Starting to Journey Together
2 • Becoming Aware of God in my Life
3 • Called to be Christians
4 • Empowered by the Spirit
5 • Gifted to Serve
6 • Remembering
7 • Alive!
8 • Watching . . . Waiting . . .

The exploration will be carried out in a manner which offers each person opportunities to experience various ways of growing in faith. Each person learns in many different ways, although most people learn *something*, whatever 'method' is used. Exploring a given topic in a **variety** of ways enables **everyone** to deepen their personal experience of that topic—hence the statement made earlier that 'each ray of colour is important to the formation of the rainbow as a whole'.

The design of the project

The development of faith is a process or journey which continues for the whole of our lives. The project, therefore, is also a journey: a journey which begins but never really finishes.

Most of us usually look for some kind of assistance when planning a journey. In this book we offer a choice of routes through eight stages of the faith journey. We recommend that as you select the paths you will follow, you bear in mind both the principle of 'S • P • R • I • N • G • S' and the needs of the particular group concerned.

At each stage of the journey people may be involved through:

a • meeting with others for planned sessions
b • celebrations
c • activities

a • **The sessions.** The group meets for a series of sessions, the number of which will be adapted to meet the needs of the particular group. Usually this will be at least one session for each stage—but some well-established groups have found that they preferred to spread the material over many more sessions. Never be afraid to start in a small way! Many thriving groups began with only three or four people who met together regularly, and welcomed newcomers who came to join them.

b • **Celebrations.** The group may meet for a series of special Masses, usually with the rest of the parish on Sundays. Again, adaptation will be needed to suit the local situation, using the guidelines provided.

c • **Activities.** A variety of ideas are provided for parish activities, related to each stage of the project.

Getting the project started

If you have not done anything like this before you will, no doubt, feel a little nervous of making a start on the project. The ideas that follow have all been tried and tested, usually by people who felt as nervous as you, and on the whole they proved to be successful. What many people have done is to 'go by the book' for their first run through the project, noting down what went well, things that were particularly successful, what was not so good and, indeed, those things that failed—along with possible reasons for the results. Their future planning was then based on their own personal experience of the material. With that behind them they then found it much easier to adapt to the specific needs of a variety of groups within the parish.

Some people started this project in a very small way in order to familiarise themselves with the material and gain confidence in the process. Others plunged straight into full–scale parish programmes. In one parish, over 140 people of all ages and nationalities were involved in the project meetings for the initial run through the material. (They have since adapted it for all kinds of adult groups.)

Planning your parish programme— an overview

As we have already mentioned, the project is closely related to the Church's liturgical year. Many parishes have, therefore, started the project just before Advent and concluded it after Pentecost. However, it is not dependent on this factor, and may be run at any time of the year.

The plan that follows is one that has proved useful to those parishes that have run the project from Advent to Pentecost. Others have adapted it to suit their particular situation.

STAGE OF PROJECT	LITURGICAL PERIOD	THEME OF EACH STAGE
A	September or earlier	Form team
B	Sep/Oct	Team meeting – plan programme; inform parish; advertise
1	Oct/Nov	'Open evening' for all. Starting to journey together
2	Advent	Becoming aware of God in my life
3	After Christmas	Called to be Christian
4	Before Lent	Empowered by the Spirit
5	Beginning of Lent	Gifted to serve
6	End of Lent	Remembering
7	Eastertide	Alive!
8	Pentecost	Watching . . . Waiting . . .

Note: The following pages are particularly relevant to those people who wish to run a parish-based project. If, however, you decide to begin in a small way, with six or seven people, you may prefer to move straight on to page 17 ('Groups in Action') and return to these pages at a later date.

Are you embarking on a parish programme?

If you are embarking on a parish programme, there are two things you need to do:
form a 'service' team;
invite people to join the group.

Form a 'service' team

Before you do anything at all you need to be quite clear about your reason for running the project and the nature of the group to be involved.

For example, is it to:

• help the parish prepare for Confirmation?
• support a parent group?
• help adults in general who want to grow and develop in faith?
• help and support engaged couples?
• support parishioners who are involved in various church ministries?
• help and support elderly people?

Having decided 'for whom' and 'why', **write it down**.

Personally contact as many people as possible.
Speak to as many people as you can, sharing your idea of the project with them and inviting them to 'come along, explore the ideas and see what is involved—but don't feel under any obligation'. Jesus never asked for volunteers but always approached people personally and invited them directly. Follow his example!
Write to people and groups, such as the parish council, catechists, parish clubs and societies, and leaders of various kinds. Make use of the parish newsletter and the church notice–board.
Hold a meeting for those you have contacted and anyone else who expresses interest. The purpose of this meeting is to:

• discuss ideas and feelings in general;
• present the specific task of running the project with a particular group;
• share thoughts and ideas on the above and clarify what might be done;
• invite people to be involved in the project in one way or another.

If it is possible, try to hold this meeting in a comfortable place, keeping it informal, hospitable, friendly and informative—but with the clear focus on the project. Close with a short period of prayer together. (When this prayer period has been well prepared and attuned to what has taken place, we found that many people considered it to be the most valuable part of the meeting and a deciding factor in their choosing to be involved in the project.)

Hold a second meeting for all those who have shown an interest in the project since the first meeting, as well as anyone whose talents have since come to your attention. This meeting should be well planned and directed, the purpose of it being to:

- provide information about the project: when, where, how long, why, for whom;
- allow time for sharing thoughts and ideas on the above;
- provide time for the team members to get to know one another, perhaps using some of the material from Stage One of the project;
- provide time for praying together as a team;
- give time for people simply to be together socially, for tea, coffee etc.

Supporting and strengthening the service team
If you have time and are able to do so, it is well worthwhile exploring the material further AS A TEAM. This may be done with one or two of you acting as leaders while the others participate as group members. Over a period of time meet to share, pray and reflect, using the material for the eight sessions. In this way members of the team will get to know one another and grow in their own individual understanding of their faith, while at the same time becoming experientially and technically familiar with the material and some of its possibilities. Teams that have tried this found that they began the 'real' work with genuine confidence.

If this is NOT possible, do try to encourage the team members by meeting a few times before you begin the actual project, to do such things as pray, socialise, plan diaries and simply get to know one another. Building up their self-confidence, and your own, is most important!

During these meetings natural leaders usually emerge. You need to look for the following:
1 • **a Director for the project**. This should be someone who is a good organiser/director/manager—and NOT a priest—to manage and direct the overall programme. It is NOT the task of this person to prepare or lead the sessions. S/he will break the project down into specific tasks of a manageable size which other individuals will carry out.

2 • **a Group Leader**. This person should have the ability to lead as well as to put people at their ease, the latter being essential if groups are to share in any depth. It will be this person's responsibility to lead each one of the group meetings.
3 • **a Priest** to minister to the group in prayer and sacrament.

The team is presented publicly to the **parish** and may be commissioned, usually during one of the Sunday Masses. This is an important sign to the parish of the growth and development of faith that is taking place within it: a sign that something is happening. It is also a visual invitation to the rest of the parish to become involved in one way or another. This may be as a leader, helper or group member, through the parish Masses and/or activities, or simply through their own personal prayer.

The director and the Service Team work out a diary or calendar of events. In it, they allocate time for group meetings, team meetings, special parish Masses and parish activities, noting when, where and for how long. We have found that it has proved very useful when one or two people have previously recorded such things as school and public holidays as well as special parish functions. This preparatory work should be done well in advance of starting the project in order to give you time to invite people to join the group, either as participants or as helpers.

Invite people to join the group
The personal approach is always best. As a team, you may draw up a list of people you feel should be involved, e.g. possible candidates for confirmation along with their parents and sponsors; parents of children preparing to celebrate Reconciliation; or whatever other group of people for whom you decided to run the project. You may then divide this list among yourselves and have each one personally invite the people allocated to him/her.

Draw up a simple, concise statement about the project, stating:
- who it is for
- why it is important
- when, where and for how long
- a brief outline of what will happen—perhaps referring to the stages of faith, the variety of approaches, the masses and the parish activities

• a contact name, address and telephone number for further information.

Have the statement typed out, attractively illustrated and printed or photocopied.

Use your description as a basis for
a newsletter
a poster
a press release to local newspapers, local radio etc.
a handout for those who show interest.

Simplify the description so that it will fit on a small card, being sure that the details of the contact person are included, and place the card as an advert
in local shop windows
through letter boxes
in local newspapers (including local free advertising papers).

Our experience of such advertising has been that it has led to the involvement of many lapsed Catholics as well as many other people who wanted to grow in understanding their faith.

An 'open evening'

At this stage some parishes have found it helpful to invite all who are interested to a general 'Open Evening' which is informative, sociable, reflective and prayerful. This has enabled people to acquire a sense of what the project is about without any feeling of obligation. Their questions are answered and they have the opportunity to experience being part of a group that shares the common desire to grow and develop in faith.

If you do decide to do this, be sure to organise the evening well, perhaps using some of the material from Stage One, 'Starting to Journey Together'. Inform people of this meeting in your initial descriptive statement of the project.

ALTERNATIVELY, by inviting people who wish to know more about the project to meet team members after the Masses on one particular Sunday, personal contact may be made and queries answered. Both printed information and on-the-spot clarification can be provided.

Some parishes advertise well in advance and then hold a thirty-minute meeting after ONE of the Sunday Masses, at which they explain and clarify ideas, as well as encourage and pray with all who come. This latter approach has proved to be particularly useful where Confirmation candidates are involved as, at such a meeting, they are able to register their request to receive the sacrament.

Inviting people to help

The Service Team should be made up of people with a variety of skills. Some of the parishioners who show clear interest may be able and willing to help you. Take note of them and invite them to help in specific ways, especially if your team is small. Do NOT try to do everything yourself but DELEGATE AS MUCH AS POSSIBLE. **By allowing others to do something, however small, you enable them to be more deeply involved in the project and thus help them in developing their faith.**

Invite them to use specific gifts and talents as their contribution to helping others grow in faith—their service to others and to the Lord. Be precise and let them know that it is only for a set of time—not for ever!

You will probably be looking for the following:
• a designer or artist to illustrate handouts and your initial statement
• a writer for the statement
• a typist or two—preferably not the people already committed to the weekly parish newsletter
• people to see to the advertising
• tea and coffee makers
• a group who meet to pray and reflect on the readings related to the special Masses so that they may share their insights with the priest to help him with his homily
• people to help prepare the Masses: eg music planning, designing, writing a special leaflet for the Mass
• people to provide and/or arrange flowers for the sessions
• someone to help with prerecorded materials, either for the sessions or the Masses
• someone to work the projector or video recorder
• people to help produce 'live' music
• people to arrange furniture for the sessions
• drivers to help with transport
• people to shop—for candles, oil, incense, charcoal, paper, pens etc.
• a photographer to keep a visual record of memorable aspects of the project
• baby-sitters.

Although the involvement of these people may sometimes seem to be minimal, it is often such small beginnings that engender future community leaders. The 'helpers' of today become the 'leaders' of tomorrow, whilst many of those who simply participate in a group gain the confidence to return later as 'helpers'. It is a special opportunity to invite young adults to help. In this way we invest in the future, making a practical act of faith and hope.

Planning and preparing to run the sessions

Each session, liturgy and activity has to be planned. The following pages may help you to do this. They are suggestions based on the experience of others—but adapt them to suit your own situation. The ideas are gathered together under the following headings:

1 • Initial preparation
2 • Preparing as a team
3 • Evaluating each session.

1 • Initial preparation

The eight stages of faith for which you will, at some time, be preparing are:

1 • Starting to Journey Together
2 • Becoming Aware of God in my Life
3 • Called to be Christian
4 • Empowered by the Spirit
5 • Gifted to Serve
6 • Remembering
7 • Alive!
8 • Watching . . . Waiting . . .

For which stage are you preparing?

a • Give yourself time to read the introduction to this stage in a leisurely way, perhaps taking notes of points that strike you as being particularly important.
b • When you have finished, sit quietly and jot down ideas, feelings or memories as they come to you. Listen to how the Lord is speaking to you through these feelings, ideas and memories, and respond to him in your own way.
c • After spending some time with the Lord, carefully look back over the notes and jottings. Highlight or draw circles around whatever seems to be most important for you about this stage at this moment.
d • Are you preparing to help the group with a session, a Mass or an activity? Turn to the relevant material in this book and look through it leisurely

and prayerfully. Hold in mind that whatever you do to help the group is a gift to them: it is NOT about controlling them! Note down the part you would like to lead or with which you would like to assist, then jot down any of your ideas, feelings, thoughts and stories related to this.
e • The theme will be presented to the group using the seven different ways in which growth is stimulated, ie S • P • R • I • N • G • S. In which of these ways will your particular contribution be communicated? Write these down.
f • Spend a little time with the Lord reflecting upon what you have chosen and the ways involved in your presentation. What does he say to you? How do you feel? What do you say to him?
g • Now write down how you will present your chosen material, indicating what you will say and what the group(s) will do.
h • Share your thoughts with the Lord. Pray both for yourself and for the other members of the team who, like you, are spending time preparing to help others grow in faith. Ask the Lord to bless all the people in the group and all those who help the project to take place or support it with their prayers (e.g. the housebound). Pray in your own way, perhaps trying different approaches to prayer. For example:

Read Scripture slowly, pondering over the words.

Light a candle and in its light
be still before the Lord.

Sit very quietly and relaxed, listening to God.

Use some reflective music.

Use a familiar prayer (for example, the 'Jesus Prayer').

Simply sit and talk to God.

We DO appreciate the busy-ness of life and know, only too well, how difficult it is to 'find time' to prepare in the way we would like. Do what you can, but whatever you do, let it be reflective and prayerful. Read the material in this book as an indication of how God has led others, and see where he leads you. We are NOT offering a structure to be followed slavishly, but are simply pointing to a familiar pathway which you will discover and explore for yourself and help others to find as well.

Some people who are just beginning to work in this way may not find these steps of initial preparation easy or even possible at first; but just do whatever you are able and offer that to the Lord and to your team. Some new teams have benefited by having one person direct them through the steps in a quiet and comfortable way, explaining each step to the group but allowing people time for their own thoughts and prayers.

2 • Preparing as a team

The Service Team meets to plan sessions, Masses and activities. What follow are guidelines for preparing a session.

1 • Either the director of the project or the session leader formally opens the meeting by welcoming everyone and checking for absentees, then invites free sharing of thoughts and ideas arising from each person's individual preparation. 10–15 mins.

2 • Brainstorm the contents of the session, making a list of what people have selected to do or assist with, in any order. Look to see if anything essential is missing. There may be many new ideas, stories that people have or things that might be done that are not included in this book. Take note of them all on your list. 20–25 mins.

Note: By 'brainstorm' we mean that everyone contributes any ideas, thoughts, etc.—however daft they may seem! No comment is passed at this stage. They are simply noted down on a board, flip chart or large sheet of paper— placed, if possible, so that everyone may see it.

3 • Estimate the time needed for each part, including the break, the introduction, and the time which may be needed before the session is concluded to give information concerning future events. Be generous in the estimates; things usually take a lot longer in practice than we anticipate. 10 mins.

4 • Add up the estimated times and compare the total with what is available for the session. Then adjust the list to fit the available time, holding S•P•R•I•N•G•S in mind throughout. Be patient with one another, listening and trusting, willing to help and, when necessary, willing to give way to one another. 10–15 mins.

5 • Have a social break, during which the session leader decides on an order for the list and timetables it, indicating the times at which different parts of the session will begin and end. 20–30 mins.

6 • After the break, the leader presents the final timetable for the session to the team. Individual names are entered beside each part of the session, indicating who will lead it and who will help. 10–15 mins.

7 • Pause for a moment while everyone considers the shape of the session as it now stands. Are all the ways of stimulating growth in faith included?

You may also consider some or all of the following:

a • Are you clear about which stage of faith (e.g. 'Empowered by the Spirit' or 'Gifted to serve') is to be the central focus of this session? Is that evident throughout the timetable?

b • Is it clear which specific truth about God, people and/or life is central to the session.

c • Do you have in mind some particular direction for the group, to help them make a specific response to life and to God? This may be, for example, facing into the fear of change, or a practical way in which to serve God.

d • Have you left sufficient space for the group participants to share among themselves; to ask questions; to tell their stories to each other—remembering that this is a most important part of the session, enriching the faith of us all?

e • Are YOU leading the group—or is GOD? Be quite clear about this in your own mind! Are you involved with them, learning with and from them, or are you inclined to give directions and then sit back and watch?

f • Are you keeping directives and explanations brief, clear and precise?

g • Is everyone getting a chance to share and discuss what they feel? And are they doing this one at a time!

8 • In the light of your considerations, make any alterations you think may be necessary to your programme. 10 mins.

9 • Spend some time in prayer together, perhaps using the prayer of the session for yourselves. The support of the priest is most important for the Service Team and while he need not be present for the whole of this meeting it is desirable that he should be there towards the end so that he may minister in prayer to them. 10 mins.

Note: The team's own growth and development in faith is central to the project. This group is as important as any other and each individual should, within the preparation period, be experiencing all of the different ways in which growth is stimulated. If this is not happening, then the leader or director needs to consider why and try to do something about it. It is natural for there to be a certain amount of tension as the team itself grows, but this can be alleviated if the right approaches are used. Ideas arising from 'Evaluating the service team' (pp.16–17) may help.

3 • Evaluating each session

In our planning we have already referred to our use of 'seven ways in which growth in faith is stimulated' (ie S • P • R • I • N • G • S). The same seven ways make an equally valuable 'tool of evaluation' by which you may reflect upon and assess your work. Evaluation is essential. It is not always easy to do, but it is an important key to growth. To help you evaluate each session you may consider the following, preferably as a team:

1 • Stories
- Did everyone, including yourself, have an opportunity to share some of his or her own story —without any feeling of pressure?
- Were people able to listen attentively as others shared?
- What was the experience of the group in sharing their own personal stories?
  the stories of our Christian heritage, e.g. Scripture, tradition, doctrine, lives of saints living and dead, sacraments, prayer etc.?

2 • Prayer
- Did the prayer truly relate to the theme of the session?
- Was it introduced briefly, simply and reflectively?
- Was the prayer expressed simply and directly so that it was directed to the needs and understanding of the participants?
- Was the atmosphere of prayer attractive and non-threatening? Were such things as flowers, sound, scent and visual images well used? Was there a caring atmosphere? Was there enough space—both of area and of time?

3 • Reflection
- Apart from the time spent in prayer, was there sufficient time allowed for people to reflect without having to share?

- Were silent moments supported as being pauses for thought or were team members inclined to fill them? The right balance is not always easy to achieve. Leaders need to be very sensitive to the group as a whole.

4 • Input
- Was input given in a variety of ways?
- Was each form of input suited to this particular group?
- Were the doctrinal or theological points conveyed in a way that enabled the group to understand them—or was the session too complex?
- Did the input manage to convey a sense of unity and development within the session?
- Was the amount of time allocated for periods of input accurate?
- Did the team tend to dominate or talk too much?
- Was input using audio or visual materials well planned or did it occupy too much time?
- Was audio-visual material used to support sharing, reflection and prayer, or was it insufficiently explored and developed?

5 • Now
- Were you aware of moments when there was a real sense of God at work or a real sense of the presence of God? Were you sufficiently flexible with your schedule to support these moments?
- Are people in the group recognising their own stories as part of the greater Christian story—that the Gospel continues to be written today—in their own lives?
- Each person present is part of a far wider community than simply that of the parish. As members of God's family we belong to a community that embraces the whole world, 'people of every tribe, tongue, people and nation' (Rev 5:9). Do your sessions reflect an awareness of that fact? Do you refer to the issues affecting today's world, your neighbourhood, this group — or do you ignore them?

6 • Groups
- What was the general atmosphere like?
- Were people able to share their own observations and their own understanding of faith?
- Were there any 'awkward' people? In what ways were they awkward? How did you cope with them? What might help at future sessions?
- If strange or unusual points of view or belief were

aired, what happened? How were they received? Were they rejected, argued about, corrected? Are you happy with the end result, or do you feel the issue should have been handled differently? Does it need to be followed up? What have you learnt from the experience?

- Did you allow or invite people to help with things such as flower arranging, visual aids, music, refreshments or moving furniture, or did members of the team do it all themselves? Remember, involvement at ALL levels is an important means of building up relationships.

7 • Socialising

- Was there time for refreshment and general chatter? Was the right amount of time allowed?
- Did the break occur at the right moment or would it have been better at some other part of the session?
- Who provides the refreshments? Do people bring food and/or drink to share?

Evaluating the service team

The growth and development of faith among the team members should reflect whatever is happening in the larger group. Team meetings should mirror all the other meetings, so the evaluation tool is as useful for considering these as it is for the sessions and Masses. Always evaluate your team meetings when you have concluded the final part of the project. If it is possible, however, as the project proceeds try to look once or twice at the relationships forming within the team and at the way in which the team is functioning. You may do this, perhaps, after Stage Three and again after Stage Six, as well as once the project has been concluded. As a team, you may like to consider the following:

Stories

- Have you had time, as a team, to share with one another your stories and experiences of the project?
- How important are the Scripture stories to you now?
- Are you aware of any change in your sense of God's presence in your life: at work, at home, shopping, with friends etc.?

Prayer

- Are you praying together as a team?

- Is a priest ministering to the team in prayer and sacrament?
- When you prepare initially, on your own, do you pray for guidance and insight; for the other team members and for those in the group(s)?

Reflection

- Have you found time to be alone, to think, to listen, to ponder and to reflect upon your own place within the project? Or do you feel it's all just one mad rush?
- Are there silent moments for thought and recollection within the team meeting, or do you tend to let the silences be filled by eager interjections and new ideas? Both are needed, but in balance.

Input

- After each planning meeting do you go home feeling clear about what you have been asked to do?
- Do you feel supported enough by other team members whenever you give your input?
- Do you feel you are all really working as a team—that everyone feels their contribution is a necessary part of the whole?

Now

- As a team, are you able to recognise, accept and support the natural feelings of uncertainty, doubt, and tiredness, as well as those of gladness and joy?
- When mistakes have been made and they are almost inevitable! are you able to explore them together? If not, why not?
- Are challenging, new ideas explored or rejected?
- Are you able to have a good laugh together; to share funny (and perhaps not so funny) situations with good humour?

Groups

- Is there a growing sense of 'community'?
- Do you ever work through any of the material as a group: e.g. the Scripture stories?
- Do you ever work in pairs on a particular part of the session, or are you inclined to work individually?
- Is everyone comfortable about asking for help when it is needed?
- Do members of the team meet outside the project work?
- Is there any anxiety concerning leadership? Are you able to discuss this? Some teams prefer to

take the leadership role in turn; perhaps this is something your team should consider?

- Do you feel more at ease sharing your own doubts, fears etc. than you did when the project began?

Socialising

- Are your preparation meetings purely 'business', or do you have time to relax, chat and have some form of refreshment?
- Do you ever go out together simply to enjoy one another's company, perhaps for a meal, a drink or a show?

Groups in Action

Each section of this book contains material to help you explore different aspects or stages of faith. SELECT and ADAPT the material for your own particular circumstances. We are simply sharing with you ideas that you have been tried and tested. We would not wish you to feel bound by them, nor should you follow them slavishly. Feel free to design your own approaches!

The examples given show a variety of ways in which you may work with groups of people. **Please note, however, that each section contains far too much material for any one session. You must select whatever is most suitable for the group with which you are working, always holding in mind the principle of** S • P • R • I • N • G • S.

As was stated at the very beginning, this is a RESOURCE book, so we hope you will dip into it for ideas to suit all kinds of situations. The things you omit now will be of use at some other time, either with the same group or with different ones.

Using the Illustrations

The illustrations used in this book are an essential part of the project and may be used in a number of different ways. Many groups have found them very good as discussion starters or as focal points for story-telling, reflection or prayer.

Often visual images are able to convey much more than words . . . but **not everyone sees the same** thing because each person interprets the image in the light of his or her own understanding and experience of life. In sharing thoughts and ideas about the visual images, therefore, everyone's understanding is greatly enriched.

Illustrations appropriate to the earlier stages of the project have been grouped together for discussion. There are many more than you need so choose one or two that are appropriate for your particular group, or disperse a number of them throughout the session. Invite people to comment upon them, saying what the picture conveys to them . . . perhaps most especially in the light of whatever task they have just completed. It is unlikely to happen but should you find there is little or no response, simply move on to another picture.

By the time you reach the latter stages of the project, you will have discovered the most appropriate way for **you** to use the illustrations, so a specific amount of time for their use has not been allocated. As with all other aspects of this project, **select** them for use in whatever way is most appropriate for the particular group with whom you are working, either from those illustrating the part of the project upon which you are working, or from elsewhere. Our experience is that it is helpful to have more than one illustration to hand as a great deal of thought is stimulated by them, discussion tends to be lively and responses are sometimes quite different to those anticipated!

Starting to Journey Together

Introduction

The relationships we form with other people are central to our growth and development as human beings and hence to our growth and development in faith. It is in our ordinary everyday encounters and activities that we meet God.

Our earliest notions of the meaning and purpose of life, and hence of our awakening to God, arose out of our childhood relationships with parents, family and friends. They enabled us to respond to life and taught us how to cope with various situations. As we grew, it was usually other people who helped us to understand, to change, to see life differently, to grow.

In the Scriptures we see many examples of this kind of growth, mostly notably when people meet Jesus for the first time, or when the disciples share their understanding of their faith with others.

There may be several people in your group for whom this session is their first experience of meeting others—and Christ—in this way. It is a significant moment of faith. Being with others to live and share our faith is an important feature of the life of the Church. Through such encounters we grow in understanding our personal relationship with God.

Meeting in this way is not only our starting point but it is central to the way in which the whole project proceeds. Adults meet together to share, to listen, to pray and to grow in faith through reflecting upon each other's stories and understanding of ordinary, everyday life.

Materials you may need for Stage One

table cloth • flowers • large candle • small candles
felt-tip pens • background music • paper • table
sticky labels • tape recorder • thick tipped pens
sticky spots • map • Blu-Tack • copies of pictures

1 • A welcoming atmosphere is essential.

The atmosphere throughout the whole session should be friendly, warm, welcoming and non-threatening. A number of things can help to create such a feeling, including the following:

Arrange the furniture carefully, placing chairs in small groups or semicircles rather than straight rows.

Lighting can be used to great effect, but be careful to consider your group before you make any decisions. Younger people often express a preference for subtle lighting whereas older people generally prefer bright lights, especially if there is any reading to be done. If you have a cross-section of age groups vary the way in which you use the lights for different parts of the session, always making sure you provide some form of light for anyone who may be reading.

Arrange a focal point. This may be a table which you cover with a cloth and decorate with an arrangement of flowers and candles. One large, decorated candle (perhaps the Easter candle) surrounded by smaller ones can be very effective, as can be night-lights fixed at differing levels within an arrangement. Do be careful not to place the candles **too** close to one another or you may end up with a blaze!

Background music helps create a good atmosphere. Again, consider the people in your group and select your music accordingly. Instrumental recordings of a **variety** of types of music are very useful at this stage.

Be there to welcome people! Members of the team should be there well ahead of time so that they may welcome people as they arrive. Many individuals will come feeling a little nervous, so be sure to put them at their ease and introduce them to one or two others.

2 • Names are important.

At the first meeting (and even at later ones if the group is large) it helps if everyone wears a label with their name on it. This may be done very simply, by providing coloured sticky labels and felt-tip pens at the door so that people can make their own labels as they come in. Some teams have found it helpful to provide a separate colour for the team members so that they may be identified easily.

3 • Make a prompt start and finish on time.

Always begin the session right on time.
Some of your group may have baby-sitters looking after their children and they will become anxious if you run over your stated time, which is inevitable if you do not begin promptly.

Ideas for your first session

Welcome and introduction 10–20 mins

a • Welcome everyone, and state why everyone has come:
e.g. — to grow in faith together through sharing our present understanding of life and of God.
or — to grow in our own understanding of faith so that we may help our children as they prepare to (. . . . .)

b • Remind everyone that God is here with us and will help us as we share, listen, reflect, and pray.

c • Members of the service team introduce themselves—briefly.

d • Be relaxed, humorous and informal.

e • It may help people to know who is here. This group is special—but who, exactly, are we? The group may respond to questions of the following kind by a show of hands:
how many are Catholics?
how many are Christians of other denominations?
how many are of other faiths?
how many have connections with Asia? Ireland? Africa? the Caribbean?
how many are employed? . . . unemployed?
how many are students of any kind?

f • Give a very rough outline of the schedule for the session, being sure to include:
when there will be a break for tea or coffee;
what time the session will end;
where the toilets are situated, etc.

Use a large scale map of the area 10–15 mins

Provide small, sticky, coloured paper 'dots'. Invite each person to place their dot on the map, indicating where they live. Encourage people to get up, move around and talk to one another as they do this, thus giving them the sense that these sessions are not about lectures and presentations but about meeting one another.

Once all the dots have been placed on—or to the side of—the map, invite everyone to have a look at it and, if they wish, comment upon it. You may have comments to make yourself, or questions to raise concerning the distribution.

Small 'buzz' groups 5–15 mins

One member of the team invites everyone to move their chairs so that they are sitting in groups of three or four, preferably with people they do not know so well. Insist that there are no more than four in any group! Once the chairs have been rearranged, direct them to find out a little about each other—e.g. 'Why have you come?' 'What kind of family do you have?'

After a few minutes, stop the 'buzz' and ask the group to reflect on what was happening. Point out that everyone should have an opportunity to speak and that some people need to be encouraged and supported, especially by the way we listen to them. Then invite the groups to continue for some minutes longer.

Hopes, expectations and fears 10–30 mins

Using either large sheets of newsprint or an overhead projector, invite people to express their hopes, expectations and fears concerning the project. These may be 'brainstormed' and listed under three headings. Allow a few moments' 'buzz' on whatever has been written down, then invite any further comments.

Once you have completed the lists, you may like to have a look at copies of some of the following pictures. In small groups, share with one another whatever the picture is conveying to each person.

Illustration 1

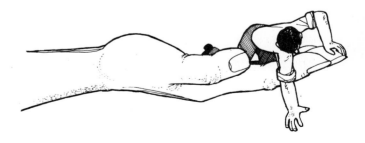

Illustration 2a(&2b)

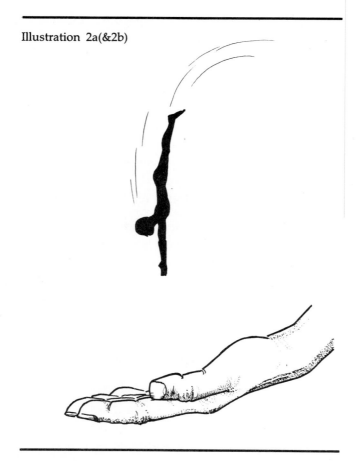

Illustration 3

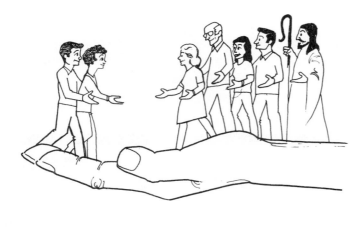

After a few minutes' discussion of one picture, the session leader invites each group to offer a comment to the large group. The small groups then proceed to discuss the next picture before again sharing their thoughts with the large group.

Moments of life 20–30 mins

Have everyone seated in groups of three or four. One of the team invites everyone to be quiet, to remember that many important things happen in our journey through life and to recall one moment that was in some way important for them. It may be something that happened today, yesterday, last week or a long time ago. Ask them to recall where they were, who was with them, what happened that made that moment important. Some people are helped by recalling the sounds, smells, feelings or sights of that moment.

After a few moments one of the team tells the group about an incident in his or her own life. This should be fairly brief and, if possible, about an 'ordinary' occurrence.

For example:

> I was feeling really low—despairing, really, about what is happening in the world. I was walking along the roadside, dragging my feet as I went, when suddenly I saw a falcon. It seemed to hover for ages and ages. I stood transfixed, fascinated. 'Miss, is that a kestrel or a peregrine falcon?' I turned to see a young boy of about eleven beside me. 'I honestly don't know,' I said, 'but isn't it beautiful?' His eyes never left the bird as he nodded and said in an awe-filled voice, 'I've never seen one before.' Then, 'Look, look! There it goes! Just look at it!' It's difficult to explain the feeling, but I found I almost skipped the rest of the way home. Something about the awe and wonder in that child was so uplifting.

A team member then explains how the essence of the story may be captured in one word; and then suggests one for the story that has just been told. (For example, for the story above we may suggest 'awe', 'wonder' or 'uplifting'.) The chosen word is then written in large letters, using a thick felt-tip pen, on to a strip of paper. (A4 sheets cut in half lengthwise are about the right size.)

Each person is then invited to return to their own important moment. Encourage them to try to think of one word that encapsulates the essence of that moment and write it down in big letters, using the pens and paper provided.

In their groups of three or four, find out what words have been written. Encourage people to share something of that moment with the others in their group, but stress that they need only share the details with which they feel comfortable. If people prefer to remain silent, that must be respected.

Once the session leader feels that all have had an opportunity to share their story, people are invited to place their words where they can be clearly seen by all, preferably on a wall. (Blu-Tack is useful for this and it helps if little bits have been arranged somewhere beforehand.) Try to encourage people to move and stick up their own paper so that they can have a good look at the other words.

Read out some or all of the words that have been written—depending on the size of the group. You will probably find they include some of the following: LOVE • WONDER • JOY • FEAR • TOGETHER • SUPPORT • FORGIVENESS • CHANGE • LIFE • BIRTH • BEGINNING • RISK • FRIENDSHIP • DECISION • CARE • STRENGTH • BELONGING • SHARING • COURAGE • SECURITY

• Remind them that each word is the essence of a story. They know the stories behind some of the words: their own, the one you told them, and one or two others.

• Ask them:
• if the words are about stories of life.
• if they would describe the words as 'religious' words.
• if they think God is in any way involved in these stories.
• if they think there is any connection between these words and the sacrament of Baptism—Confirmation—Reconciliation—Eucharist. (Focus upon the sacrament which is particularly relevant to the group; eg if the group is preparing for Marriage, then focus upon the sacrament of Marriage.)

Allow a few moments for people to discuss this in small groups, then gently try to focus the discussion by asking:

Do we agree that these words are about life? Do we also agree that they are about the sacraments? Suggest that God is revealed to us in and through all the ordinary as well as extraordinary events of life—and the sacraments are Christian celebrations of life.

What do you see? 15–20 mins

Visual images often convey a lot more to us than any amount of words. But do we all see the same thing? Do we all receive the same message? Invite discussion on some or all of the following pictures. Ask people what the picture is saying to them—especially now, as we meet to share our life and our faith.

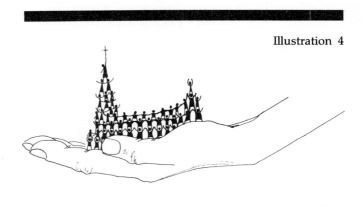

Illustration 4

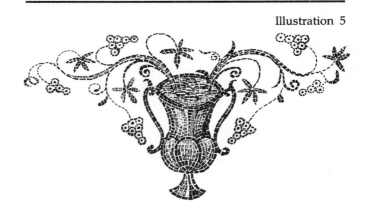

Illustration 5

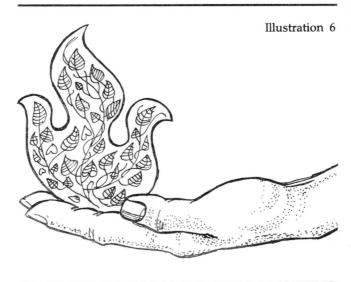

Illustration 6

Illustration 7

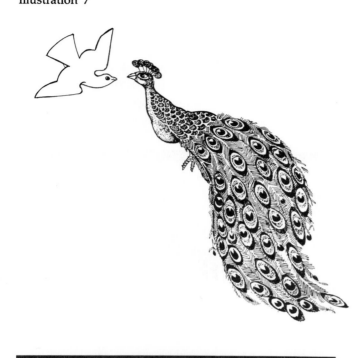

Prayer 15–20 mins

Ask everyone to form a circle around the 'focal point', the table on which there is an arrangement of flowers and candles, including the Easter candle or a large decorated candle. Dim the lights and pause for a few moments' silent recollection of the events of the evening (during which eyes will adjust to the light!). Then one or two members of the team reflect aloud on the sacrament of Baptism, perhaps using some of the following ideas.

Most of us were baptised as babies and we have no recollection of the event. For many of us that was a long time ago! Our parents, in loving and caring for us, brought us to the Lord of Life and offered us to him. They gave us life and wanted us to share in their 'new life' in Christ. There may be others among us who were baptised when we were old enough to remember the event, and those memories are precious.

Let us now remember that special moment. For most of us, other adults made promises at that time on our behalf. We are now able to accept fully those promises and their implications for ourselves. We are invited daily to enter more deeply into our 'new life' in Christ; to say 'Yes' to God's work in our lives.

The light of the Easter candle (*point to the flame*) is a symbol of the Risen Jesus who is here with us now, just as he has been at every moment of our lives. He has enabled us to feel and know his presence among us as we have shared together. These smaller candles (*point to them*) represent the 'new life' in him, which we celebrate at our baptism.

When we were baptised we were prayed for, prayed with and prayed over. There are times now when we struggle to pray, and may find this difficult or worrying. Let us now rest in the memory of our baptism and allow others once again to pray for us.

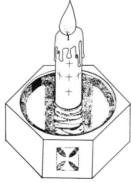

The prayer-leader prays:

God our Father, in our baptism we celebrated your call to all human beings to be members of your family and to work together for the building of your kingdom here on earth. You have brought us here to grow in our understanding of our baptism and to grow in being of service to you by building a better world for others. Strengthen us and protect us. Let us know the presence of your Risen Son here among us as you lead us in our time together.

(It helps the atmosphere to have gentle music playing in the background.)

Several priests then move among the group, laying their hands on the head of each person and praying briefly. Each one is accompanied by a team member who carries one of the small candles from the table. As they pray the priests may use these or similar words:

May Christ Jesus fill you with his presence and bring you understanding and peace.

After each person is blessed the team member gives him or her the candle to hold while the person alongside is receiving their blessing. It is then returned to the team member who hands it on to the next person.

The attitude of the priests and team members is one of love and service, silently conveying the important truth of the 'Servant' nature of the Church and of the Risen Jesus.

Once the priests have prayed with everyone, they bless those members of the team who accompanied them and then bless one another.

The candles are replaced on the table and the group sits for a few moments in silent prayer.

Turn down the music, wish people goodbye and remind them when you will meet again.

Note: Should you be in a situation where there is no priest available to minister to you at the end of this meeting, the team members may pray with the group, recalling the way parent and Godparents bless their children at their baptism.

Celebrating Stage One with the parish

The way in which you celebrate with the parish, at this stage of the project, will depend very much upon the nature of your group.

Have a social evening

For some groups it may be best to celebrate by having a social evening at which people are able to meet and chat in a very informal manner. This may be held before or after the first session.

Have a house mass

Some groups may not be ready to 'face' the parish. They may prefer to have a simple Mass or some other form of liturgical celebration—of the kind we would have in our homes.

Celebrate at a parish mass

If, however, you do decide to celebrate with the parish at a Sunday Mass there are several things you could do:

- Hymns may reflect the theme of the session (i.e. Starting to Journey Together).
- A special Penitential Rite may be composed.
- The participants may be introduced to the congregation before or after the homily.
- The homily may be related to the theme of the session as well as to the readings.
- The Easter candle used at the session—or a specially decorated candle—may be presented with the gifts at the offertory. This should be placed either on the altar or somewhere in the sanctuary where people are able to see it clearly—the main purpose of it being to remind the parish of the need to support the group through prayer. It will be lit at this time and at all of the special Masses for the group, as well as whenever the parish needs to be reminded of its supporting role.

Becoming Aware of God in my Life.

Introduction

All of us have known moments in our lives when we have been aware that God was—in some way—very close to us. We do not always find it easy to express our understanding of those moments to other people; in fact, it can be difficult to explain them even to ourselves! There have been other times, however, when we wondered just where God was when we felt most in need of his love, care and support and were unaware that he was with us throughout every single moment.

As we journey through life, our images of God change; our ability to recognise the presence of God gradually develops. Events and relationships in our lives enable us to grow in our understanding of God's love and care for us always and everywhere—some of them more than others. It may be the deep intimacy experienced with another; the sense of loss caused by death, unemployment, divorce or illness; the moment of wonder shared with a child; the sheer relief felt as a 'missing' youngster walks in through the door; the consolation given over a pint; or the unexpected kindness of a neighbour.

As human beings we are always searching for meaning in our lives, but many of us hesitate to share our present understanding because we feel others may laugh at us or think we are ignorant. We are **all** on a journey. Everyone is at a different stage of that journey—but wherever we are it is all right for us to be there. **No one** knows all the answers because no one ever completes the journey in this life. But we do need to continue searching if we are to grow.

In our searching we are greatly helped when others share with us the fruits—and struggles—of their search. There are times when our previously-held ideas seem to be blown apart or our present, familiar way of being with God no longer has meaning. At such times we often suffer a very real sense of loss before a new understanding emerges. People who are willing to share with us their images and experiences of God provide tremendous support as we struggle through what could be bewildering and lonely periods of growth and change.

It is wonderful to have the opportunity to be part of a group of people willing to share in this way. Together, we struggle to find words to express whatever is going on in the innermost depths of our being. As we do we find we gain confidence about our images of God and about sharing them with others. We also find a greatly increased awareness of the presence of God in ordinary, everyday things. What people say, what happens, television programmes, songs, books—all are full of meaning. As we awaken to this we often find that Scripture, too, has for us a new and deeper meaning.

NOTE: Many people have found that keeping a personal notebook of their life and journey in faith has greatly helped them to appreciate God's presence and action in their lives. This stage of your programme is a most suitable time to introduce people to the idea of keeping such a notebook, perhaps including some of the exercises carried out as part of the project. These may be pasted into the notebook, with the person's own comments alongside, thus providing a good basis upon which to build a personal record of events. Depending upon the nature and purpose of your particular group, you may decide that a suitable notebook be presented to the group members at the parish celebration—as their symbol of the Word of God.

Materials you may need for Stage Two

table • table cloth • large candle • flowers
olive oil, in a suitable container • towel
bowl of water • small dish(es) for mixing oils
oil of frankincense in a suitable container •
background music • paper • pens or pencils
bowl of sliced lemon • magazines • paper bags
scissors • notebooks

Copies of the following worksheets:
'Relationships' (Worksheets 1a & 1b)
'Parent-Child Relationship Chart' (Worksheet 2)
'On prayer' (Worksheet 3)
'Times when I felt . . .' (Worksheet 4)
 Appropriate pictures for 'What do you see?'
'Images of the Risen Lord' (Worksheet 5)
'A survey of prayer' (Worksheet 6)
'I called out your name' (Worksheet 7)
'Thankful leper' (Lk 17) (Worksheet 8)
'1 Corinthians 13' (Worksheet 9)
'The Road to Emmaus' (Lk 24) (Worksheet 10)
'Guidelines for reading the Bible' (Worksheet 11)

A welcoming atmosphere is always important.

At the beginning of Stage One we made some suggestions about ways of creating a welcoming atmosphere and would advise you to do similar things this time. Your **focal point**, however, should be a little different, highlighting the theme of the meeting. Use a table, again covered with a cloth and decorated with flowers and candles, but this time add oils, a dish with slices of lemon, some small empty dishes (glass ashtrays or coffee-cup saucers will do), a small bowl of water (one that has a 'cut glass' look enhances the sparkle of the water!) and a towel.

Ideas for your Second Session
To be selected and adapted

Welcome and introduction 5 mins

You may like to use some of the following ideas in your welcome and introduction to the theme of the meeting:

Last time we met we got to know one another a little as we began our journey in faith together. Some of us may have come expecting a high-powered talk on our faith, but instead we found ourselves talking about very ordinary everyday things—and then found that those things had a lot to do with our faith!

What, exactly, do we mean by 'faith'? When I talk about 'my faith' what I am really referring to is my own one-to-one relationship with God. I may try to encapsulate that relationship in words—my 'beliefs'—but they can never adequately express my own personal faith, my own personal relationship with God. Even when we are not conscious of the fact, a relationship always exists between ourselves and God because he is with us always.

Our relationship with God is closely allied to our relationship with others and with ourselves. These relationships may be expressed in moments of silence or reflection, in loving and caring, in anger, or in simply spending time together.

During this meeting we are going to try to grow in our understanding of the different ways in which God speaks to us. At times we tend to limit our understanding of relating to God to 'saying our prayers'—sometimes to the extent that instead of Samuel's 'Speak, Lord, your servant is listening' we would seem to be saying, 'Listen, Lord, your servant

is speaking'!! Prayer is not only what we say to God, or how we are with him, but is also how God is with us and how he speaks to us.

Jesus promised us that wherever we gather in his name he would be there in the midst of us. He is here with us now, helping us as we journey together.

Our relationship with God and with others 20–40 mins

We are what our relationships are. They give meaning to us, make us the sort of people we are. They are central to our very living. Each one of us is the same person with God as he or she is with other people.

Using the 'Relationships' Worksheet (1a), a flip-chart, board or overhead projector, present the following illustrations. (You may prefer to draw your own illustrations or use photographs.)

Relationships Chart Worksheet 1a

For each illustration in turn, invite comments on the following questions:
When they are this age
    what do children NEED from their parents?
    What do parents DO for their children?
    How do children FEEL about their parents?
The discussion may take place in small groups or in one large group, but as it proceeds, write down key words or phrases under the headings of:
a • child NEEDS . . .
b • parent DOES, is experienced as . . .
c • child FEELS . . .
Once you have looked at all the diagrams or pictures and written down the comments, you will probably find you have something along the lines set out in worksheet 1b.

Relationships Chart Worksheet 1b

Allow a few moments for a general 'buzz' on the words that have been written and the way the relationship between child and parent develops. Would anyone like to add anything further?

Do people think there is any similarity between the way in which our relationship develops with our parents and the way in which we relate to God? You may like to point out that sometimes we feel protected by God; sometimes we expect him to fix things for us—to answer our prayers the way we want; at times we are aware of him guiding us; or we think of him as a lawgiver whose laws control us; or we experience a deep trust, a deep love. We have different feelings about God at different stages of our lives, but can, at times, relate to him very much as the young child, while at other times our relationship with him is very much that of the adult 'child'.

Parent–Child Relationship Chart
Worksheet 2

Have the Parent-Child Relationship Chart' (Worksheet 2) prepared on a flip-chart, board, hand-out or overhead transparency and present it now to the group. Invite them to comment upon it.
Point out that:

- As adults we experience God in different ways.
- There may be times when we find this disconcerting.
- The Scriptures are very consoling! They tell us about people who complain about God or get angry with him, as well as about those who are full of amazement or plead for help.

A reflective meditation 20–30 mins
This reflection is particularly effective when it follows the last exercise, although it may, of course, be used at some other time. It allows people space and time to explore their own relationship with God more fully. Try to have the room as quiet as possible and the lighting subdued, perhaps using only candles for illumination. You may also like to have some very gentle music playing in the background, but make sure it is not intrusive.

Invite everyone to find space for themselves and to sit comfortably or, depending on your group, to stretch out flat on the floor. Ask them to be quiet—but alert!

When everyone is quiet, invite them to read all or some of the following passages which you have already prepared (and perhaps adapted) on hand-outs. Encourage them to read slowly and meditatively, allowing images and memories to drift into their minds.

(You may prefer to have different members of the team reading the passages aloud, using a gentle tone, and pausing every so often to allow time for personal reflection.)

God protects and cares
Think of all you receive from God—
    the air you breathe
    the energy you have
    the things you hear . . . touch . . . see
    the thoughts you have
    the feelings you have
    the things you value in life
    your family, the people you know, friends
    the gifts and talents you have.
Call these things and people to mind, by name.
Where are they now? How do you feel about them?
How do you use or treat them?
Tell God how much you appreciate all that you have been given.

God is all powerful, able to fix everything
Allow yourself time to wonder about:
    stars, their number
    mountains and valleys
    flowers, animals
    waterfalls, streams, lakes, rivers and oceans
    the sun, rain and snow
    the complexity of your own body.

Stay for some time with that sense of awe and wonder, amazed by God's power to arrange such a world.

You may have experienced God in a special way when, for example, you felt protected from danger; family or friends have been healed; or you have felt hurt and sought God's help.

How do you respond to so great a God—who designs and arranges even the most insignificant detail? Share your feeling with him, perhaps 'with sighs too great for words' (cf Rom 8:26)

God guides and controls you
Life is a puzzle! It has meaning but we are never sure just what that meaning is. We are always searching,

always trying to discover the meaning of our lives; that is part of being human. We know we are going somewhere, that we are on a journey through life— a journey that means we have to make choices. We want to be good, to do the right thing, but we often feel desperately uncertain and in need of help as we choose a particular path in life.

God is always there to guide us if we are attentive to his word with us, but he leaves us free to choose. Sometimes, however, we have a feeling that he is controlling things; that we have no real choice; that decisions have been made for us. Sometimes that can be very reassuring; but there are other times when we may kick against that and go our own way, and may well find ourselves down a wrong track. That can be very disturbing! We may experience the feeling and frustration of the naughty child who has been caught out—and that feeling is not comfortable!

Talk to God about the decisions and choices you make. Tell him about the things you really value. Ask him to forgive you for the times you hurt others, or yourself, through making poor choices. Let him help you to be the person he wants you to be. Listen to him. Be aware of his love for you; that he wants only what is best for you; that he cares.

God is difficult; interfering; gets in the way; is not interested
Our relationship with God can be very confusing! There are times when it seems beyond our understanding. Nothing appears to be going right. We need God, we want him to be with us, we call, but—no answer. Where is he? Does he exist at all? If he does, why isn't he doing something about the troubles in this world that he's supposed to have made so perfect? Why does he allow mothers to die; children to suffer; athletes to be crippled; marriages to break up; war; famine; tornadoes; hatred; violence? Why why why? Is he not interested? Does he not care? What kind of a God is he? Tell him how you feel. Then ask him to help you to understand, to see what he is asking of you, and to give you the courage to respond.

There are other moments, however, when God seems too close for comfort! He intrudes into our lives. We want to do things but he seems to be demanding that we do something else. He's a nuisance. He demands too much of us. He's unreasonable and we don't like

the threats of punishment! They're much too severe! Why doesn't he let us just get on and enjoy life? Don't be afraid to tell him how you feel. Then ask him to help you choose the right path, and to give you the courage to keep to it even when you would prefer to go a different way.

There were times when Jesus felt like this. He even sweated blood over it!

God respects you, trusts you and loves you. You feel the same about God
Jesus said, 'You are my friends' (Jn 15:14). To be friends with a person means we both give and receive. We depend on each other. We spend a lot of time together. We expect a lot of each other. We know a lot about each other. We share everything and do whatever we can together.

It takes time to grow in friendship with God. We have to spend time together, getting to know each other as we are now rather than as we would perhaps like to be! We have to do things together, to depend on each other, to act out of love for each other.

Ask Jesus to help you reflect upon your friendship with him. Share with him your feeling about how good this friendship is for you. Talk to him about the times you have failed to be the friend you would want to be. Recall Jesus' words: 'When you failed to do it for the least of my brothers and sisters you failed to do it for me.' Ask him to help you to strengthen the friendship between you.

Think over the different ways you have experienced God in your life. Thank him for being with you always.

On Prayer   Worksheet 3

On Prayer
Give out copies of the 'On Prayer' worksheet (3), and make sure everyone has a pen or a pencil.

Invite one person to read it slowly, clearly and thoughtfully to the group.

Suggest to the group that as the passage is read, each person may like to underline words or phrases that have particular meaning for them.

Allow a few moments' silence for people to ponder over the content.

Invite each person to say aloud, and without any comment, any one word or phrase that he or she has underlined.

Allow a short pause, then invite people to say **why** the words or phrases chosen are important to them.

Times when . . . Worksheet 4

Times when I felt . . .
Times when Jesus felt . . . 20–30 mins

Give out copies of the 'Times when . . .' worksheet (4) and pencils, biros or felt pens. Invite people to move so that they are sitting on their own and ask everyone to follow these instructions:

• Complete the sentence in the top half to the central circle with your own name.

• For the other circles recall times when you felt
  confused
  happy and content
  in a state of conflict
  aware of a feeling of companionship
  lonely

In one half of each circle put a date, place name, mark or comment about that time. (*Reassure the group that whatever they put is private—for their eyes alone.*)

• Now go around the outer circles again, but this time try to think of times when Jesus had those feeling of confusion contentment, conflict, companionship, and loneliness. Write a word about each of those times in the second half of the relevant circle.

When everyone has finished, invite them to move into small groups and share with one another the GOSPEL EVENTS they have noted for each word. Ask them to talk about the feelings they think Jesus may have experienced during each event.

You may invite the small groups to offer comment to the large group and then encourage them to share one of their own stories. Tell them to share only one with which they are comfortable. No one must feel they have to say anything. Being a good listener is a very important part of sharing!

Draw this exercise to a close by asking such questions as:
• Do you think Jesus knows and understands the feelings we have?
• Does that make any difference to you; to your relationship?

You may finish by singing *Walk with me, O my Lord* or some other familiar hymn.

Note: • Being able to identify our own lives with that of Jesus is essential to deepening our personal relationships with the Risen Lord. It provides a necessary foundation for prayer.
• Sharing faith is very much about telling each other the stories of what God had done in our lives.

What do you see? 10–30 mins
Invite people to comment on all or some of the visual images you have selected from Appendix 2. What is each image conveying to you as we share our understandings of the way in which God speaks to us in the events of everyday?

Illustration 8

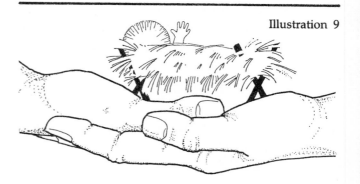

Illustration 9

Illustration 10

Illustration 14

Illustration 11

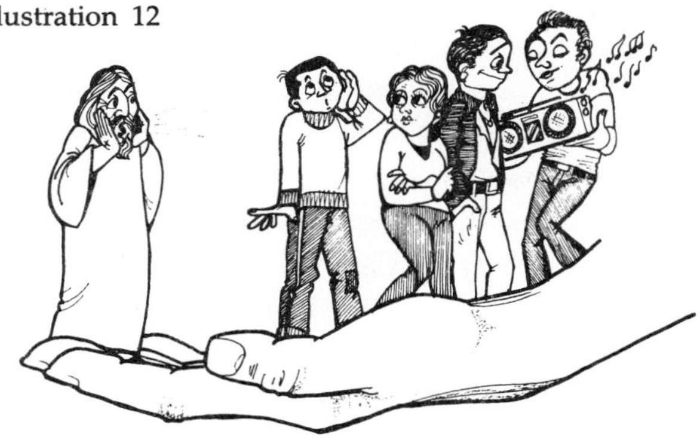

Illustration 6

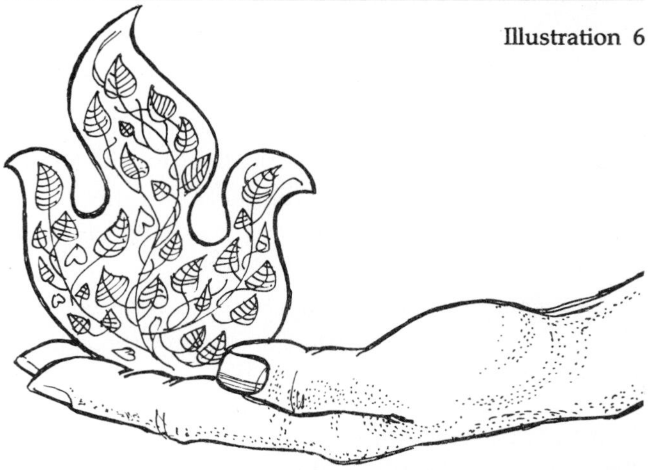

Illustration 12

Illustration 15

Illustration 13

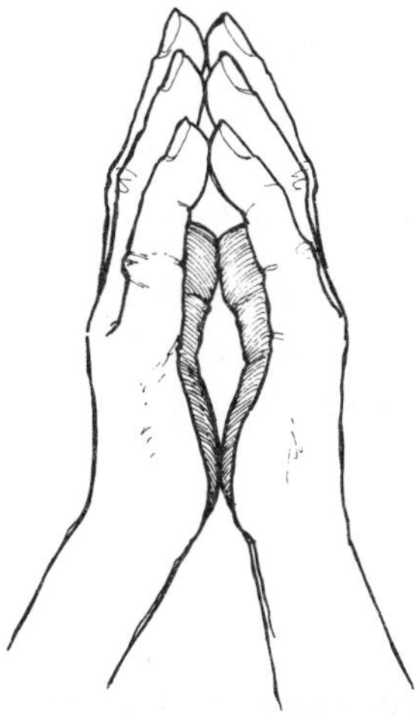

Note: You may prefer to scatter your presentation of some of these images throughout the session rather than use them all together. For example, some could be used with the reflective meditation, some may follow the discussion based on the relationship between parent and child, and/or you may choose to use some within the period of prayer at the close of the session.

You are a person who speaks
You are a person who listens

15–20 mins

Invite everyone to think quietly of a moment in their lives when someone spoke to them and, for some reason, it was important for them. You may say something along the following lines to help them:

- Who was it who spoke to you? Where were you? When did it happen?
- Did the person know that what s/he was saying meant so much to you—or was s/he unaware of the fact? Perhaps it was something you heard on the radio or television, read, or simply overheard. (Pause for a few moments.)
- What made you listen so attentively? Was it something that met your need, gave you a fresh understanding, or presented you with a challenge?
- Spend a few moments recalling everything about this time, most of all your FEELINGS. (Pause for a few moments.)
- Now share with one another how you listened, why it was so important to listen, and what your feelings were at the time.

Think of a time when you were very aware of someone listening carefully to you. Who was listening? When? Where? Why were you speaking? Was it to offer advice, help, in response to a question, a warning? What made you realise that you must speak to him or her? What were your FEELINGS at that time? (Pause to allow time for reflection.)

Again, share you stories with one another, this time sharing how you spoke, why it was important to speak and how you felt as you were speaking.

Do you think these experiences of speaking and listening correspond in any way to our relationship with God?

Images of the Risen Lord
Worksheet 5

Images of the Risen Lord 10–15 mins

Give out worksheet 5, plus pens or pencils, and have everyone complete it. Then share together as indicated.

Journeys in prayer with the risen Lord

20–35 mins

Introductory Notes—to help you present ideas or start a discussion, before you proceed with the prayer exercise which follows.

- Sometimes people are afraid of God.
- There are times when some people relate to God as if he was a 'soft teddy bear that is clutched and fondled—a method of obtaining favours' (Damian Lundy).
- To know and be close to the Risen Jesus is to have a special kind of relationship with God.
- To talk all the time when we are at prayer suggests that we are declaring. 'Listen, Lord, your servant is speaking—a condition that is in stark contrast to Samuel's, 'Speak, Lord, your servant is listening,' (1 Sam 3:9).

Note: The story of Samuel in 1 Sam 3 is worth exploring, possibly following this introduction.

- As human beings, there are times when we find it difficult really to trust others;—yet trusting is at the centre of all relationships that are loving and caring.

A prayer exercise

Ask everyone to sit comfortably (or to stretch out on the floor), to relax and to breathe deeply—but not to fall asleep!

1 • Invite them to take Jesus on a tour through part of their lives—a day, a morning, an hour or a particular incident—and to share their feelings about that time with him.

2 • After a while, invite them to let Jesus take them on a tour through an incident or day in his life—and to ask him to share his feelings about that time with them.

3 • Finally, ask them to invite Jesus to take them on a tour through part of their own lives—and to share with them something of HIS feelings about that time in their life.

A focus for prayer ... 20–40 mins

Supply each person with magazines, a paper bag and scissors.

Invite everyone to search through the magazines for pictures or words that say something to them or represent things about which they pray. These may include things for which they are thankful, things they need, things for which they themselves have been asked, expressions of love or care etc. Ask them to cut out each picture, word or phrase and place it in their 'prayer bag'.

When everyone appears to have finished, invite them to move into small groups and share with one another, as far as they are able, the contents of their prayer bags.

You may like to conclude this exercise by inviting the members of each group to pray for one another.

A survey of prayer Worksheet 6

A survey of prayer . . . 20–30 mins

Each person should be given a copy of the chart (worksheet 6) and invited to place an 'X' on each line to represent his or her opinion concerning the ideas expressed there. Do they stand close to the positive statement; do they totally resonate with the feeling expressed in the negative statement; or do they find themselves somewhere between the two? Stress that there are no right or wrong answers. These are simply statements that have been made when people were talking about prayer. The idea is to see the stance we take as individuals and as a group. Encourage people, therefore, to answer as honestly as possible.

Once the 'survey' has been completed, it may be followed by a debate. Ask all those whose X's have been placed consistently on the positive side to form one group, and the rest to form a second group. They then proceed to debate the validity of the following or similar statements, one group trying to convince the other, using examples, personal experience, scripture references and any other evidence they have.

God does answer prayer.
God answers prayer in three ways: yes, no or wait.
Prayer should not be governed by feelings.
Public prayer is important.
A mature Christian needs to pray without ceasing.

I called . . . Worksheet 7

I called out your name and you answered me. I called upon you to help and you stepped forward

20–30 mins

Distribute copies of the 'I called . . .' worksheet (7) to the group members.

The exercise proceeds in a similar way to the one already fully described in worksheet 4, and outlined on worksheet 7.

Alternatively, you may choose to focus entirely on incidents or moments in the lives of the individuals in the group.

Be sure to respect the fact that some people may wish to listen rather than speak.

The Thankful Leper Worksheet 8

The Thankful Leper . . . 20–30 mins

Provide each person with:
1 • a copy of 'The thankful leper' (worksheet 8)
2 • paper, coloured felt-tip pens or paint, and biros

When the exercise has been completed, invite everyone to move into small groups and share his or her answers concerning the story of the lepers. If they wish to do so, they may also share something from their cards perhaps simply explaining the illustration.

(The cards may be kept by each person to place inside their personal notebooks.)

It would be appropriate to close this exercise with a prayer of thanksgiving.

---

1 Corinthians 13   Worksheet 9

Using Scripture (20–30 mins)

Many passages of scripture may be used in the way illustrated by worksheet 9 (1 Corinthians 13).

Key words and phrases have been omitted, but the key ideas are still communicated.

Encourage the group to fill in the blanks as appropriate to them as individuals. Then invite group comment and comparison.

Hospitality to the risen Lord 15–20 mins

- Invite everyone to be alone, to relax and to breathe deeply. Pause for a few moments, then ask each person to imagine s/he is with his/her closest friend.
- Allow a short pause before encouraging everyone to enter more deeply into the situation for a little while, perhaps with the assistance of these or similar questions:

    Where are you meeting your friend?
    Is the place in any way special for you?
    Are you alone, or with other people?
    Where are you going?
    What are you saying to each other?

- Once they have had sufficient time to explore the situation, ask them to return to the present moment and to imagine they would very much like to see their special friend now. You may encourage them by asking questions such as:

    How do you let your friend know you want to see him or her? Do you write, telephone, call at the house, go and look for him/her, or what? How do you actually express your invitation?
    Do you do anything special before meeting your friend? What are your feelings as you prepare?

- After a pause, invite them to return to the present moment and discuss with one another:

    how invitations to friends were made;
    what preparations were made and how;
    where they were with their friends.

- Now invite them to think of the people and places to which they go during an ordinary week and, in their imaginations, to visit those they particularly like. It may be for work or for fun.

- While they are still imagining these events and experiences, ask them where, when and with whom they would invite the Risen Jesus to be with them.

    How would they invite him?
    How does he reply to the invitation?
    Would they make any special preparation?
    How does he feel when he is there?
    Does he say anything?
    Does he do anything?
    How do they feel about him being there?

Approaching Scripture 20–35 mins.

Most people welcome help in both understanding and sharing Scripture. This is dealt with very fully in a number of books, but the following is offered for those who have little time to spare.

Introduction

Scripture is 'good news' that was written down by people who were changed by the action of the Holy Spirit. Some of these people lived before the birth of Jesus and their writings have been collected together to form the Old Testament. The New Testament is a collection of the works of those people who wrote several years after the life, death and resurrection of Jesus.

Scripture is a verbal account of the way God changes both individuals and groups of people.

'Gospel' means 'good news'. To meet the Risen Lord and to be changed by the power of the Holy Spirit is good news.

The way God acts in our lives is this same good news. He is with us at all times, in the events and people in our lives.

It is truly wonderful to know God is with us, at work in our lives, helping us to become the persons he wishes us to be, until we are 'filled up with God himself' (Eph 3:19).

Reading Scripture is exciting because it is full of this wonder while, at the same time, helping us to recognise the work of God in our own lives.

An exercise to help you in your reading of Scripture

The people who wrote the Scriptures were trying to explain many different things about the way in which God is at work. The following three points are very important:

1 • The work of God in your life is good news for you. Your life can be changed; it is possible for it to be different, for you and for others. Your problems can be experienced in a new and peaceful way.

2 • God is always active in your life. He is very near, showing himself to you even at this very moment. This is good news.

3 • As you grow in understanding the way God is at work in your life, you also grow in your ability to say 'Yes' to him and his work. As his activity and your understanding of it develops, your life appears to be different. His work seems to turn things upside down, changing the values that you had before. This has a stunning effect, arising from the fact that you recognise that God has done this for you.

The group leader may display a summary of these three points.
   For example:

1 • God can change your problems.

2 • God is with you now and will show himself to you.

3 • God will change the way things seem to be.

'The Road to Emmaus'   Worksheet 10

Now have the group do the exercise on 'The Road to Emmaus' worksheet (10).

Guidelines . . .   Worksheet 11

Guidelines for reading the Bible

The guidelines given on worksheet 11 may help people who want to develop their relationship with God through prayerful reading of Scripture. They may be handed out at the end of the 'Approaching Scripture' for session use at home.

Prayer—remembering Baptism . . .

15–20 mins

Introduction

(Because a priest will be more familiar with handling oils, mixing them and anointing people, you may prefer that he leads this particular prayer service. Apart from this practical consideration, there is no reason why a lay person should not lead the prayer.)

We need the ability:
• to hear God speaking to us;
• to speak to others of his work in our lives.
The Church prayed for this during our baptism, and God always answers such prayer.

'Whatever you ask my Father in my name he will do.' Our confidence in this fact is often weak! We are uncertain of the power of God to change us and draw us more and more deeply into the risen life of his Son Jesus.

When we were baptised, we were anointed with chrism, a perfumed oil mixed with olive oil. The rich scent clung to us as an outward sign of the sacredness of the risen Christ, and of his presence with us always, throughout our lives.

Frankincense is the perfumed oil most frequently used today. It is a richly scented oil, obtained by distilling the resin from certain trees in the Eastern world. Because the trees grow in high-altitude deserts, their growth is slow and husbandry is difficult, making the oil expensive.

Mixed with olive oil, this oil is one of those blessed by the bishop on Maundy Thursday. As chrism, it is used for sealing at Baptism, Confirmation and Ordination. It is also used to anoint kings and queens when they are crowned.

The perfume of frankincense is striking. It symbolises the power and kingship of the Risen Christ, who is with us always and everywhere. It is a sign of his priesthood—a priesthood he shares with us.

We are now going to remember the celebration of our own baptism. We will ask the Lord to renew in us the anointing we received at that time, and thus confirm his promise to enable us to hear him speaking to us, to be with us and to empower us to share the good news with others. So often we behave like the disciples before the day of Pentecost—hesitant, uncertain and fearful. We will ask the Lord to transform us, and to give us the confidence we need to speak of his work in our lives.

Pause for reflection

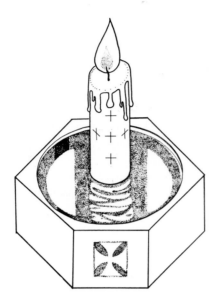

Prayer for God's blessing on the oils
Prayer over the olive oil

God our Father, you made all that exists and freely created us so that we might know and love you. As we remember the celebration of our baptism, make us fully aware of your presence here with us now, and let us know your power to change us and strengthen us.

May this oil be for us a sign of your continuing protection from all that would harm us, and of your constant healing in our lives.

We ask you this in the name of Jesus Christ, your Son, our Risen Lord.

All: **Amen.**

Prayer over the perfumed oil of frankincense

Father, we remember that through the life, death and resurrection of Jesus, your Son, our lives have been transformed. You have given us your life.

Bless this perfumed oil so that, in clinging to us, it may help us to know the abiding presence and action of Jesus in our lives. Grant that as the scent touches us and surrounds us, we may become certain of his closeness, his holiness and his authority, and that we may really know Jesus as Lord in our lives.

The oils are mixed.

May these oils remind us of our sealing with Christ at our baptism and how we were called to be holy, enabled to hear him speak to us in our lives, and sent to speak of him to others. We ask this through Christ our Lord.

Each person is anointed
(You may like to have some gentle music playing in the background.)

As he anoints the first ear, the prayer-leader says:
May his power protect you from evil.

As he moves from the first to the second ear, says:
May your ears be opened.

As he anoints the second ear, says:
May you forever hear him speak to you.

As he anoints the mouth, says:
May your mouth be opened.

With his hand on the person's head, he says:
May you speak to others of his wonder and power.

Close the period of prayer with a few moments of silence.

Note: This celebration is a paraliturgy and the oil used is not chrism.

Celebrating Stage Two with the Parish.

Becoming aware of God in my life

Note: It is important that people meet in small groups to share, receive information, reflect and pray together. However, they also need to celebrate their lives within the context of the Christian mysteries. One way of enabling them to do this is to plan and celebrate special Masses.

By incorporating the special celebration into one of the normal Sunday Masses, the whole parish community is given the opportunity to celebrate the growth in faith that is taking place within the group.

At this stage of the project, the special Mass should celebrate and draw attention to our awareness of God's presence in our lives, always and everywhere; that he reveals himself to us through all the people and events of our lives; and that he speaks to us in a very special way through the Scriptures.

During the Mass, the members of the group are entrusted with the Word of God. They may be given a Bible, a copy of the New Testament or a copy of one Gospel, or they may simply be given a particular passage of Scripture (perhaps suitably decorated). Symbols of faith may also be used, such as a decorated candle, the parish seal or a personal notebook. What is given and how it is given will depend very much upon the nature of the group. You may, for example, have a parish Confirmation group, parents preparing their children to receive a sacrament, or a retreat group.

The following suggestions may help you as you prepare your celebration. **Select and adapt them to suit your local situation**.

1 • Near to the ambo or the lectern place a specially decorated table on which are arranged the books, texts or symbols to be presented.

2 • Make the ambo or the lectern a strong focal point. Decorate it with lighted candles, flowers, an icon, hangings, drapery and/or spot lights.

3 • Cense the books, texts or symbols to be presented—preferably at the beginning of the Mass, after the censing of the cross and altar.

4 • Highlight the Liturgy of the Word:
Present the Lectionary to the celebrant, who then shows it to the people while saying:

May the Word of God always be heard in this place, as it unfolds the mystery of Christ before you and brings you salvation within the Church. *(Rite of Dedication of a Church.)*
With both hands, readers point to or raise the Lectionary after each reading.
Sing 'This is the Word of the Lord'—perhaps using the tone given in the Missal.

5 • Sing the Responsorial Psalm, the verses being chanted by a cantor while the whole congregation sings the response. (On this occasion the psalm should not be replaced by a 'suitable hymn'.)

6 • The deacon says aloud:
May the Lord be in my heart and on my lips that I may worthily proclaim the holy Gospel.

7 • Have a solemn Gospel procession with an extended, elaborate setting of the Gospel Acclamation, accompanied by musical instruments.

8 • After a brief explanation of the readings of the day, the preacher concludes in these or similar words:

The sacred Scriptures, which are proclaimed at all our celebrations, are the very basis of our Christian life. Over the course of more than a thousand years the wonders which God worked for his chosen people of Israel, his love and care for them and his messages to them sent through the prophets and kings, were passed on orally before being written down in books which we call the Old Testament.

The first followers of Jesus passed on, by word of mouth and through preaching, the truths which Jesus taught as well as the great reality of his life, death, resurrection and ascension. These traditions were eventually written down in the books of the New Testament.

God still speaks to us through the Scriptures. He is present in our midst when his word is proclaimed. It is through the Bible that we hear and receive the words of eternal life because it is the Lord of heaven and earth who speaks to us, today and for ever.

9 • After the homily each member of the group is presented with a Bible, New Testament, Gospel, Scripture passage or symbol. They stand, either in

their places or in front of the priest, who remains at or near the ambo. The celebrant addresses them, saying:

As baptised Christians you are given the mission of witnessing to Jesus Christ and proclaiming the Gospel wherever you go. In order to carry out this most worthy mission you must first take the Word of God into your hearts and minds through study, prayer and reflection. Are you resolved to do this?

I am.

One by one the members of the group approach the celebrant who says, as he presents the Scripture or symbol:

N., receive the Word of God, the source and rule of your life as a Christian. Ponder upon it in your mind, reflect upon it in your heart and let all your actions be inspired by it as you bring the Good News of Christ our Lord to the world.

All: **Amen**

10 • Some of the group carry the gifts at the Offertory.

11 • A solemn blessing is given, for example:
May God who reveals himself to you
grant you wisdom and understanding.
All: **Amen**.

May his Word be alive in your hearts
and lead you to lasting joy.
All: **Amen**

May he inspire you and guide you
all the days of your life.
All: **Amen**.

May almighty God bless you,
the Father, Son and Holy Spirit.
All: **Amen**.

12 • Carrying their books, texts or symbols, the group joins the Recessional Procession.

13 • The parish holds a social gathering after the Mass.

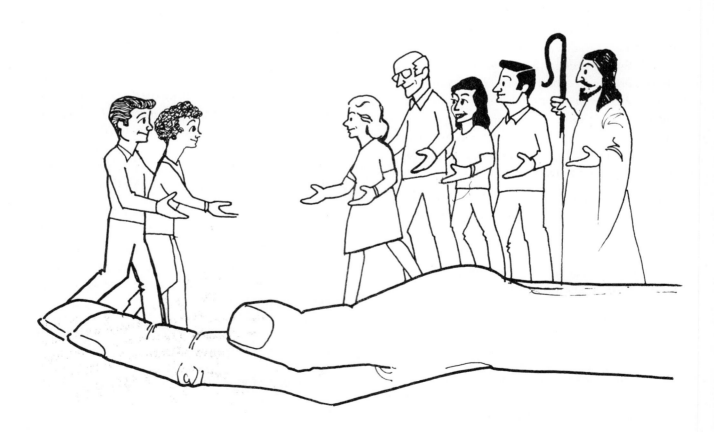

Stage Three

Called to be Christians

When we become aware of the way God is working in our lives and hear him speaking to us, whether through persons or events, we feel moved to respond in some way or other. We may have a sense of being 'called', but often we are not very clear about the direction we are to take.

Our experiences have often been shared by many other people in the past, and some of them have recorded their understanding of these events in their lives. Reflecting upon their stories, sharing our understanding of the Christian story and tradition we have inherited, and sharing our own stories in the light of these helps us to understand all that is happening to us. In doing so, we often find we are enlivened by the energy and companionship generated. We come to realise that what we are sharing is very much a living tradition. We begin to experience and welcome others, not only as friends, but as people whose gifts and talents are different from our own—people who, as Christians, each have a unique 'call'.

Materials you may need for Stage Three

table • bowl(s) of water • flowers • large candle(s) towel(s) • pens/pencils • background music paper strips (half of A4) • Blu-Tack large felt pens • blank paper (A4) • salt

Copies of: 'The Trial' script for each performer (Worksheet 12)
The 'Journey of Faith' (Worksheet 13)
The 'Diamond' (Worksheet 14)
The 'Baptism' (Worksheet 15)
Pictures for 'What do you see?'

Appropriate hymns eg *Love is flowing like a river; Oh living water, refresh my soul; Come down, O love divine; God's Spirit is in my heart; Follow Christ and love the world as he did; I heard the Lord call my name; My God said to me 'Follow'; Oh the word of my Lord.*

The Trial   Worksheet 12

The Trial . . . 40–50 mins

1 • Arrange the seats so that everyone will be able to see the scene being portrayed.
2 • Invite four people to dramatise 'The Trial'. Give out copies of the script and allow the characters sufficient time for them to look over the script before beginning their presentation.
3 • Introduce the drama, explaining that:

• the scene about to be performed is set in the year 2025.
• it is a criminal offence to be a Christian and we are witnessing a trial which is now in its second day.
• Mrs Wright claims, most emphatically, that she is a Christian and that she has never made any attempt to conceal the fact.
• but—is there enough evidence to convict her? All of you here are the Jury.

Note. Only the four performers need copies of the text. They should dramatise the parts wherever possible, using physical movement and facial expressions to help convey the message.

The dramatisation ends with the Jury – ie the large group – being instructed by the Judge to consider the evidence and give their verdict.

One of the team now directs the 'members of the Jury' to discuss the evidence they have heard. (This should be done in small groups of four or five.) S/he reminds them that—their task is to decide whether or not Mrs Wright is a Christian, and they must consider all the evidence placed before them. **If some groups appear to be getting bogged down with one or other particular issue rather than keeping to the task in hand, it would be wise to repeat this instruction as discussion progresses.** (You may decide to take note of the issues causing concern, and discuss them in depth at a later time.)

After sufficient time has been allowed for discussion, a team member says:

> Would all those members of the Jury who consider that Mrs Wright is a Christian, as she claims to be, please raise one hand.

The hands are counted—and the number recorded where everyone can see it.

> Would those members of the Jury who consider that Mrs Wright is not a Christian please raise one hand.

Again, the hands are counted and the number recorded.

• Invite everyone to discuss the results of the trial.

• Have slips of paper in equal quantities of two colours eg twenty blue and twenty pink. (A4 paper, cut in half lengthwise, would be suitable. You may need more than one strip per person.) Distribute these so that everyone in any one group has the same colour. A member of the team then gives the instructions immediately below to all the groups with one colour (eg blue), while another team member gives the second set of instructions to the groups with the other colour (eg pink).

1 • The instructions for the groups of one colour (eg blue) are as follows:

> Imagine you are sitting in a crowded room, perhaps a cafe, club room or waiting room. You can overhear two people talking to each other and, from their conversation, you begin to think that they may belong to the same Church as yourself. You listen more carefully to see if they say anything further to confirm your thoughts. For a few moments imagine yourself to be in that situation and notice what is being said that convinces you that they do belong to **your Church**.

• Allow a few minutes for reflection, then invite everyone to indicate—on their papers—the type of things about which the two people may have been speaking. *We have found that people are encouraged when the team member first writes down an example in large letters. Thus, a team member who is a Roman Catholic may write down 'Rosary' or 'Mass'.*

• When everyone has completed this, invite them to discuss, in their small groups, what they have written. You may encourage them to think, together, of other things and write these down also.

2 • The instructions for the other groups (ie those with pink strips of paper) are as follows:

> Imagine you are sitting in a crowded room, perhaps a cafe, club room or waiting room. You can overhear two people talking to each other and, from their conversation, you begin to think that they may be Christians. You listen more carefully to see if they say anything further to confirm your thoughts. For a few moments, imagine yourself to be in that situation and notice what is being said that convinces you that they are Christians.

• Allow a few minutes for reflection, then invite everyone to indicate—on their papers—the type of things about which the two people may have been speaking. *People are encouraged when the team member first writes down an example in large letters, such as 'Visiting the sick' or 'Caring for a neighbour'.*

• When everyone has completed this, invite them to discuss, in their small groups, what they have written. You may encourage them to think, together, of other things and write these down also.

After sufficient time for sharing, invite each person to come with his/her own paper and display it in the space you have provided—one for each colour—perhaps using Blu-Tack or simply scattering on the floor.

• Read aloud the words and phrases produced by one group. Then have another person read aloud the words and phrases produced by the second group.

• Invite comments from the entire group about whatever has been written. Support, encourage and invite clarification of the comments—but do not interfere, contradict or agree. Simply allow people to express their thoughts.

Have a cup of tea. A break at this time is essential! You need a **minimum** time of forty minutes for the drama and follow-up work. The exercise is both powerful and challenging—and a break encourages further discussion to take place in a relaxed atmosphere.

Using Scripture—
related to Baptism, Call,
or Journey   15–20 mins

There are many ways of using Scripture. The following may help you.

1 • Scripture contains stories that are told to us by another person. It is helpful, therefore, if texts are provided for each person to read while at the same time **listening** to one person reading the passage aloud. This enables everyone to **hear** the word as well as read it.

2 • Invite each person to pick out a word or phrase that has meaning for him/her and write it in large print on a strip of paper (A4 cut in half lengthwise).

3 • Ask each person to display the word or phrase. They may use Blu-Tack on a wall or scatter the papers on the floor.

4 • When all the words can be clearly seen by everyone, allow a few moments for observation; then invite people, if they wish, to share the importance or significance of their chosen words or phrases.

As we talk about Scripture and listen to others sharing their thoughts and ideas we acquire the language of Christians. At the same time we grow in our knowledge of God and become more confident about speaking of him with others.

Suitable passages for this stage include:
   John 3:1–8
   Matthew 3:13–17
   Romans 6:1–11
   Matthew 28:16–20

For example: Matthew 28:16–20 reads as follows:

The eleven disciples went to the hill in Galilee where Jesus had told them to go. When they saw him, they worshipped him, even though some of them doubted. Jesus drew near and said to them, 'I have been given all authority in heaven and on earth. Go, then, to all peoples everywhere and make them my disciples: baptise them in the name of the Father, the Son and the Holy Spirit, and teach them to obey everything I have commanded you. And I will be with you always, to the end of the age.'

The following words and comments were among those produced by one group of people after reading, listening, reflecting upon and sharing that passage:
'Eleven'—One is missing. Not all are successful.
'Told them'—I trust even when I don't know fully why.
'They worshipped him'—He is God.
'Some of them doubted'—That's reassuring. Sometimes I doubt.
'Jesus drew near'—I want him to be near to me.
'Go, then'—We are sent. We should reach out more to others.
'Make them my disciples'—We have a responsibility to recruit non-believers.
'Teach them to obey'—People don't know the meaning of obedience today!
'Baptise'—This is important to me because . . .
'I will be with you always'—That's encouraging. No matter what we do or where we are, Jesus is with us always and everywhere.

Comparing other people's stories with my own

It sometimes helps us to look at the stories of other people, and to consider the way in which they responded to God and to life's journey. The Scriptures contain a multitude of suitable stories. You may like to consider the following at this particular stage of your project:

OLD TESTAMENT
Genesis 1, 2 & 12
Exodus 3; 12:1–14; 19 & 20
Isaiah 16
NEW TESTAMENT
Luke 1:26–35
Luke 3:1–18

• Offer each passage of Scripture as a story of God's work in the life of the person concerned.

• Ask the members of the group to describe how they think the person(s) in the story would have felt.

• Ask them if they ever experience similar feelings themselves. Encourage them to share stories from their own lives.

• Invite them to discuss the way in which the Scripture stories relate to their own lives and journeys in faith.

Journey of Faith
Worksheet 13

No one makes the journey of faith alone: we are helped by others ...

20–25 mins

1 • Give each person a copy of the 'Journey of Faith' worksheet 13 and pen or pencil, and assure everyone that whatever he or she puts on to the paper, it is for his or her eyes alone.

2 • Tell everyone to write his or her own name at the top of the central circle.

3 • Ask each person first to consider the circle which says, 'When I was a baby ...'. Reflect with everyone along the following lines:

When you were a baby who helped you most? Who fed you, cared for you, helped you grow into life? Write the name of that person in the circle—or put some symbol for him or her.

4 • Repeat the process for the remaining four circles, encouraging people to think back to times, people and places—and reflect on them. Do not rush; take one circle at a time. Adjust your reflection to suit the age range upon which you are dwelling, eg:

As a young teenager, who was important in your life? Who explained things, supported you, listened, understood you, shared things with you?

Note: Adjust the age ranges and your reflections to suit the group; eg if you are working with senior citizens you could alter the circles to include middle age and perhaps old age; whereas if you are working with young adults, four-to five-year blocks of time would be more appropriate.

5 • Once the five outside circles have been completed, ask each person to look back over the names or symbols and consider who has been the most important person for him or her and to write the name or symbol of that person in the central circle.

Note: This name may or may not be already on the paper.

6 • Invite each person to reflect upon:
What did the person **do**?
How did that help?
(It is important to reflect on the difference between what a person **does** and the **way in which that helps**.)

7 • People may now be invited to share with one another examples of **things that people do and how this helps**. This is best done in small groups of three or four. You may begin the discussion by sharing with everyone one of your own experiences.

Assure people that although they may share something from their paper, they must not feel that they have to do so. Their examples may be taken from any part of their lives.

What do you see? 20–25 mins

Choose a selection of visual images from Appendix 2: for example, numbers 17, 18a & b; or some of those used in the earlier stages (numbers 2a & b, 5, 6, 7, 16).

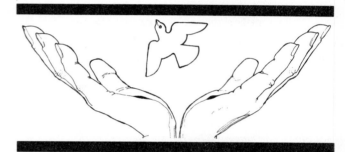

Ask the group:
What is each image conveying to you as we share our understanding of what it means to be called Christian?
What does it say about the nature of that call?
What does it say about the help and support we both give and receive as we try to come to terms with the way in which we respond to that call?

Reflections 15–30 mins

There are moments when it is important for people to have space and time to be alone so that they may think and reflect without any pressure. Material for four such periods of reflection is offered here. (You may, of course, decide to use it in some other way, eg for the period of prayer or for the final session.) Select one piece—or use some other material that you feel would be appropriate for the people with whom you are working. Some songs and hymns can provide very useful material, especially if they also have a melody that sustains a reflective atmosphere. The material may be presented to the group as a whole—but allow people time to reflect upon it on their own.

1 Jesus once said, 'What you have hidden from the learned and the wise, you have revealed to the merest children.' Remembering those words, let us reflect on something that was said by a child who never reached the age of eight. The extract is taken from the book *Mister God, this is Anna* by Fynn.

'Mister God made everything, didn't he?'
'Yes.'
'Even the dirt and the stars and the animals and the people and the trees and everything, and the pollyiogs?'. . . .
I said, 'Yes, He made everything.'
'Does Mister God love us truly?'
'Sure thing,' I said, 'Mister God loves everything.'
'Oh,' she said. 'Well then, why does he let things get hurt and dead?' Her voice sounded as if she had betrayed a sacred trust, but the question had been thought and it had to be spoken.
'I don't know,' I replied. 'There's a great many things about Mister God that we don't know about.'
'Well, then,' she continued, 'if we don't know many things about Mister God, how do we know he loves us?' . . . she hurried on: 'Them pollyiogs, I could love them till I bust, but they wouldn't know, would they? I'm a million times bigger than they are and Mister God is a million times bigger than me, so how do I know that Mister God does?

'Fynn, Mister God doesn't love us.' She hesitated. 'He doesn't really, you know, only people can love. I love Bossy, but Bossy don't love me. I love you, Fynn, and you love me, don't you?
'You love me because you are people. I love Mister God truly, but he don't love me.
'No,' she went on, 'no, he don't love me, not like you do, it's different, it's millions of times bigger. 'Fynn, you can love better than any people that ever was, and so can I, can't I? But Mister God is different. You see, Fynn, people can only love outside and can only kiss outside, but Mister God can love you right inside, and Mister God can kiss you right inside, so it's different. Mister God ain't like us; we are a little bit like Mister God but not much yet.'

Allow time for quiet reflection.

2 ## God the Creator and Israel the Creature

This meditation is based on Isaiah 45: 9–12

Speak this slowly and quietly, in your own words, adapting to suit the group where necessary. Allow plenty of time between the phrases so that 'feeling' may speak to people.

Sit comfortably, relax and, if you prefer to do so, close your eyes. We are going to make use of fantasy.

Imagine you are in a pottery and you are the potter. In front of you is a lifeless, shapeless lump of clay. Have a good look at it. Pick it up.

Turn it over in your hands. Feel it. What will you make it into? Will it be something fragile or something strong; something decorative or something useful?

It is **your** choice, **your** decision. You are the creator.

Begin to shape it. Feel the sensation of power and control as you shape, form, give meaning to this clay.

Experience not only the power going out from you, from your body, through your shoulders, arms, hands and fingers, but also feel the love. You are giving something of yourself, something of your ideal of beauty and goodness to mere clay.

Without you it would be nothing more than that. Now it is in your image.

Can the clay now rebel . . . argue with you . . . question your skill or your taste . . . dictate?

Identify now with the clay. As you spin round on the wheel, feel the potter's hands and fingers touching you, moulding you, giving you shape and meaning, beauty and purpose.

Experience your complete dependence on him: 'I am in your hands.' Sense his power 'informing' you, giving you form.

Sense his love sharing something of his own life and being with you, his creature.

You may like to precede or follow this reflection with some time spent in working with clay or plasticine. Depending upon the nature of your group, it may be good for them to share their feelings—both about their task as creator and about the shapes that they create, especially if they talk about these in the first person. It will help them if, for example, you begin by stating something like, 'I am a bowl . . . unfinished . . . in need of some decoration.'

You may also like to use slides or posters during the meditation.

3 These words are taken from a song by
The Fisherfolk. You may like to use the
recording—*Celebrate the whole of it*—rather than
simply read the words. This reflection would
be enhanced by the use of slides or posters.

> The Word of the Lord came to Jeremiah saying:
> Go down to the house of the Potter.
> Watch him work the clay.
> Listen to what I say as you watch him.
> Go down to the house of the Potter.
> Watch him turn his wheel.
> Know that's how I feel as I'm working.
>
> That is how I need to mould you,
> Form a vessel in my hand.
> Just to let me have and hold you,
> Break you, mould you to my plan.
>
> Go down to the house of the Potter.
> Watch him work the clay.
> Listen to what I say as you watch him.
> Go down to the house of the Potter.
> Watch him turn his wheel.
> Know that's how I feel as I'm working.
>
> For I need these earthen vessels
> filled with life that overflows.
> Put my treasure in earthen vessels,
> then the skill of the Potter shows.
>
> So I went down to the House of the Potter
> and there he was working at his wheel.
> Sometimes the vessel would spoil in
> his hands . . .
> and he would rework it as it was fitting
> for him to do.

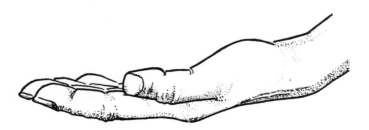

The Potter's Song, words and music by Jonathan Asprey.
© Celebration, administered in Europe by Thankyou
Music, PO Box 75, Eastbourne, E Sussex BN23 6NW.
Reprinted by permission.

4 Read and discuss the Gospel for the second
Sunday of Advent. (Whichever year it is, the
reference is to John the Baptist baptising in the
River Jordan.)

Play *Bridge over troubled water* or some other
suitable music.

Show various slides of water and baptism.

Spread posters, photographs and magazine
pictures about the room.

Invite people to spend some time alone with
their thoughts—to ponder. They may make use
of whatever illustrations they like, to help them
to focus their thoughts, if they so wish.

The Diamond, Kite, Eye or Mirror 20–25 mins

1 • Give each person a copy of the 'Diamond'
worksheet (14). Ask each one to write his or her name
inside the top corner of the diamond.

Diamond . . .   Worksheet 14.

2 • Invite everyone to be alone and to imagine that
they have a special mirror which enables them to
look into places so that they can see and hear people
without being seen.

3 • **First Section: FRIEND**
Encourage each one to imagine that s/he can see
and hear her/his best friend talking to someone else
about her/her . . . What is the friend saying? How
does the friend feel about him/her?
Allow a few moments for thought, then invite
each person to put in the appropriate section—in
sign, symbol or words—whatever was being said or
expressed. Reassure everyone that whatever is put
on the paper, it will be for his or her eyes only.

4 • When all have completed that section, move on to the others in turn, each time setting the scene.

Second Section: PARENT

What do your parents say about you?
How do they feel about you?

Third Section: BOSS

What does your boss / headteacher / social worker / employment officer / foreman / etc (ie whichever 'authority' figure is relevant) say about you? How does s/he feel about you?

Fourth Section: MYSELF

What would you say about yourself?
How do you feel about yourself?

The Diamond: GOD

This is the Ojo de Dios – the Eye of God. It is seen in a variety of art forms in many different cultures. Red Indian tribes often weave them, in wool or beads, as prayers, each colour expressing a feeling, making a statement about life or asking for help. Very small ones, for example, are attached to arrow heads, asking God to guide them in the search for food. Among the most beautiful are the large ones seen in churches.

The diamond, then, is God. Look into your special mirror. What is he saying about you? How does he feel about you?

5 • When everyone has completed the paper, invite each person to look back over whatever s/he has written—as if s/he was reading a report about him or herself. Suggest that for each section they give themselves a mark out of twenty—twenty being perfect!

6 • Ask each person to add up the marks and write down the total out of 100.

7 • Being sure to keep the tone light-hearted, invite each person to indicate his or her mark. For example, how many scored between zero and fifteen? fifteen and thirty? Do this in the large group. Have a few moments' 'buzz', holding in mind that a low mark **may** be the result of honesty and courage; but very often it reflects a lack of self-worth. Be ready, therefore, to provide support should this be needed. Each one of us is, after all, 'God's work of art,' (Eph 2:10), and who are we to criticise his work?

8 • **Encourage reflection on the report,** but be sure to respect people's privacy about what they have written. This exercise will be done best in small groups, each one led by a team member who may use the following ideas to help discussion. Present only one idea at a time, allowing some discussion before proceeding to the next idea.

• Does God's view differ from our own? If anyone expresses difficulty about this area, point out that although God does know everything, it is important for us sometimes to let him tell us that he knows and understands; that he does not form opinions about us, nor does he ever leave us.

• How do you feel about your report?

• Did you learn anything about yourself as you completed the report? Indicate that we learn a lot about ourselves by noticing how we behave in different situations and how different people respond when we are with them. The opinions of others convey a lot to us.

• Part of us is hidden—not only from others, but also from ourselves. Occasionally something happens that throws a light upon those hidden areas—and we understand a little bit more about our own being. People, especially those who love us, help us to grow in our understanding of those hidden parts—but such growth is rarely easy, comfortable or predictable. Life is full of surprises! (You may like to share an example of such a moment of growth in your own life.)

• We come to understand life slowly, gradually. When we were conceived, each one of us was but a single cell with little, if any, understanding of a vast universe of life. The whole universe was there before we came into existence. We had to grow into it gradually, and, indeed, are still doing so! This includes our growing in the knowledge and understanding of God. It is all right to feel confused and unsure at times; it is a normal part of growing and maturing in life and in faith.

Prayer Celebration 10–15 mins

Three different prayer celebrations are offered for the end of this stage of the project. Select and adapt whichever one you feel is most suitable for your particular group.

1

Through our Baptism we are called to be Christians

You will need: a table, covered with a cloth, on which is standing a large candle, a bowl of water, some salt and some flowers (*probably this will have formed your focal point for the session*); and copies of the 'Baptism' worksheet (15).

Baptism. . .   Worksheet 15

1 • Invite everyone to move his or her chair to form groups of four or five. Ask that the chairs be arranged in semicircles around the table, with the open end of the semicircle nearest to the table.

2 • Distribute copies of the 'Baptism' worksheet (15).

3 • Allow a short time for people to complete the papers individually and quietly.

4 • Invite them to share their responses with one another—in their small groups—for five or six minutes.

5 • After sufficient time has been allowed for discussion, direct attention to the table upon which there is the water, salt, candle and flowers.

6 • A priest or one of the team sprinkles salt over the water, as a symbol of savouring the blessings we received at our baptism.

7 • He or she then prays over the water:
God our Father, we ask you to bless this water. It is a sign of our baptism, the sacrament that celebrated our new life in Jesus. May we remember that we are called to share that life with others. Grant that, through our sharing, we may be made one in the

Spirit who calls us to holiness. We ask this through Jesus Christ, our Lord.
All: **Amen.**

8 • Each person is then invited to share his or her life in Christ with others. In pairs, all—in turn—go up to the water. One by one, each dips his or her thumb into the water and then signs the other on the forehead, saying:
Name, remember the life to which you were called through your baptism. In the name of the Church, I send you forth to share that life with the people of God.
All: **Amen.**
(While this is happening, you may like to sing a hymn such as *Love is flowing like a river* or *Oh living water, refresh my soul*; or you may prefer to play some gentle music.)

9 • When everyone is once again seated in the semicircles, a priest or one of the team concludes with these or similar words:
The water has reminded us of our baptism and of the call made to each one of us to be Christians. Let us renew our 'YES' to that call and live as true followers of our Lord and Saviour, Jesus Christ.

Pause for a few moments.

May God our Father inspire us to follow the example of his Son and give witness to the truth before all peoples.

May he renew us and keep us in his love.

May almighty God bless us, the Father, and the Son and the Holy Spirit.

All: **Amen.**

End with a hymn, eg *Come down, O love divine*, or *My God said to me, 'Follow'*.

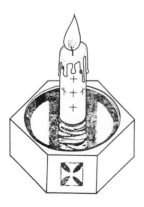

2

All our family, our friends, all we do, try do to, all we fail in, succeed in, all are important to him. We are given his life and become like him

You will need: a table, covered with a cloth, on which are standing a bowl of water and a large candle in a steady holder. (You may be able to use the baptismal font and/or the Easter candle.) If you have a large group, provide extra bowls and candles, eg one for every twenty people.

(Be prepared to darken the room for the period of prayer.)

1 • **A member of the team introduces the prayer**:
• Each year a new Easter candle is blessed and lit at the beginning of the Easter Vigil. Its new flame, flaring to life in the darkness of Easter Night, is a symbol of the new life of Jesus, risen from the dead.
• At our baptism we celebrated the fact that we share in this new life of Jesus. Symbolising this, each of us was given a candle, lit from the flame of the Easter candle. Most of us were too young to hold this candle ourselves, so it was held for us by one of our parents or Godparents.

2 • Someone now lights the large candle.

3 • The lights of the room are turned off and everyone is invited to sit for a few moments in silence, reflecting upon the light cast by the candle flame.

4 • A team member picks up the lighted candle and continues:

We and all the people in our lives are blessed by God and are always close to him, even though we or they may not always appear to recognise that fact. All we do, try to do, and succeed in doing—everything and everyone is important on our journey in life and in faith. Through them all, we are slowly being made more Christlike.

At this moment in time, are you willing to hold your baptismal candle **yourself**? Are you willing to say 'YES' to God and to all that has happened since you celebrated being part of his family?

For a few moments, think about all the people in your life. Silently, in your mind, name them.

Think about where they are now and what they are doing.
(Pause)

Now reflect upon all your own hopes and dreams, both for yourselves and for your families and/or friends, at home, at work, at school. Think especially about those who are in greatest need of love and support at this time, for whatever reason.

5 • A priest or one of the team members then raises the bowl of water and prays in these or similar words:
God our Father, you are our creator. We ask you to bless this water. It is a sign of our baptism, the sacrament that celebrated our new life in Jesus, your Son. May we always remember that you called us to share that life with others. Grant that we may be filled with the Holy Spirit who gives life to this water and continue to grow in holiness. In sharing your life with others may we be made one in the Spirit. We ask this through Jesus Christ, our Lord.
All: **Amen**

6 • One of the team explains that each one, in turn, is invited to immerse the candle in the bowl of water, symbolising the fact that we bring our lives—with all our experiences and relationships—and place them in Christ.

7 • Another team member moves from her/his seat and takes hold of the candle which s/he then places slowly and deliberately into the water. S/he pauses, holding it steady, then removes it, dries it with the towel and hands it to the next person, saying,
This is the light of Christ.

8 • Those who so wish, come forward and do the same.
You may like to have soft, reflective music in the background.

9 • When all have finished, the priest or one of team holds the candle in one hand and sprinkles the water—the bowl being carried by a second person—over all the people present. S/he then prays in the following or similar words:

May God bless us and make us holy. May he give us health of mind and body and help us to be always faithful to him. May he protect us from all that is evil and fill us with his peace. We ask this through Jesus Christ, our Lord.
All: **Amen**

3

Praying together

1 • Towards the end of the session, people sit in pairs and each person writes down ONE thought arising from the material through which the group has worked.

2 • Using their two thoughts together, each pair prepares a short prayer.

3 • Everyone gathers around the focal point (eg a table on which are arranged flowers and a candle) and the lights are dimmed.

4 • The prepared prayers are shared and, depending upon the group with whom you are working, you may also like to allow some time for spontaneous prayer.

5 • A priest or one of the team members closes the period of prayer with a blessing, possibly using one of those suggested for the prayer celebrations above.

Celebrating Stage Three with the Parish
Called to be Christian

The special focus of this Mass is the Renewal of Baptismal Vows and the commitment of each person to a time of renewal or preparation. The whole congregation is asked to support those taking part in the project by both their prayer and their encouragement.

As with all Masses, this is a community affair. A symbolic expression of 'belonging' may help to develop a sense of community. For example, the parish may present each person with a decorated baptismal candle, a copy of the seal or crest of the parish, or a photograph taken on some special parish occasion.

Suggestions to help you prepare your Celebration

Select and adapt those that suit your local situation.

1 • The opening prayer may focus on the Christian family to which we belong.

2 • The Renewal of Baptismal Vows follows the homily. Because this involves a turning away from sin and turning in faith to God, this replaces the Penitential Rite and the Creed.

3 • After the renewal of baptismal promises, the people may be sprinkled with blessed water. You may like to have the members of the project group sprinkled individually at the chair, after which the priest moves through the church sprinkling the rest of the congregation. Alternatively, **everyone** in the church may be invited to come forward to the blessed water, dip their hands into it (allowing it to flow through their fingers) and bless themselves. A suitable hymn or chant may be sung while this is happening.

4 • The following Rite of Commitment may follow the sprinkling with water. The wording of it should be adapted to suit the particular group with whom you are working.

Rite of Commitment

All sit. The president addresses all:

> The faith we have proclaimed is God's gift to us and when we gather together as a community of faith we are guided and inspired by the Holy Spirit. Those of us who have been baptised in water and the Holy Spirit have received the gifts which the

Spirit pours out upon his people for the building up of the Body of Christ which is the Church. They include the gifts of wisdom, understanding, right judgement, courage, knowledge, love of God and awe in his presence. These gifts are given to us that we might share them with others and thus spread the love of Christ throughout the world.

We have all been made one with Christ in Baptism. When we celebrate the Eucharist we are celebrating the presence of the Risen Lord with us and within us. Today we welcome in a special way this group of people, members of our parish family who are ....

....

(eg preparing for the sacrament of Confirmation)
We must support them with our prayers and encouragement as they continue on their journey of faith.

Those who are NOT *taking part in the project are invited to stand.*
The president addresses them as follows:

Do you acknowledge that the gifts of the Holy Spirit are given for the good of the whole Church?
All: **We do.**

Do you, therefore, joyfully receive and accept these members of our parish who are..

....
All: **We do.**

Do you promise to support them during their project?
All: **We do.**

Do you promise to share in their project by your prayers, your encouragement and your example of Christian living?
All: **We do.**

All sit. Those involved in the project are invited to stand.
The president addresses them:

Dear sons and daughters, the Church invites you to grow ever more deeply into Christ. God, through us, makes that invitation. Only YOU can decide how you will respond.

In the initial stages of the project you have been involved in sharing your faith with others, in learning about your faith, in activities and in sacred celebrations. These have all marked your progress on your own personal journey in faith.

Our forefathers in faith, the people of Israel, entered into a covenant with God. Likewise, you now commit yourselves to living and sharing your faith as fully as possible with this parish community and with all those with whom you come into contact. We thank God for you, that you have made this commitment and, as you continue to grow and develop in faith, we wholeheartedly support you with our prayers and our help.

I now ask you to declare before us all your firm intention to ....
'..
Do you realise that the project in which you are involved will lead you to a deeper commitment as a member of the Church?
Those involved in the project: **We do.**

Do you understand that we, the Church, want you to participate as fully as possible in the project?
Those involved in the project: **We do.**

Do you willingly enter into this commitment with our parish, eager to cooperate and share in the development of the project?
Those involved in the project: **We do.**

Do you acknowledge that the gifts of the Holy Spirit are to be used for the service of others and for the building up of the People of God?
Those involved in the project: **We do.**

May God, who has begun this work in you, give you the strength and determination to bring it to fulfilment.
All: **Amen, amen, amen.**

Applause, possibly followed by the sign of peace, would be appropriate at this time. (In fact, historically the sign of peace came at this point in the Mass, as a bridge between the liturgy of the Word and the Liturgy of the Eucharist.)
President: In the name of this parish, I accept your commitment, which you will shortly sign and place on the altar, thus signifying the solemnity of your undertaking and your oneness with Christ whose sacrifice we celebrate.

Those involved in the project now come forward, one by one, as their names are called out by a member of the team. They go to the altar where they sign a copy of the commitment they have made. (While this is happening, a suitable hymn may be sung quietly or background music may be played softly.)

5 • The celebration continues as usual, hymns following the themes of 'belonging' and 'discipleship', e.g.

God's Spirit is in my heart;
Follow Christ and love the world as he did;
I heard the Lord call my name;
My God said to me 'Follow';
Oh the word of my Lord.

6 • The parish holds a social gathering after the celebration.

7 • Produce greetings cards to be sent by those members of the parish not directly involved in the project to those who are. They may be designed by one of your parishioners. Inside them have simple words of encouragement and an assurance that someone is praying for the person to whom the card is sent. The cards may be left in the porch of the church to be taken by members of the congregation, but they may also be taken to those members of the parish who are house-bound – thus giving them an opportunity to play an active role in the life of the parish. (Be sure to devise some means by which everyone involved receives a card! You may, for example, type out the envelopes or leave a list of names and addresses to be ticked by those who send the cards.)

Stage Four

Empowered by the Spirit

Introduction

People all over the world use many signs and symbols which express something of their understanding of life. **Symbols are often expressions of profound thoughts or ideas** that cannot be explained adequately in a few words. This means that, although we may try to convey our own personal understanding of a symbol, each person will interpret it in his or her own way, the interpretation being subject to such things as culture, age and experience of life. Thus the **meaning** of a symbol may be enriched with the passage of time; it may change completely, or it may disappear altogether.

As Christians, we use many powerful signs and symbols. It is important, however, that we try to develop our understanding of them—otherwise they become empty, meaningless expressions of our faith.

At this stage of the project, time and space are provided for people to examine, experience and be challenged by some of the signs and symbols used by their own parish community—a group that is familiar with them as expressions of God's transforming power and authority. This also enables the group to discern the way in which events and material things are transformed, changed or take on new meaning when experienced within a powerful, living relationship with the Risen Lord.

Jesus Christ, the Risen Lord, is THE most amazing sign of all time! Jesus of Nazareth was executed, died and was buried. But by rising to new life—to a life filled with great power and authority, he completely transformed the meaning of those events and thus became **the** sign of God's presence and power in the world.

Christians who know and love the Risen Lord are also radical signs of God's presence and power in the world, because they have come to understand life in a very different way from those who have not yet experienced the transforming nature of the power of God. They joyfully celebrate their understanding of this truth in a number of different ways, using the many signs and symbols of the sacraments.

Sacraments are not merely **signs** of grace but are **agents** of grace. They do not simply inform, but also transform. They both celebrate realities already present in our lives **and** give those realities a new dimension. They are powerful, creative symbols that manifest the presence and glory of God and effect change in all those who are touched by them. For example, **the water used to celebrate the sacrament of Baptism** is a sign of rebirth; of new life; of a new beginning—in and through the community. **Those of us who enter this water are made whole, our consciousness is transformed and we share in the renewed, risen life of Jesus Christ, our Lord.** Water, however, can be a means of salvation or destruction. It can be a sign of life or of death—an important aspect of baptism. Jesus twice referred to his future death as 'a baptism' (Mk 10:38; Lk 12:50). His death was the climax of his service, the moment of total baptism. The same is true for all of us who are baptised into Christ. Following his example and filled with the strength of his Spirit, we endeavour to respond positively to Jesus' question, 'Can you drink the cup that I must drink? Can you be baptised in the way I must be baptised?' (Mk 10:38). When we understand this, we realise that baptism is not something that is completed with a celebration at the font! It is, rather, **a new beginning**.

During baptism we are anointed with **chrism**, a holy oil that is an important symbol with profound meaning. It is a sign that each of us is called upon to become another Christ, sharing in the prophetic, priestly and kingly mission of Jesus. As we are anointed, we hear the words 'Be sealed with the gift of the Holy Spirit'—a sign that our relationship with God has been sealed by the Holy Spirit, who is with us always and everywhere, to protect us from all that would harm us, and empower us with spiritual gifts.

The celebration of the Passover meal is a very special occasion for the Jews, rich in symbolism. When he celebrated this meal with his friends, Jesus invested it with new and important meaning. Over the bread and wine he said, 'This is my body . . . This is my blood.' Then, 'Do this in remembrance of me.' What Christ declared is true, and this truth is fulfilled every time the Eucharist is celebrated. **Bread and wine are transformed, becoming the body and blood of the Risen Lord Jesus Christ, truly present, in and among us, with power and authority**. The bread and wine are symbols of the **reality** we receive in Communion: the Risen Jesus, who comes to us in order to feed us and transform our entire being. There is no limit to his ability to act, restore, heal, guide or forgive, and he calls us to follow in his footsteps.

Jesus chose wine—a drink that gladdens the heart, **a sign of life and joy**—as the sign of his blood, shed for us. Life and joy are interwoven with sacrifice. 'A grain of wheat remains no more than a single grain unless it falls to the ground and dies'(Jn 12:24). On the cross, Jesus poured out his life so that we might live. When we remember Jesus in the breaking of bread and the drinking of wine, we take part in the Paschal mystery, directly sharing in the great mystery of his life, death and resurrection. If we have truly grasped even a fraction of the meaning of this mystery, then it is something we celebrate with joy.

Our illustration of this stage of the project is based on a small group celebration of the Eucharist. Signs and symbols of this central mystery of our faith are explored, allowing people time to reflect upon them and be challenged by them. Most of the prayers suggested are those of Eucharistic Prayer IV, as used by the Roman Catholic Church. The general format, however, can be adapted easily for use with non-communicant members of the Church who are exploring the rich symbolism of our faith, or by members of other churches, should they so wish. The Liturgy of the Word is suitable for use with any group.

Materials you may need for Stage Four
- low (coffee) table, with flowers and baptismal (Easter) candle
- the parish's phial of chrism oil
- cassette or record player, and suitable music

For the Eucharist:
table, covered with a cloth • paten(s) • chalice(s) corporal • stole • altar breads • wine purificators • finger towels • water • flowers

For each person:
- three small cards or pieces of paper
- OR two of the above and the Worksheet (16) 'I am gifted'
- pen or pencil
- one small candle
- hand-out of host drawing

Welcome and Introduction 5 mins
Arrange the room so that your focal point for the first part of the evening is the large (Easter) candle, set on a low table with a floral arrangement. Another table should be prepared ready for the celebration of the Eucharist. Have it ready so that, when you begin the second part of the session, either people may easily move their chairs around that table or it may be moved easily to a more suitable position.

Welcome everyone and then light the large candle.

Explain that, during this session, we are going to explore the way in which the Christian, in meeting the Risen Lord, enters a new world where both events and things have new meaning. We are going to look at the way in which God transforms and empowers our lives if we allow him to do so. (*If you are going to celebrate the Eucharist during this session, be sure to tell people that fact either at the beginning of your session or at the end of the previous one.*)

A story of Change 25–30 mins

The first four Disciples are called (Luke 5:1–11)

Before presenting this story to the group be sure to reflect upon it yourself, and notice how it relates to your own journey in faith. The notes given below are to help you both in your own reflections and in your preparation for the session.

Some notes about this story

In this story Luke is at pains to show us what happens to Peter when he first experiences who Jesus really is. The evangelist tells similar stories about other people who all experience the same pattern of emotions, feelings and changes in their lives when they meet Jesus.

We need to remember that Luke wrote this story with hindsight—**after** Jesus had risen from the dead. Peter's experiences are shared by all of us who meet the Risen Lord.

Luke himself has experienced being changed by knowing Jesus Christ, and he identifies with others who have also been transformed and converted. He has a deep understanding of the Christian life and all its mysteries, and is very perceptive about the way these affect the mind and heart. This is the reflected in the way he describes the changes that occur as men and women progress, step by step, on their spiritual journey.

In this story we see that the **first step** is that Peter is **chosen** by Jesus. The **second step** is that Peter **listens as Jesus speaks**. He is there, on the side, looking and listening, and somehow being drawn towards this man.

The **third step** is that Jesus issues an **invitation** to Peter—but it has a **challenging** edge to it! 'Put out into deep water,' says Jesus. But Peter is a professional! He knows there are no fish out there! What should he do? The crowd know he has been invited to move out into deep water; what will they think if he refuses? And what will they think if he goes?

Peter finds a compromise. 'But if YOU say so . . .' Despite his feelings of unease Peter wants to stay with Jesus, so he decides to take a risk, even if he does end up looking a fool in front of the others.

The **fourth step** is that Peter **does** go out into deep water. The move made by Peter is crucial; it is a

personal act. Each one of us responds in his or her own way once we have been chosen, have listened to the Lord and have been invited by him – to move out into deep water. The calm, unruffled water of the harbour is so much safer, so much more secure, than the deep water!

Illustration 19

The **fifth step** is that there is **a manifestation of the power of God**. In Peter's case there were fish where, previously, there had been no fish. For other people, the manifestation may be made in the form of forgiveness, or a change in relationships or circum▮▮▮▮, or healing. Whatever happens, the impo▮▮▮▮▮g is that the individual senses, in a very▮▮▮▮ both the close presence of God and a h▮▮▮ awareness of God's power.

The ▮▮▮▮p is that Peter is overwhelmed by fear. So▮▮▮▮g new, unpredictable, powerful and challengi▮▮▮as happened – and he is there in the middle of it! His familiar world has suddenly changed, and he is shaken! The fear pervades his whole being and he wants to get away from it, to escape. 'Leave me, Lord,' he says to Jesus, seeing him as the cause of his terror. But that is not the case. The fear has been inside Peter all the time.

He is not free to rejoice or respond to the truth he sees before him, because it exposes his state of sin, alienation, damage and hurt. 'I am a sinful man,' he says, falling on his knees.

'Do not be afraid,' Jesus says to Peter. His words have an authority and power that is absolute. What he says will take place, does take place. The truth of what Jesus says is fulfilled, and Peter is free of all fear. This powerful action of Jesus is the **seventh step** of Peter's spiritual journey.

It takes a long time before the **eighth step** is fully realised, but this is the moment of initial transformation. Peter is changed. His giftedness, personality and experience of life are going to be used by God in a very special way. He has qualities of leadership; a shrewd way of judging people; and the fishing skills of patience, determination, survival in moments of danger and persistence in times of hardship. All are needed for the work Jesus wants him to do.

Not one of these skills is wasted when Peter leaves all to follow Jesus. Instead they are taken up by Jesus and used in a way that Peter never dreamed would be possible. What makes this story so compelling is that this pattern of spiritual development is true for all Christians when they respond to Jesus' invitation, risk all and 'pull out into deep water'.

Presenting the story of Peter to the group

1 • Ask everyone to locate the story in his or her Bible (Luke 5:1–11)
2 • Invite one person to read the story aloud, clearly and slowly, while everyone else listens and follows the text.
3 • Allow a short period of silence for the story to be received.
4 • Invite people to offer any word o̶ ̶ ̶ ̶that seems important to them. They need n̶ ̶ ̶ ̶ny explanation; the word or phrase is, itse̶ ̶ ̶ ̶t. Be sure to offer your own word or phra̶
5 • Invite each person to explore the ̶ ̶ ̶ perhaps identify with what is happenin̶ ̶ Peter. Do this in small groups of three to five. The questions below are offered as a guide.

*(We have found it better to present the questions one at a time, allowing sufficient time for discussion before proceeding to the next one. When we have given a hand-out with all the questions printed, people have not moved through the story but have remained discussing one particular aspect. The intention here is that people see the **overall** pattern of this part of Peter's spiritual journey and recognise its relationship to their own journey in faith. The notes given on the previous page and the following questions should help you.)*

Questions for discussion

1 • Why does Peter hesitate about going out again to fish?
2 • There is a crowd on the lake shore. What thoughts do you think this fact may cause to run through Peter's mind as he tries to decide what to do?
3 • Is Peter sure about what he is doing when he decides to pull out into the deep water again?
4 • What kind of character do you think Peter has?
5 • The huge catch of fish is dramatic! Why is Peter overcome by it?
6 • What causes Peter to say, 'Leave me, Lord, for I am a sinful man'? What feelings do you think he has as he says that? Of what is he aware?
7 • Peter is briefly exposed to the truth but the feelings and awareness that he experiences do not last long—because Jesus is quick to act. What does Jesus do?
8 • This event was a very special moment in Peter's life. His experience and giftedness as a fisherman are very important—but Jesus changes the way in which they are to be used. A major upheaval occurs in Peter's life. He, himself, is changed. What gifts, talents and experiences would Peter have as a fisherman? In what ways would these be important to Jesus? How would Jesus use them? How is Peter changed—and what does he do about it?

Recognising our own gifts and talents

After the group has had time to discuss Peter's gifts and talents, as well as the change that took place in him, and his response, give each person a plain piece of card or paper. Invite each one, alone, to reflect upon his or her own God-given gifts and talents.

Note: Depending upon the nature of your group, you may find the 'I am gifted' worksheet (16), suggested below, helpful at this time.

After a short while, ask each person to focus his or her attention upon one gift in particular. Invite each person to write this gift down on the card or paper, perhaps suggesting that this be done in the form of a sentence in which God is thanked for his gift and the use the person is able to make of it.

Each person may like to sign his or her statement—then ask that it be put aside, in a safe place, until later.

AN ALTERNATIVE APPROACH

I am gifted   Worksheet 16

'I am Gifted';
a list of gifts which may help your group

All of us have many gifts and talents that we take very much for granted—unless, by some misfortune, we lose them. Some of us have also been taught to feel we are being 'proud' or are 'blowing our own trumpet' if we dare to acknowledge any of our personal gifts and talents. Yet every single one of them has been given to us by God, and to deny them is to deny the God who created them. We have found that a list, such as the example offered in worksheet 16, has not only helped people to overcome the psychological barrier they have to recognising and acknowledging their God-given gifts and talents, but it has also caused them to be filled with an overwhelming sense of gratitude. You may find it helpful to use such a hand-out at this time, adapting the list of suggested gifts to suit your own group if necessary.

A story of the Christian mystery of Faith 20–30 mins

Through Baptism each one of us is called and empowered to work for the transformation of the society in which we live and the building up of the kingdom of God. The following true story is about Maximilian Kolbe, a Polish Franciscan priest who was born in 1894 in Lodz and died on 14 August 1941, having given his life for a fellow prisoner.

At the time of his death, Maximilian was 47 years old. He had been a stubborn man, a fact that often caused an awkwardness in his relationships with others. Some people were irritated by his dogmatism and moral righteousness; by his blunt way of stating facts and by his rather self-centred manner. It took almost his whole lifetime for him to grow more and more into Christ, and for his view of life to be transformed to embrace everyone, irrespective of his or her morals or beliefs. Gradually he became more loving and loyal to the people in his life. His qualities of tenacity became a rich source of goodness in serving others. In the death camps there was a very clear growth in his ability to survive, to hang on, to remain beside people, and to enter into the pain and fear of others.

Maximilian's true qualities like Peter's, had been his from the day of his birth. The Risen Lord, however, called them forth and empowered them in a very special way. The way in which Maximilian accompanied others in their pain and terror is a striking example of God's abiding ministry to us. In him we see the priesthood of the Risen Jesus, who walks with us into death and new life.

The story shows us a particular aspect of priesthood that hints at an inner meaning of the sacraments as signs of transformation. It also serves to remind us that, through our baptism, we are all called to fulfil a priestly role of service among the people of God. This we do when we remain with those who are sick, depressed, dying, afraid or hurt—gradually growing more and more into Christ.

The story of Maximilian Kolbe may be read aloud to the group, as it is written here, or you may prefer to tell it in your own words.

Note: A 'hunger cell' was a tiny concrete box in which there was a small air vent—only 10 cm × 6 cm. Ten people were stripped naked and packed into it to starve to death.

We come to 30 July 1941. In Block 14 where Fr Kolbe is, a prisoner is missing, another escape. And the prisoners remember with terror the head officer's threat that for each fugitive twenty men of his block would be condemned to die of starvation.

That night no one in the barracks slept. Those wretched men, broken down with the most refined tortures, who often longed for death as a release, were overcome with mortal fear. To die by the executioner's bullet, well and good; but to die of hunger is the most dreadful of all deaths. In the camp tales were told on this subject which froze the blood in their veins. Sometimes they heard howlings like animals coming from the torture cell. Fr Kolbe comforted them and heard their confessions. To a boy trembling at his side he whispered, 'Are you afraid, my child? But death is nothing to be afraid of.'

The next morning at roll-call the head of the camp announced that the fugitive had not been found. He gave orders to disperse the ranks of all the blocks except Block 14. Hours passed, midday came, then in the evening when the men came back from work, Block 14 was still there, standing to attention, awaiting the sentence.

The Camp Commandant, Fritz, stops before the ranks. He calls out, 'The fugitive has not been found. Ten of you will die for him, in the hunger cell. Next time twenty of you will be condemned.' He passes along the front ranks, he looks each one in the face, seems to consider, then chooses, 'This one.' The man leaves the ranks. In the silence their hissing breaths sound like a moan. 'This one and this one' and then 'that one'.

Ten of them. Ten condemned to death. One of them cries out in a stifled voice, 'My poor wife, my poor children.' Those remaining in the ranks breath again. Suddenly the unexpected happens.

A prisoner leaves the ranks. How daring he is! His head is slightly to one side, his great eyes stare into the amazed face of Fritz. That officer seizes his revolver, steps back a pace, shouts out, 'Halt, what does the swine want?' Fr Maximilian stands before him. He speaks so quietly that his comrades in the front rank hardly hear him. 'Will you allow me to die in the place of one of the condemned men?' Fritz looks at him, dumbfounded. He is silent for a minute.

Then he asks, 'Who are you? A Catholic priest? Whose place do you want to take?' 'That one's.' Father Kolbe points to the man who has just complained. 'And what for?' 'Because I am old and useless. My life is no longer of any account, whilst he has a family.' The Camp Commandant thinks for a minute, then makes a sign with his hand. It means 'Yes'. Father Maximilian joins the condemned men. For a brief moment there is a profound silence. No one quite understands what has just happened. Father Maximilian is calm and radiant.

In the death block, kept to this day, there is a cell where the condemned were locked up, naked. From this moment nothing more is given them to eat and what is much more dreadful, nothing more to drink. They will stay shut up until they die. A martyrdom of hunger is nothing compared to a martyrdom of thirst. In condemning himself to die of hunger during his famous strikes, Gandhi stopped eating, but he did not stop drinking. Up to this time the hunger cell (a miniature hell) resounded with the howlings of the condemned men. But this time there is something different. The SS men are not pleased about it. In this hell the condemned are praying and singing. Every day their voices become weaker, moans are heard, but they are not cries of despair. What is going on there? On 14 August, a fortnight after their confinement, Fr Kolbe was the sole survivor. The prison warder finished him off with a carbolic injection. The gang of men sent to clean up found him sitting on the ground, his head leaning against the wall, 'his body clean and his face radiant'. 'To see him,' continued the witness, 'you would easily have taken him for a saint.'

(From The life of the Spirit)

Discussion points

1 • What sacraments have been celebrated in Maxmilian Kolbe's life?

2 • What understanding do you think Maximilian has of the events that lead to his death?

3 • Why do you think Maximilian remained so calm and peaceful before the Camp Commandant, Fritz, and later, when he was discovered still alive in the hunger cell?

4 • In what ways is Maximilian a sign of God's power in our world—both then, in 1941, and today?

Liturgy of the Eucharist
Preparation

Now is the time to arrange all that is needed for the eucharistic liturgy:

• the eucharistic table may be moved to a more suitable position

• the gifts are prepared.

In this celebration the 'gifts', for which we give thanks, will be represented not only by the bread and wine, but other symbols of the gifts God has given us. These are:

• our natural and spiritual gifts, represented by 'I am gifted' cards;

• our faith, represented by the candle;

• our baptismal calling, represented by the oil of chrism.

Invite everyone to gather around the table which is now prepared for the celebration of the Eucharist.

Ask each person to have his/her 'I am gifted' card ready, and give two more pieces of paper or card to everyone.

Introduce the next stage of the session/celebration using the ideas suggested below.

1 • Preparing Ourselves

A member of the team lifts up the phial of chrism oil and shows it to the people, telling them:

> This is a special oil that was blessed by the bishop at the Chrism Mass on Maundy Thursday.
> It is a sign of the Lord's power and a symbol of his anointing.
> It is not an ordinary oil. It has been invested with power by the Holy Spirit, that we may be transformed and grow into Christ. We were each anointed with chrism when we were baptised and when we were confirmed, as a sign that we are called upon to share in the prophetic, priestly and kingly mission of Jesus Christ, the 'anointed one'.
> The oil in this phial was brought from the cathedral to be used in this parish, to seal with the gift of the Holy Spirit all those who are baptised and confirmed here, thus empowering them to work for the building up of the kingdom of God.

The phial of oil is now placed on the eucharistic table.

> *Celebrant:*
> Lord, we thank you for your presence and power in your Church. We praise and thank you for all the ways in which you change and empower us. We praise and thank you for the multitude of signs and symbols you have given us, that we may come to know and love you and make your life among us manifest in our world.
> *All:* **Amen**

The celebrant now carries the phial of oil to one of the team members and gives it to him/her to hold, saying:

> This is the chrism oil, blessed by our bishop. It is a sign that we are sealed and empowered with the gift of the Holy Spirit.

Holding the phial, the team member says aloud and clearly (thus setting the example for others to follow):

> Lord, I believe. Help my unbelief.

S/he now returns the phial to the celebrant, who repeats the same action and words with each person in turn.

(You may like to have some very gentle, meditative music playing in the background, depending on the size of the whole group and how long the above action will, therefore, take. Allow time for reflection here, as the tension and fear caused by belief and unbelief is often faced and supported in these few quiet moments.)

2 • Preparing to 'Make Memory'

Invite everyone to have ready the two pieces of paper/card they have each been given.

One of the team members then

reflects aloud briefly on the presence of the Risen Lord here among us now;

reflects briefly that the presence of the Risen Lord extends beyond those present, to the whole Church, which is his body;

invites the members of the group to think of people still living—family, friends, sick, needy— for whom they would particularly like to pray during this celebration of the ucharist;

invites the members to list these people on ONE of the pieces of paper/card.

Be careful to allow sufficient time for everyone to think and write down a list of names, then

invite the members to think of dead friends and relatives for whom they would like to pray; invite the members to list those names on the SECOND piece of card/paper.

When everyone has completed both cards, invite each person to place the cards on the eucharistic table. (We have found small bread baskets make practical holders for these—marked appropriately one for the living and one for the dead. Each one may then be raised later by the celebrant at the appropriate moment of the eucharistic prayer.)

3 • Preparing our Gifts

Introduce this next part of the session, using the ideas suggested below:

a • Jesus, our Risen Lord and Saviour, is here —with us—now—just as he has been whenever we have met together before. During the Easter Vigil, a fire is lit and a special single candle is lit, as a symbol of Christ's light shining in our darkness and the experience we have of his living presence among us. The candle is carried into the church and from it each person lights his or her own small candle. The dark church becomes a sea of light as each person holds in his or her hand what he or she has become—pure light—not of his or her own making, but through Jesus. The lighted candle given to us at our baptism reminds us of that fact, and of the invitation to carry that light out into the world.

One of the members of the team now brings the large lighted candle from the low table and places it on the eucharistic table. S/he then stands back a little, points to the candle and, in a clear voice, states:

This is the light of Christ

A small candle is given to each person. While the following hymn is sung, each person comes forward to light his/her individual candle from the large one, returning then to his/ her place. (If possible, dim the lights for this so that the room is eventually illuminated by candlelight only.)

The light of Christ has come into the world.
The light of Christ has come into the world.

1. We all must be born again,
   to see the kingdom of God.
   The water and the Spirit,
   bring new life in God's love.

2. God gave up his only Son
   out of love for the world
   so that ev'ryone who believes in him
   will live for ever.

3. The light of Christ has come to us
   so that we might have salvation
   from the darkness of our sins we walk
   into the glory with Jesus Christ.

When the hymn has ended allow a few moments for silent reflection, and then invite everyone to blow out his or her candle.
A member of the team continues:

b • It is important—and natural—that we should celebrate these truths, joining ourselves to him, allowing his authority and power to act in and through us.

c • In sharing the bread and wine of the Eucharist we meet and receive the Risen Lord in a very special way. Through the power of the

The light of Christ, words and music by Donald Fishel, © Word of God Music, PO Box 8617, Ann Arbor, Michigan 48107. Reprinted by permission.

Holy Spirit, the bread and wine we offer are taken and transformed, becoming the body and blood of our Risen Lord Jesus Christ. The bread and wine are symbols of the reality we receive: the Risen Lord, who comes to us to feed us and transform our entire being. We have been sealed by the gift of the Holy Spirit, protected from all harm and evil; and even if we reject this gift and damage ourselves or others, Jesus is there to heal us and restore us to life: to change us, day by day, until we become truly other Christs.

At this, the bread and wine are presented to the celebrant, who accepts them. He places the bread on the eucharistic table, without any prayer. He then prepares the chalices, and places them on the eucharistic table, again without any prayer.

A member of the team continues:

    d • We offer not only bread and wine to be transformed, but also ourselves. On our 'gift cards' we have noted the gifts that God has given to us. We give them to him now and ask him to take them, transform them with his power and use them in whatever way he wishes. We ask him to take our entire being, to transform us and give us the courage to respond to his invitation, whatever it may be, in the way he would wish.

Each person is now invited to place his or her 'gift card'—ie his or her self—beside the bread and wine on the eucharistic table. (A small bread basket makes a suitable container for this.)

When all the gifts are ready on the eucharistic table, the celebrant raises the basket and, speaking in our name, asks the Father to accept our gifts.

    Lord, accept the gifts we bring of ourselves
    which we entrust to you with love and joy.
    May the skills created in us be transformed
    by your power to be of service in building
    your kingdom today.
    We ask this through Christ our Lord.
    All: **Amen**.

The Eucharistic Prayer

We begin the great prayer of praise and thanksgiving, of offering and of memorial. The celebrant speaks the prayer on our behalf: as the introductory dialogue reminds us, we all join together to lift up our hearts and give thanks to the Father, through Jesus Christ.

Introductory dialogue
    Celebrant: The Lord be with you.
    All: **And also with you**.
    Celebrant: Lift up your hearts.
    All: **We lift them up to the Lord**.
    Celebrant: Let us give thanks to the Lord our God.
    All: **It is right to give him thanks and praise**.

Preface and acclamation
    Celebrant:
    Father, all-powerful and ever-living God,
    we do well always and everywhere to give you
       thanks.
    We thank you now for this house of prayer
    in which you bless your family
    as we come to you on pilgrimage.
    Here you reveal your presence
    by sacramental signs,
    and make us one with you
    through the unseen bond of grace.
    Here you build your temple of living stones,
    and bring the Church to its full stature
    as the body of Christ throughout the world,
    to reach its perfection at last
    in the heavenly city of Jerusalem,
    which is the vision of your peace.
    In communion with all the angels and saints
    we bless and praise your greatness
    in the temple of your glory:

All join in the acclamation:
    Holy, holy, holy Lord, God of power and might,
    heaven and earth are full of your glory.
       Hosanna in the highest.
    Blessed is he who comes in the name of the Lord.
       Hosanna in the highest.

Praise of the Father for creation and salvation
    Father, we acknowledge your greatness:
    all your actions show your wisdom and love.
    You formed man in your own likeness
    and set him over the whole world
    to serve you, his creator,
    and to rule over all creatures.
    Even when he disobeyed you and lost your
       friendship
    you did not abandon him to the power of death,
    but helped all men to seek and find you.
    Again and again you offered a covenant to man,
    and through the prophets taught him to hope for
       salvation.

Father, you so loved the world
that in the fullness of time you sent your only Son
    to be our Saviour.
He was conceived through the power of the Holy
    Spirit,
and born of the Virgin Mary,
a man like us in all things but sin.
To the poor he proclaimed the good news of
    salvation,
to prisoners, freedom,
and to those in sorrow, joy.
In fulfilment of your will
he gave himself up to death;
but by rising from the dead,
he destroyed death and restored life.
And that we might live no longer for ourselves
    but for him,
he sent the Holy Spirit from you, Father,
as his first gift to those who believe,
to complete his work on earth
and bring us the fullness of grace.

Invocation of the Holy Spirit

Father, may this Holy Spirit sanctify these
    offerings.
Let them become the body and blood of Jesus
    Christ our Lord
as we celebrate the great mystery
which he left us as an everlasting covenant.

The Lord's Supper

He always loved those who were his own in the
    world.
When the time came for him to be glorified by
    you, his heavenly Father,
he showed the depth of his love.
While they were at supper,
he took bread, said the blessing, broke the bread,
and gave it to his disciples, saying:
Take this, all of you, and eat it:
this is my body which will be given up for
    you.

All sing:

This is my body, broken for you,
bringing you wholeness, making you free.
Take it and eat it, and when you do,
do it in love for me.

In Love for me, words and music by Jimmy Owens.
© Lexicon, administered by Cherry Lane Music, 75
High Street, Needham Market, Suffolk IP6 8AN.

The celebrant alone continues:
In the same way, he took the cup, filled with wine.
He gave you thanks, and giving the cup to his
    disciples, said:
Take this, all of you, and drink from it:
this is the cup of my blood,
the blood of the new and everlasting covenant.
It will be shed for you and for all
so that sins may be forgiven.

All sing:

This is my blood, poured out for you,
bringing forgiveness, making you free.
Take it and drink it, and when you do,
do it in love for me.

The celebrant alone continues:
Then he said to them:
Do this in memory of me.

He sings or says:
Let us proclaim the mystery of faith.

All sing:

You are Lord, you are Lord!
You are risen from the dead
    and you are Lord!
Every knee shall bow,
every tongue confess
that Jesus Christ is Lord!

Father, we now celebrate this memorial of our
    redemption.
We recall Christ's death, his descent among the
    dead,
his resurrection, and his ascension to your right
    hand;
and, looking forward to his coming in glory,
we offer you his body and blood,
the acceptable sacrifice
which brings salvation to the whole world.
Lord, look upon this sacrifice which you have
    given to your Church;
and by your Holy Spirit, gather all who share
    this one bread and one cup
into the body of Christ, a living sacrifice of praise.

For the Church

Lord, remember those for whom we offer this
    sacrifice,
especially N. our Pope,
N. our bishop, and bishops and clergy
    everywhere.

For the living

Remember those who take part in this offering,
those here present and all your people . . .
*The celebrant raises the basket containing the names of the
living for whom we wish to pray*
and all who seek you with a sincere heart.

For the dead

Remember those who have died in the peace of
Christ . . .
*The celebrant raises the basket containing the names of
those who have died for whom we wish to pray*
and all the dead whose faith is known to you alone.

In Communion with the Saints

Father, in your mercy grant also to us, your
children,
to enter into our heavenly inheritance
in the company of the Virgin Mary, the Mother
of God,
and your apostles and saints.
Then, in your kingdom, freed from the corruption
of sin and death,
we shall sing your glory with every creature
through Christ our Lord,
through whom you give us everything that is good.

Doxology (Praise) and Great Amen

Through him,
with him,
in him,
in the unity of the Holy Spirit,
all glory and honour is yours,
almighty Father,
for ever and ever.
All: **Amen.**

COMMUNION RITE

Lord's Prayer   *(Stand)*
Celebrant:

Let us pray with confidence to the Father
in the words our Saviour gave us:

All:

**Our Father, who art in heaven,
hallowed be thy name;
thy kingdom come;
thy will be done on earth as it is in heaven.
Give us this day our daily bread;
and forgive us our trespasses
as we forgive those who trespass against us;
and lead us not into temptation,
but deliver us from evil.**

Celebrant:

Deliver us, Lord, from every evil,
and grant us peace in our day.
In your mercy keep us free from sin
and protect us from all anxiety
as we wait in joyful hope
for the coming of our Saviour, Jesus Christ.

All:

**For the kingdom, the power, and the glory are
yours, now and for ever.**

Sign of Peace
The celebrant says the prayer for peace:

Lord Jesus Christ, you said to your apostles:
I leave you peace, my peace I give you.
Look not on our sins, but on the faith of
your Church,
and grant us the peace and unity of your
kingdom where you live for ever and ever.
All:

Amen.
Celebrant:

The peace of the Lord be with you always.
All:

And also with you.

Deacon or Celebrant:

Let us offer each other the sign of peace.
Before eating the body of the Lord and drinking
from the one cup of salvation, let us express,
deepen and restore our peaceful, by exchanging
a sign of peace.
All exchange a sign of peace and love.

Breaking of the Bread

Christians are gathered for the 'breaking of the bread', another name for the Mass. In Communion, though many we are made one body in the one bread which is Christ.

The celebrant breaks the host over the paten and places a small piece in the chalice, saying quietly:

May this mingling of the body and blood of our Lord Jesus Christ bring eternal life to us who receive it.

Meanwhile, the people sing or say a version of the 'Lamb of God', which should last as long as it takes to break the bread.

Communion

We pray in silence and then voice words of humility and hope as our final preparation before meeting Christ in the Eucharist.

Celebrant:

This is the Lamb of God,
who takes away the sins of the world.
Happy are those who are called to his supper.

All:

**Lord, I am not worthy to receive you,
but only say the word and I shall be healed.**

Communion, in form of both bread and wine, is now shared.

Silent pause for reflection and private prayer.

Thanksgiving reflection
Worksheet 17

Experience shows that the following exercise helps people, perhaps not used to long periods of silent prayer, to reflect on the meaning of the Eucharist for themselves and in their lives.

A member of the team now guides the group through the following reflection.

This Mass celebrates what is always happening in our lives. Every moment is Eucharistic. All we do, all we say, all we are: everything is caught up in the life, death and rising to new life of Jesus Christ, our Lord.

After everyone has had sufficient time to reflect upon the material in the worksheet, a member of the team invites people to share part of their reflections with one another, preferably in groups of three or four. (Privacy must be respected, people being encouraged to share only as much as they so wish.)

(We have found that it helps to have the refreshments while this discussion and reflection is in progress. This means the final blessing can become the conclusion to the entire session.)

Finally, the celebrant draws all this private prayer into the prayer of the Church.

Father, you make your Church on earth a sign of new life which will never die.
By sharing in this sacrament may we become temples of your presence and the home of your power and glory.
Through Christ our Lord
All: **Amen.**

Concluding Rites

Celebrant: May these sacraments you have celebrated tonight continue
to show you God is love.
All: **Amen.**
Celebrant: May he continue to change
your lives.
All: **Amen.**
Celebrant: And may the Risen Christ make
you signs of love and power
in the world tonight.
All: **Amen.**
Celebrant: May the blessing of Almighty
God, the Father, and the Son
and the Holy Spirit, come upon
you and remain with you
forever.
All: **Amen.**

Celebrating Stage Four with the Parish

Empowered by the Spirit

In this parish celebration we focus on the fact that **through our baptism we are called and empowered to transform the society in which we live.** As Christians, we are called and empowered to build a better world. This special Mass enables the members of the Christian community to identify specific 'areas' where they could, and indeed should, be visible signs of God's love, care and compassion for his people.

Being servants to others is a visible sign of God's presence in our world. Those who serve others show, in a tangible way, the love and care of God. We need, therefore, to be aware of the aspects of life within our own society that are the consequences of sin: unjust structures, ignorance, unemployment, poverty and prejudice, to mention just a few. Having identified those aspects, we need to consider **what** should be changed and **how** it can be changed. More important still, **what must I, personally, do** to help bring about the necessary change—or, at least, to help alleviate someone's pain and suffering? Major issues may seem beyond the reach of an individual, but every one of us is able to reach out to a neighbour, or perhaps simply to someone under our own roof who is in need of that tangible expression of the love and care of God.

Suggestions to help you prepare your Celebration

Select and adapt those that suit your local situation.

1 • The celebration needs to be practical and relevant to the circumstances in which your parish is situated. Careful planning is needed by those preparing it.

2 • The parish newsletter may carry information concerning areas of need within the boundaries of the parish—but NOT restricted to members of the particular Christian community! It may also carry information concerning groups within the community that already try to meet some of those needs—such as 'Justice and Peace', AA and SVP.

3 • A homily may be prepared, emphasising the presence and sign of God in and among needy people.

4 • The main focus may be on two moments during the celebration, the **first** occurring just before the Offertory and the **second** occurring after Communion.

The First Moment

Different people (of all ages, all nationalities, male and female, individually or in groups) make public statements to the community. They may begin with words such as:

'I have heard . . .'
'I know . . .'
'We know of . . .'
'It has come to our notice that . . .'

Obviously their statements would concern your own particular situation, but the following may give you some ideas:

- Some elderly people are lonely.
- Some/Many people are without work.
- Some people are ill and in pain.
- Some men and many women are alone at home struggling to look after their children.
- There are men and women who are divorced or separated and are in anguish.
- Some young people are in need of companionship and understanding.
- Some men and women have left religious life or the active priesthood and feel rejected and alienated.
- Some parishioners are cold and hungry. They find it impossible to make ends meet.
- Some young people feel alienated from the parish and find the parish Mass irrelevant.
- Some young people need help in preparing for examinations or seeking employment.
- Some of our brothers and sisters suffer addiction to drugs and alcohol.
- Some of our families are suffering tension caused by breakdown in relationships. Some of them are also suffering from violence.
- Some people long to meet others who will talk with them about the meaning of life and God. They want someone to pray with and for them.
- Some of our neighbours are in prison/hospital and have no one to visit them.
- Some of our neighbours have been evicted from their homes, and no one seems to care.

After these statements prayer may be offered by the priest, reminding us that, through our baptism, God calls and empowers us to respond to these needs.

The Second Moment

Another group of people respond to some, if not all, of the statements made earlier in the celebration. Each person may begin his or her response with such words as:

'I want to . . .'
'We are trying to help . . .'
'I am trying to respond to . . .'

eg 'I am trying to help and support a friend who is addicted to alcohol.'

'We are trying to help our very elderly neighbours. We call in every day to make sure they are all right, shop for them and occasionally take them out for a run in the car.'

Stage Five

Gifted to Serve

During Stage Four of the project we looked at the nature of some of the signs and symbols which we, as Christians, use. We explored something of their **potential to bring about change**, each one being a powerful encounter with the Risen Lord. As human beings, however, we do not find it easy to change, often because that would mean stepping out into the unknown—and **we are afraid of the unknown.**

Fear and anxiety are experiences that are common to all of us. They indicate our inability to control and understand our lives—and we can be quite energetic in our attempts to escape from the discomfort they arouse within us. John's statement, **'The truth will set you free'** (Jn 8:32), is a penetrating insight—yet, rather than seek the truth, we immerse ourselves in work, seek solitude or company, drink, take drugs—including those prescribed—or pursue other comforting activities.

Fear can cause severe debilitation. It consumes a great deal of energy, and is often a root cause of such things as war, torture, racialism, sexual discrimination, brutality and other perversions. **Truth** is revealed to us in and through the action of the Holy Spirit, liberating us from the darkness and depression caused by our fear. **Full, absolute truth,** however, is beyond our reach. It is something that is mysterious and sacred, being part of the mystery of God himself. It is, therefore, something freely given to us by him. Through the relationship we have with him who is the centre, source and designer of all life, we are enabled to grow in truth.

We interpret events, draw conclusions and form models of living based on a frame of reference constructed out of the experiences of a particular time and culture—but how **true** are our conclusions? our interpretations? our models of living? More especially, how true are they when they are carried forward into each new day, into a NEW time and a NEW culture? As we grow older we may reconstruct our frame of reference and adjust our explanations; yet we always remain with the problem that our new picture of life is never wholly true.

Sometimes we catch a glimpse of life that touches our innermost being: something we may explain as a religious experience. Somehow it sends us into a state of turmoil, seeming to tear us emotionally apart. We **want** to search for the truth, but—for some reason—we are afraid. The Holy Spirit casts light into our darkness but, in doing so, our **darkness** is made dramatically apparent, and we are uncomfortable with what we see. It takes courage to face the truth, and the change for which that truth calls. How much easier to ignore it and to carry on as before!

At this stage of the project, we take a look at this familiar human condition. Many of those who met Jesus were afraid. The truth revealed in Jesus does not **cause** their fears—but it does **surface** them. (Cf. the story of Peter explored in Stage Four.) This exposure of our inadequacy and fear, however, is a **prelude** to their being dispelled and our being freed from their binding power, thus instigating a change which brings understanding, an overcoming of shame, removal of guilt and a reordering of life. It is **a change that brings peace and joy.** Liberated by this gift, we experience a 'newness' about life. We sometimes label this action of God in our lives as 'remission of sin', 'reconciliation', 'conversion' or 'forgiveness'.

The awareness of being free and of life having new meaning is something that is personal and intimate. **A sense of self-worth, thankfulness and giftedness occurs.** For many people an event that harmed them, a relationship that caused them to be hurt, or a feature of personality that somehow diminished them, **now** is accepted and becomes wholly part of their lives. **The ability to accept and live with ourselves embraces those aspects of ourselves that could be fearful and harmful and makes them creative.**

The remission of sin does not wipe out our past; it does not waste our actions and involvements. Rather, **it reveals an understanding and liberates the skills and giftedness that were there all the time.** The loving nature of Mary Magdalene, the prostitute, was liberated—to be used in a new way for the building of the kingdom. Peter's fishing skills—of judgement, energy, storytelling and courage—were redirected to proclaiming the Good News and enfolding the hearts and minds of others into the kingdom.

When we experience healing and forgiveness, we should expect our essential giftedness to be directed in a new way. **The energy previously being used to contain our fears is now free to be used creatively.**

We find we have a new capacity to act. Seeing and understanding life more fully, we also grow in our understanding of God's work in ourselves and in our relationships with others—and we begin to change our behaviour accordingly.

We find that we are now free in ourselves and, being more liberated, **we see the needs of others more clearly, and want to respond**. This giving of ourselves is a sign of God's work in us. **We are gifted and empowered by the Holy Spirit so that we may do as Jesus did: so that we may serve others.** We are called to be agents of change, signs and actions that free others from anxiety and help bring them forgiveness and peace.

Our actions with and for others bring them **his** healing and peace. We are becoming like him who poured out his life for us. We are becoming the servants of others. We, who were fearful, are being **transformed** into loving and trusting persons. We become **daily signs** of all that we celebrate in the Eucharist in our relationships at home, work and play.

Being converted and changed by the Holy Spirit is a lifelong process. Through the cycle of spiritual, emotional, moral and intellectual development, we are called and challenged many times to reorder our lives. Each time we step forward on the Christian journey—be our steps big or small—we become more confident about the presence of the Holy Spirit, always with us. We begin to live more fully our own **individual** lives and to express more clearly the **unique giftedness** each one of those lives brings to the world.

The general purposes of this stage of the project is:
- to enable people to understand more deeply the way in which the Holy Spirit **gifts** each one of us and **empowers** us to act;
- to help people be **less afraid** of whatever happens in life and to **respond more trustingly** to the work of the Holy Spirit in their own lives;
- to help people grow in understanding of the **work of Jesus** and the **mission entrusted to each of us** through his Church.

Materials you may need for Stage Five

table • cloth • flowers • candle • bowl of water
towel • slices of lemon • oil of myrrh • olive oil
shallow dish for oil • grains of incense •
container in which to burn incense • matches
brazier • paper/pens

Copies of:
   Scripture (Jerusalem or Good News Bibles) for
   'The presence of the Holy Spirit . . .'
   'Scripture stories of gifts'
   'Spiritual gift list'
   'Journey of faith' (Worksheet 18)
   Teenagers' letters to God (Worksheet 19)
   Appropriate pictures for 'What do you see?'
   'Fruits of the Spirit' (Worksheet 20)

The Presence of the Holy Spirit in the Life of Jesus 15–45 mins

The Holy Spirit and Jesus are always together. It is a creative, powerful union, a relationship from the moment of conception and throughout his life. His baptism in the Spirit is fulfilled in his death and resurrection, when the Spirit's work in him is complete.

The same is also true for us. From the moment of conception, the Holy Spirit is constantly at work in all people. Being privileged to dunderstand this is a special grace, a gift that God gives to us—to share with others.

In this exercise we are going to examine some passages of Scripture that describe the action of the Holy Spirit in the life of Jesus. These passages are:
1 • the conception of Jesus (Luke 1:26–38)
2 • Jesus is baptised—and tempted (Luke3:21–22, 4:1–14)
3 • Jesus begins his Ministry (Luke 4:14–30)
4 • the agony in the garden (Luke 22:39–46)
5 • Jesus dies on the cross (Luke 23:39–46)
6 • Jesus is risen (Luke 24:36–49)

You may decide to examine all of those suggested here, all of which have been selected from St Luke's Gospel, or you may decide to **select one or two** of the passages. On the other hand, you may prefer to use parallel passages from the other Gospels. **Do whatever is most appropriate for your particular group.**

Note: We would recommend that, for this reflection, you use the translations that appear in either the Jerusalem Bible or the Good News Bible.

In examining these passages, we want to help people **understand the relationship** between Jesus and the Holy Spirit, and to recognise that the same is also true for each one of us. We also want to help them **explore the pattern** of being drawn into a relationship with the Risen Lord and being gifted and empowered by the Holy Spirit. This pattern, already seen when we considered the story of Peter in the previous stage of the project, is that:

- a person is chosen and spoken to by God;
- fear and anxiety are revealed;
- fear and anxiety are dispelled and peace is given;
- the person is then empowered to do the same for others—to proclaim the Good News—that fear, shame, and guilt can be removed. The person is a witness of this—and is empowered by the Holy Spirit to proclaim this.

Select the passages you wish to explore.
Taking one passage at a time:
  invite one person to read the passage aloud;

  invite people to say aloud the words which, for them, appear to be important or to have special meaning (you may then invite people to share with the group **why** they find those words important or special);

  recall the pattern (referred to above) which we have already seen in the story of Peter's encounter with Jesus (Lk 5:1–11), and discuss the way in which the same pattern is repeated in the text being explored.

1 • The Conception of Jesus
Luke 1:26–38

Read the account of the conception of Jesus as presented to us in Luke 1:26–42. You will notice that the pattern here is just like the one we saw when, during the last stage of the project, we considered Peter's encounter with Jesus:

- God speaks (v 28).
- Fear and anxiety are expressed (v 29).
- The fear is commanded away (v 30).
- The Holy Spirit makes possible that which seems to be impossible (vv 35 and 37).

2 • Jesus is Baptised—and Tempted
Luke 3:21–22, 4:1–14

Read aloud the account of the **baptism** of Jesus by his cousin John in the River Jordan—as told in Luke 3:21–22.

You may notice that Luke's words seem to suggest that the Holy Spirit was not revealed at the moment of baptism, especially if we look at the translation which appears in the Jerusalem Bible. We are told that 'while Jesus **after** his own baptism **was at prayer**,. . . the Holy Spirit descended on him'. Luke is making a point which he actually makes several times in his writings, the most obvious one being the story of the apostles gathered together in prayer on the feast of Pentecost. His point is that things do not always happen as and when we expect and it is often only in retrospect––and especially when we are at prayer—that we come to realise and understand what has, in fact, already happened. This experience is something that happened. This experience is something that is common to all of us.

Discuss ways people have experienced this in their own lives.

The way in which you now proceed will depend upon the nature of your group. You may:

- invite people to recall what Jesus did immediately after his baptism (ie he was led by the Spirit into the desert–a place of 'emptiness').

- read the account of the temptations as given in Luke 4:1-14, making sure that you include verse 14!

- Invite people to reflect upon **why** they think Jesus went into the desert. Have they ever known moments when they have been filled with a great awareness about something in their lives, and yet have had a terribly 'empty' feeling and have not felt sure about the path they should take? Were they aware of a 'struggle' within themselves at that time?

- Reflect with everyone that one aspect of Jesus' experience in the desert was that he was being tempted to repress the gift that was his own unique personality—and be like the rest of people; to feed on bread, wealth and worldly prestige. How often do we find ourselves in a similar situation? 'Don't make a nuisance of yourself. Why rock the boat? We're quite happy as we are. Join us. This is the way it's always been done—and when in Rome do as the Romans. You'll only get people's backs up, and no one will thank you.' It is not easy to ask searching questions or to challenge established ideas. It is not easy to stand alone, even when we know in our hearts and minds that what has 'always been done' is not necessarily right. It is so much easier to do exactly what others want and be flattered for our efforts, even when, deep down, we know that another path is closer to the truth. **Invite people to discuss this —in small groups.** What feelings do we experience when we do, eventually, respond to what we know to be right?

• St Luke situates the temptations between Jesus' **baptism** (Lk 3:21–22) and the inauguration of his **mission** (Lk 4:14). He places emphasis upon the role of the Spirit, telling us that Jesus returned from the Jordan 'full of the Holy Spirit', was 'led by the Spirit into the desert' and that when he returned to Galilee 'the power of the Holy Spirit was with him'. The baptism, the time spent in the desert and the mission of Jesus are very closely related, and it is when we reflect upon these episodes together that we see a most profound link with our own lives. **Reflect upon this in your small groups**, noting the overall pattern emerging once again and the way in which it relates to our own lives.

3 • Jesus begins his Ministry
Luke 4:14–30

Jesus begins his ministry and preaches in his 'home town' of Nazareth. Read the account of this as told in Luke 4:14–30.

(Note: The 'Year of the Lord's Favour' or 'Jubilee' occurred every fifty years: cf. Leviticus 25:8–55, especially v 10. During that year all property was to be restored to the original owners, slaves were to be free to return to their homes and debts were to be wiped out. By the time of Jesus, however, this law was no longer properly observed.)

Jesus' mission is to free people from fear and hurt. This is also our mission. Filled with the power and authority given to us by the Holy Spirit, we are empowered to do the same as Jesus. We, too, are 'anointed' and 'sent'.

• Invite each person to share how s/he would (or does) feel when s/he has to stand before her/his 'home crowd'? Is it easier to face strangers? What

difference would it make if his/her name has gone before him/her? How does s/he think Jesus felt? What was the role of the Spirit in this episode? How does this story relate to his/her own life?

4 • The Agony in the Garden
Luke 22:39–46

Read the account of Jesus' experience in the garden on the Mount of Olives as told to us in Luke 22:39–46. You may notice that it is almost a mirror image of his earlier experience in the desert (Lk 4:1–14).

Jesus celebrated the Passover meal with his disciples (Luke 22:14–38) and then 'went, as he usually did, to the Mount of Olives'. Twice, in this short passage, Jesus commands his disciples to, 'pray that you will not fall into temptation', words that echo the concluding petition of the Lord's prayer (Lk 11:4b). Disciples of Jesus are called to follow in his footsteps —footsteps that will lead through death in a life of service—to resurrection.

a • Jesus is faced with the challenge of the passion. He moves away from his disciples to pray (v 41).

b • He expresses his fear and anxiety (v 42). At the Passover meal, Jesus had accepted the cup (v 20) as 'God's new covenant, sealed with my blood, which is poured out for you', but he is afraid. (Mark tells us that 'distress and anguish came over him', and that he 'threw himself to the ground' Mk 14:33, 35). Perhaps here more than anywhere else we see Jesus as one of us.

c • 'Not my will, however, but your will be done'—and, precisely as he sheds his blood, an angel appears to strengthen him (v 43).

d • Jesus returns to the disciples, ready to fulfil his mission.

• Many of the group will, at some time, have had the experience of tossing and turning, trying to make a major decision about life, while others sleep, apparently totally unconcerned. Discuss the feelings one experiences at such a time. Discuss, also, the feelings of apprehension mixed with deep peace, knowing that the choice made is the right one, but that the consequences of that choice will not be easy. Invite people to share their own stories of such feelings.

5 • Jesus dies on the Cross
Luke 23:39–46

Read the account of Jesus' death as told in Luke 23:39–46.

You will notice that the thief expresses his fear of death as well as anxiety about his feelings of guilt (vv 40–41). Jesus' response, once again, clearly expresses his mission of proclaiming the Good News, and of forgiving and healing.

The complete commitment of Jesus and the pouring out of his breath (v 46) show the finalisation of the work of the Holy Spirit in the life of Jesus. He is now totally baptised and pours out his life-giving Holy Spirit upon the whole world. (St John also adds that blood and water poured from his side, thereby indicating the life-giving nature of the Holy Spirit as it is released to flow out upon the whole world.)

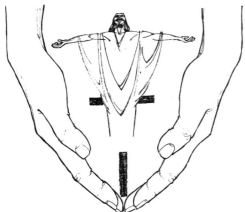

6 • Jesus is Risen
Luke 24:36–49

Read about Jesus' appearance to the disciples as told in Luke 24:36–49.

You will notice that the same pattern emerges yet again:

a • Jesus speaks (v 36).

b • Fear, terror, alarm are expressed (v 37).

c • These feelings are dispelled by Jesus (vv 38–43). The disciples now experience great joy—but not understanding. Jesus opens their minds (v 45) and they now understand his real mission. They also realise that they, now, have the same mission (vv 47–48).

d • The disciples must wait to be led and empowered by the Holy Spirit so that then they can go out and fulfil their mission (v 49).

Giving and Receiving Gifts 30–45 mins

Introduction

The following words are to be found in Eucharistic Prayer IV (used in the last session), leading up to the Consecration.

He was **conceived through the power of the Holy Spirit,**
and born of the Virgin Mary,
a man like us in all things but sin.
To the poor he proclaimed the good news of salvation,
to prisoners, freedom,
and to those in sorrow, joy.
In fulfilment of your will
he gave himself up to death;
but by rising from the dead,
he destroyed death and restored life.
And **that we might live no longer for ourselves but for him,**
he sent the Holy Spirit from you, Father,
as **his first gift to those who believe,**
to complete his work on earth
and bring us the fullness of grace.

The proclamation of the Good News is an action that sets people free and brings joy and peace to those who are burdened with certain aspects of their lives. As we respond to both his call and his action in our lives, we are being empowered by the gift of his Spirit so that we, in turn, may be bearers of the Good News. It is his anointing action in our lives that enables us to 'live no longer for ourselves but for him'.

Jesus, in death, poured out upon us his Holy Spirit, 'his first **Gift** to those who believe'. Why? 'To complete his work on earth and bring us the fullness of grace.'

'His first **Gift** . . .' But—the experiences involved in either giving or receiving gifts are not always easy! Both actions can be fraught with their own difficulties. It would be useful to examine those experiences.

What is it like to receive Gifts?
What is it like to give Gifts?

Receiving Gifts

The following points may help you encourage discussion on the experience of receiving presents.

1 • When do we receive presents/gifts?

2 • Sometimes we sense that a present can manipulate. Have you ever had that experience? How did you **feel** about that?

3 • Young courting adults often offer tokens to one another. An object may be broken, cut or torn in half, each person then keeping a part of it. Why do they do this?

4 • What are your feelings when you receive a present? Are there ever times when you find it a difficult experience?

5 • What are your feelings when you have to open a present in front of others? . . . family . . . friends . . . the giver?

6 • Presents often have little material value. The real value is that the gift expresses, in a very special way, the presence of the giver. Even a person who is miles away, somehow, can be truly present to us through the gift. Have you experienced this? Can you recall a time when a relatively worthless object became important when given as a gift?

7 • There are times when the 'gift' involves having something done for or to us, such as being fed, bandaged or washed. How do we feel when we find ourselves in that kind of situation, or when someone offers to help us in this way?

8 • Recall the most important present you have ever received.

> Think about:
>
> who gave it to you;
>
> why that person gave it to you;
>
> why the present is important to you;
>
> when it was given to you;
>
> how you felt on that occasion;
>
> how the giver felt when you received the gift.

Giving Gifts

1 • When do you give gifts?

2 • How do you decide what to give a person?

3 • Do you find it easy to give gifts? What things may make the giving of a gift difficult?

4 • When a person shows little interest in what you give him or her—stores it away . . . breaks it . . . gives it away—how do you feel?

5 • Recall the most special gift or present you have ever given.

> Think about:
>
> the person to whom you gave it;
>
> why you gave it;
>
> why it was so special a gift;
>
> when you gave it;
>
> how you felt at the time;
>
> how the recipient felt when s/he realised what you had given.

Scripture stories of Jesus

Recall a gift that Jesus gave.

> Think about:
>
> the person to whom he gave it;
>
> why he gave it;
>
> the kind of feelings Jesus may have had about this;
>
> when he gave it;
>
> how it was received.

Recall a gift that Jesus received.

> Think about:
>
> the person who gave it;
>
> why it was given;
>
> why it was important to Jesus and the feelings he may have had;
>
> when it was given;
>
> how the giver felt at the time.

An alternative approach

You may prefer to reflect on some of the aspects of giving and receiving gifts in the following way. Give everyone a sheet of A4 paper, which is then folded to provide spaces as illustrated.

1.	2.
3.	4.
5.	6.
7.	8.

One, or more, of the team members asks questions based on the ideas in 'Giving Gifts' question 5 (p.68), and those in the 'Stories of Jesus' (p.68). Personal experiences of giving and receiving gifts are recorded in the upper half of each space, while the lower half is reserved for Jesus' experience of giving and receiving.

Some responses may then be shared with the group **insofar as the individual feels comfortable**, the others being there simply for personal reflection.

Journey of faith
Worksheet 18

No one makes the journey of faith alone

We are always part of the way other people grow in faith; we have helped others 25–30 mins.

We are, and always have been, ministers of faith to one another. We are gift to one another. We accompany one another on the journey of faith—both giving and receiving along the way.

1 • Give each person a copy of the 'Journey of faith' worksheet (18) and pen or pencil, and assure everyone that whatever he or she puts on to the paper, it is for his or her eyes alone.

2 • Tell everyone to write his or her own name at the TOP of the central circle (eg 'I, Lynn').

3 • Begin with the circle marked 'When I was a baby . . .', and reflect with everyone along the following lines:

> When you were a baby whom did you accompany on his or her journey of faith? For whom were you a source of wonder, a gift? Write the name of that person in the circle—or put some symbol for him or her.

4 • Repeat the process for the remaining four circles, encouraging people to think back to times, people and places—and reflect on them. Do not rush; take one circle at a time. Adjust your reflection to suit the age range upon which you are dwelling, eg:

> As a teenager, who was important in your life? To whom did you explain things? Whom did you support, listen to and understand? With whom did you share things?

Note: Adjust the age ranges and your reflections to suit the group; eg if you are working with senior citizens you could alter the circles to include middle age and—perhaps —old age; whereas if you are working with young adults, four-to-five-year blocks of time would be more appropriate.

5 • Once the outer circles have been completed, ask each person to look back over the names or symbols and consider who has been the most important person for him or her. Then, in the central circle write the name or symbol of that person.

Note: This name may or may not be already on the paper.

6 • Invite each person to reflect upon:

> What he or she **did**;

> **How** what was done helped the other person.

(It is important to reflect on the difference between the action itself and the way in which the action helps.)

7 • People may now be invited to share with one another examples of **things they have done and how this helped another person.** (This is best done in small groups of three or four.) You may begin the discussion by sharing with everyone one of your own experiences. *Assure people that although they MAY share something from their papers, they must not feel that they have to do so. Their examples may be taken from any part of their lives.*

Scripture stories of Gifts 20–30 mins

Invite the members of your group to select, individually, one or two (or more) of the following passages of Scripture, and to read them slowly and reflectively—allowing themselves to be challenged by God's Word. While they are reflecting by themselves, each person may also be invited to make a list of his or her own special gifts.

Exodus 31:1–11	Exodus 35:30–36:1
Romans 12:1–8	1 Cor 12:4–11
1 Cor 12:12–26	Matt 25:14–30
Matt 25:31–46	Eph 3:14–21
Eph 4:1–16	John 6:5–15

When they have had sufficient time to reflect individually, you may then invite them to share a few of their thoughts with one another.

You may then invite them to reflect together upon Paul's comment (an incredibly loaded sentence!) to the Romans (12:6a) – 'We are to **use** our different gifts in accordance with the grace that God has given us' – perhaps alongside the example Jesus sets before us, as related in John 13:1–17. Our gifts are the means by which the grace of Christ expresses itself in OUR place and in OUR time. They are not personal possessions to be polished and stored away. They are **to be used** in service—**for the building up of the Body of Christ**.

Teenagers' letters to God
Worksheet 19

A letter to God 20–25 mins.

Provide:

space for people to sit alone;

paper and pen for each person.

• Invite each person to write a letter to God about his or her individual gifts – telling God how he or she feels about those gifts and the way they are or are not used. Emphasise that the contents are for the eyes of the individual only. Depending upon the nature of the group and your choice of exercises preceding this, you may find it helpful to reflect briefly on this before they begin to write, perhaps using some of the ideas given in the pages introducing this stage.

• When the letters have been completed the group may be encouraged to share their feelings concerning the experience of writing such a letter – but do be sure NOT to encourage disclosure of content.

• The group may then like to look at and together reflect upon the examples of such letters written by teenagers (published in *New Review* with their permission) reprinted in Worksheet 19. They indicate something of the fears that are common to all of us at one stage or other in our lives.

The Fruits of the Spirit Worksheet 20

Spiritual gift list 20–25 mins

Make a list of all the 'gifts of the Spirit' found in: Ephesians 4, Romans 12 and 1 Corinthians 12. Invite everyone to:

a • list the gifts in order of importance, beginning with the most important and ending with the least;

b • explain why s/he has chosen that particular order.

Discuss the choices made in the light of Paul's advice to 'set your hearts on the more important gifts' (1 Cor 12:31) and his discourse on love (1 Cor 13). The 'Fruits of the Spirit' worksheet (20) may help and can be handed out.

Prayer Celebration 15–20 mins

Theme of the prayer:
We are Gifted, Free of Fear, Commissioned to Serve Others

The illustration shows you all that you need for this celebration. Candlelight should provide sufficient illumination, and will help to create a prayerful atmosphere.

Note: Place a thick, protective table mat—or something similar, under the container in which you burn the incense.

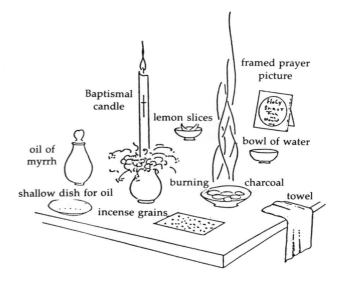

Check that you have some suitable music ready. The following suggestions may help you:

Lord, have mercy; We come to you, Lord; Here I am, Lord; Come, come, follow me.

Arrange the seats in semicircular groups of three-to-five people. Place the semicircles so that the 'open' ends are towards the prepared table.

We are Gifted. One of the team members invites the group to reflect upon the fact that each one of us is gifted. We do not always find it easy to give presents—but there are times when we find it even more difficult to receive them.

• Invite each one, for a few moments, to reflect upon the varying gifts there are among the members of each small group. Ask them to name the gifts of each person quite specifically, in their minds.

• Remind everyone that the gifts are given to us by God. They are his work in us. We may be uneasy about displaying our goodness and embarrassed when good things are said about us; yet we have been given our gifts so that we may **use** them for the building up of the kingdom of God.

• Now invite each one to tell the other members of the group the specific gifts that they recognize in each individual person. You may do this by having the whole group focus on one person at a time, with everyone else offering his or her insights about that person. (Take your time doing this—and do not rush in to fill moments of silence! People often, initially, feel uncomfortable. We are much more practised in pointing out another's faults rather than their good points! You may find that someone cries. Don't worry about this. Sometimes we have a strange way of

expressing our joy! Always, you will find that there is a growing sense of community, appreciation and reverence.)

• Finish this sharing by praying together in the small groups, inviting each person to thank God for one of his or her gifts. Lead the way by example, thanking God for one of your owns gifts.

• **One of the team members** now lights the charcoal and places it in the holder. The grains of incense are scattered on a white cloth as s/he explains that they are all kinds of shapes, colours and sizes—just like us! Not one is the same as another.

• Each person is invited to select a piece of incense that represents his or her self, and return to his or her place with it in the palm of his or her hand.

• One of the team members invites everyone to look at and feel the piece of incense. As they do so, s/he explains that the incense looks like a bit of grit . . . useless . . . without value . . . something that could easily be forgotten . . . to be discarded. It feels hard, brittle and small—with sharp edges. We often feel like that: useless . . . forgotten . . . afraid . . . hard . . . brittle . . . small . . . perhaps with a few sharp edges!

• Invite each person to focus upon one aspect of his or her self which he or she finds most difficult. Encourage them to entrust these difficult areas to the Risen Lord, asking that his love and care will heal and transform them.

A priest or one of the team members prays:
Lord God, you made us and know us. We praise and thank you for the gift of your Son, Jesus, and for all you have done for us in and through him. We thank you that, in pouring out of his life for us, he has freed us. And we thank you for the constant presence of both of you in our lives.

You know our hearts and how afraid we are. We ask you to fill us with the gift of your Holy Spirit. Take away our fears and renew our hearts. Take away the stoniness and coldness in them. Fill them, instead, with your love, with the warmth of flesh, with joy and with trust in you.
We ask this through Christ our Lord.
All: **Amen.**

Each person is now invited to come forward and burn his or her grain of incense – to be transformed by the fire from a simple, apparently useless piece of 'grit' to rise as an offering of oneself, a prayer, to the Lord, the perfume of which lingers in the air, in the same way that we, too, are transformed if we allow our apparently useless selves to be consumed in the fire of God's love.

While each person burns the incense, either [softly] play or sing a suitable hymn, such as 'Lord, have mercy'

• St Paul, in his letter to the Romans, helps us to see our lives together, as gifted people, as reflections of God's fundamental gift of Christ. Together, in Christ, with each one fulfilling his or her own particular function, we ARE the Body of Christ. Paul tells us that the source of our gifts is the Holy Spirit, that we can do what we do through the Holy Spirit, and that we do what we do so that we may build up the Body of Christ. We are gifted so that we might serve (Rom 12:6a).

• Reflect for a few moments upon the different ways each one of us might use his or her individual gifts. In what ways might we try to share them with others? How could we use our time, our ability to care, our skills?

• Indicate the oil on the table and explain that it is oil of myrrh, mixed now with olive oil. Myrrh is a precious oil with a bitter perfume. It was given to Jesus as a gift at the time of his birth, as a sign of reverence and respect. It is, however, also a sign of death, and reminds us that Jesus gave his life for us so that we might live in the new life of the Spirit. This is a life in which we, like him, become loving servants to others, bringing them peace, joy and forgiveness.

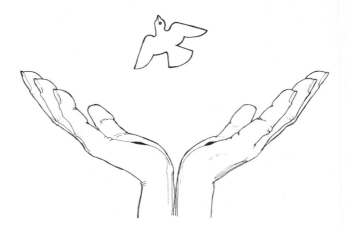

A priest (or one of the team) then prays over the oil, using these or similar words:

Father, we remember your Son and the way he showed us, in his life, how we, too, are to be good news to others, by helping and caring for them.

Bless this oil of myrrh and send us your Holy Spirit that, being free now of fear, we might bring your love and peace to others as we try to serve their needs.

We ask this through Christ our Lord.

All: **Amen.**

Each person is now anointed with the oil on the forehead and hands while the following words are said:

May the Holy Spirit empower you to bring love and peace to all whom you serve. **Amen**

A suitable hymn or piece of music may be play the anointing, eg *Here I am, Lord.*

When everyone has been anointed, remind the group
• of their need to ask the Holy Spirit to empower them each day;
• that Jesus prayed and the Holy Spirit guided him constantly;
• that people in the parish are praying for them, also.

As a reminder of these facts, you may give each participant an appropriate card or picture to keep at home, possibly in their bedrooms. This 'gift' may first be blessed by your priest before being distributed to the members of the group.

Celebrating Stage Five with the Parish

Gifted to Serve

A Celebration of Healing and Reconciliation

The focus of this parish celebration is the essential mission of God's people—to bring health of soul, mind and body to the world. It celebrates Christ's reconciling and healing work among his people, emphasising the care that the Church has for the WHOLE person. Such compassion and love must first be experienced within the local community so that, from there, it may spread to the world.

Suggestions to help you prepare for your celebration
Select and adapt those that suit your local situation.

1 • Invite all the parish who are ill in any way and arrange transport for them. People involved in the project may do this as a practical expression of their response to the call to serve others, assisted by other parish groups such as SVP, CWL, doctors, nurses, hospital services and ambulance services.

2 • Make or provide a low brazier in which incense may be burned. (A round 'barbecue' stand would do, or you may like to ask your local secondary school or youth group to design and make one.) This should be placed in the sanctuary, in front of or to the side of the altar, where it is accessible for people in wheel chairs. *Be sure to put some form of heat protection beneath the brazier if the floor is wooden or carpeted.*

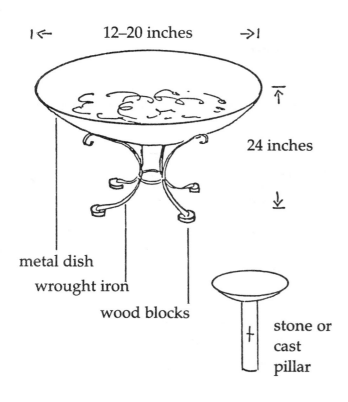

12–20 inches

24 inches

metal dish
wrought iron
wood blocks

stone or cast pillar

3 • An abundant amount of fresh olive oil may be carried in the entrance procession. It should be carried in a glass container so that it may be clearly seen. The oil should be placed on a specially prepared table, near the altar and visually connected with the brazier. You may decide also to place on this table (on a cloth) the grains of incense that will be burned during the Rite of Reconciliation and Healing.

4 • If possible, the Liturgy of the Word should highlight the theme of healing and reconciliation.

5 • Visuals, film-strips or slides may be used during the reading(s), showing the effects of sin and selfishness in suffering; or the Gospel may be dramatised.

6 • An elaborate Rite of Reconciliation and Healing may follow the Liturgy of the Word, thus showing that it is in hearing God's word and taking it into our hearts that we are called and led to conversion. This rite emphasises the ongoing need of the Christian community to be converted and forgiven.

7 • During the Penitential Rite, incense may be burned in the brazier or in some other suitable container, to symbolise penance and 'sin-offering'. Each person is invited to place a piece or pinch of incense on to the burning coals. This may be done in processional form, accompanied by suitable psalms or other chants.

The following Rite of Reconciliation and Healing may help you. Adapt the wording to suit the people with whom you will be celebrating.

Rite of Reconciliation and Healing

President:

It is through hearing God's word that we receive the message of life and our faith is nourished; through the presence of Christ in us that the Christian community is formed and built up. By giving his life on the cross Jesus, by a selfless act of love, brings forgiveness and reconciliation to mankind. By sharing in his life we are called to share in his death and resurrection and this way we become a people of forgiveness and reconciliation—we become the Easter people who go on dying with Christ to selfishness in order that we may continue to rise with him to a newness of life.

Let us pause for a moment, examine our lives and acknowledge before God and each other our sinfulness.

(*All pause in silence*)

President: Lord, you reveal yourself to us and through our blindness we fail to recognise you.
Lord, have mercy.

All: **Lord, have mercy.**

President: Lord, you open wide your hands in compassion and mercy and we, with stubborn hearts, reject you.
Christ have mercy.

All: **Christ, have mercy.**

President: Lord, you pour out upon us your Spirit of power and yet we try and be self-sufficient.
Lord, have mercy.

All: **Lord, have mercy.**

President: With faith in the mercy and love of the Lord, let us now signify the offering to God of our repentance by burning incense. As we watch the grains being changed to rise as perfumed smoke, let us ask God to transform us by deepening our faith, our trust and our love.

All come forward, in procession, to the altar and place a grain or pinch of incense on the burning coals in the brazier. Meanwhile suitable psalms or hymns are sung.

When everybody has returned to their places the president then addresses the people:

The Lord Jesus Christ restored the sick to health. He is present among us as we recall the words of the apostle James: 'Is there anyone sick among you? Let him call for the elders of the Church and let them pray over him, and anoint him in the name of the Lord. This prayer, made in faith, will cure the sick man. The Lord will restore his health, and if he has committed any sins, they will be forgiven.'

Let us entrust our brothers and sisters who are sick to the grace and power of Jesus Christ, that the Lord may ease their suffering and grant them health and salvation.

The sick are brought to the front of the altar and the President stretches out his hands over them in silence. While this is being done a suitable hymn or psalm may be sung. (Members of the project group may be among those assisting the sick.)

The oil is now brought to the President, who blesses it.

Lord God, loving Father, you bring healing to the sick through your Son Jesus Christ. Hear us as we pray to you in faith, and send the Holy Spirit, our helper and friend, upon this oil, which nature has provided to serve the needs of all people. May your blessing come upon all who are anointed with this oil, that they may be freed from pain and illness and made well again in body, mind and soul. Father, may this oil be blessed for our use in the name of our Lord Jesus Christ who lives and reigns with you for ever and ever.

All: **Amen**

The President (and other priests if present) now anoints the sick, using the following words:

Through this holy anointing may the Lord in his love and mercy help you with the grace of the Holy Spirit.

All: **Amen.**

May the Lord who frees you from sin save you and raise you up.

All: **Amen.**

When the sick have returned to their places the rite concludes with the absolution:

The Lord is rich in compassion and mercy. May he forgive us all our sins and renew us in his love.
Amen.

Prayer of the faithful
The petitions should include the needs of the sick and suffering in the local community and throughout the world. A further intention should be included for those who are participating in the project.

Liturgy of the Eucharist
Prayer over the gifts
Lord,
receive these gifts of bread and wine which we offer with sincere hearts.
We ask this in the name of Jesus the Lord.

All: **Amen.**

Eucharistic Prayer
If the rubrics allow it one of the Eucharistic Prayers for Masses of Reconciliation may be used.

Prayer after communion
God our Father,
through the heavenly gifts we have received
we are made whole.
May we carry with us in our hearts
your spirit of love and compassion.
We ask this through Christ our Lord.
All: **Amen**.

Remembering

All Jewish meals

Religious, ritual acts

The night before he died, Jesus shared a festive meal with his friends; and so at this stage of the project we are going to focus our attention on a Jewish meal. All Jewish meals, and most especially festive meals, are religious, ritual acts. They are essentially communal in nature and reflect an understanding of God's action in the faith journey of a particular group of people.

The Berakah

At all meals the host, father or leader always says a blessing, a **berakah**, over each kind of food as it is served. The word *berakah* has a special, powerful meaning which is not captured by our word 'blessing'. *Berakah* means that my whole being, every breath in my body, acknowledges God as the source of every single created thing—everything that has been, that is and that is to come. It is a proclamation of God's total power and of confidence that everything is in his hands. God is life. Those who share and eat the food are thus drawn into the stream of divine life, nourished by God himself. A slightly different blessing is said each time a person's cup is refilled with wine.

The final blessing

At the end of the meal, and especially on more solemn occasions, a long concluding prayer of thanksgiving—known simply as 'The Blessing'—is recited over a special cup of wine, which is then passed around to everyone. (When St Paul wrote about 'the cup of blessing which we bless' (1 Cor 10: 16) it was probably this ritual cup to which he was referring.) It is an enthusiastic expression of gratitude to God for providing nourishment, and is a concept that comes from the Torah itself: 'You shall eat, and be satisfied, and then you will thank God' (Deut 8:10). There are four parts to the blessing, referring in turn to food; to the land of Israel and its food; to the rebuilding of the land and the temple; and finally to the whole of life itself. A special clause is inserted into the blessing, appropriate to whatever feast is being celebrated.

Shabbat Shalom
Celebrating the Sabbath

Once a week members of Jewish families gather together for the festive meals which are an essential part of celebrating the Sabbath. *Shabbat* is observed for just over 25 hours, beginning an hour before sunset on Friday and ending after twilight on Saturday, as soon as it is dark enough for three stars to be visible. Most modern Jews normally begin to celebrate the Sabbath once members of the family have gathered together, usually about 6 pm.

Preparing the table

The table is prepared beforehand. It is usually covered with a clean white cloth, and often has an arrangement of flowers upon it. Always there are two (or more) candlesticks, two loaves of braided bread (*challah*) covered with a finely embroidered cloth, a bottle of wine and a large wine cup, and a salt cellar. The two candles are a reminder of the two versions of the Ten Commandments. (Some families light an extra candle for each child.) The 'double bread' is a reminder of the double portion of manna given to the Jews on Friday in the desert, for Shabbat (Exodus 16:22–26), whilst the finely embroidered cover over it symbolises the dew which covered the manna (Exodus 16:13–14). The salt recalls the tears shed in Egypt, whilst the wine is a symbol of joy.

Lighting the candles

The lady of the house is usually the one who welcomes the Sabbath (and other festivals) by lighting the Shabbat candles. She lights two (or more) candles, known as *hadlakat haner* and says the special blessing. She then turns to the family and wishes them *Shabbat shalom*, which means 'a peaceful Sabbath'.

Creating an atmosphere

The parents may bless their children (*birchat habanim*), placing both hands on each child's head to symbolise that the blessing is given with a full heart. Gathering around the table the family then sings *Shalom Aleichem*, a poem of welcome to the visiting angels, the messengers of peace. The latter part of Chapter 31 of Proverbs is then read or sung by the father. This passage, *Eshet Chayil*, 'A woman of worth', is an allegorical poem expressing appreciation of the Jewish wife and mother. It has been interpreted in a variety of ways but many people understand it to be about the relationship between the Jewish people and God.

'Kiddush'

Having created the right atmosphere for the Sabbath meal, the family is now ready for *Kiddush*, meaning 'sanctification' or 'making holy'. *Kiddush* is said over a large cup filled with wine, the symbol of joy. The prayer recalls God's completion of the creation of the world and the fact that he rested on 'the seventh day and made it holy'. It goes on to compare the birth of the Jewish people, rescued by God from slavery in Egypt, to the birth or origin of the world, and ends with thanks to God for the gift of Shabbat itself. The family listens carefully while the father recites or sings the words, and answers 'Amen' at the end. Most of the contents of the cup are then drunk by the one who 'made kiddush', whilst the others also drink some wine.

Washing the hands and blessing the bread

As an act of ritual purity each person washes his or her hands, and says a blessing before drying them. The father then uncovers the two loaves of *challah*, says the blessing and cuts enough for each member of the family. He lightly sprinkles it with salt and each person eats a piece.

Songs of joy and the final blessing

The meal is taken at a very leisurely pace. During it songs of praise are sung, stories of life are told and passages of Scripture are shared. At the end of the meal the final blessing (see above) is recited or sung, beginning always on Shabbat with the singing of *Shir Hamaalot*, Psalm 126, a psalm of joy.

The Passover meal
An annual festive meal

The Passover meal is an **annual** festive meal with special foods and blessings. It celebrates the Exodus, the stories of that event being told not only in words—and possibly actions—but also with food. For example, a bowl of bitter horseradish is passed around when the bitterness of Egypt is mentioned, and unleavened bread is used because the people were in a hurry. In many ways the Passover meal could be considered a perfect example of an 'audio-visual lesson' with full participation of all involved.

Remembering

During the Passover meal the Jews **remember** the Exodus and their liberation from Egypt (cf. Exodus 12). It was this event that established them as a people; this event that set them free; this event to which they always refer when they want to explain rituals or institutions; this event which helps them understand the meaning of all other events. We have already seen, for example, the part it plays in the celebration of Shabbat.

Reflecting upon the use of the word **'remember'** in Old Testament passages (eg Ps 111:4), we see that people are able to remember **only because God has first remembered**. When **he** remembers, the great acts of redemption are repeated, enabling his people to experience them and thus remember the great moments of passion and glorification. When God remembers, he does much more than simply recollect the event. He effects what he recalls. **In remembering and celebrating the Passover, therefore, a past event becomes present and the Jews are able to participate in it**. Remembering and reflecting upon the past helps them to understand the present. The whole of life is seen as an exodus, a paschal moment, a journey towards the kingdom of God. The celebration of the Passover is an event which teaches that what God has done in the past he can, and does, do over and over again. It is an event that maintains hope—even when things are grim—by reflecting upon the present in the light of the past and then looking forward to the future.

The New Passover
The Last Supper

Matthew, Mark and Luke tell us that the last meal Jesus shared with his friends was a Passover meal. John, however, tells us that the final meal was shared the day **before** the Passover (Jn 13:1). He also tells us that when the Jews brought Jesus before Pilate they had not yet eaten the Passover (Jn 18:28). All kinds of reasons have been suggested for this discrepancy. The essential fact, however, is that all the Gospel writers firmly connect the death of Jesus with the Passover event. From the earliest post-resurrection days the disciples understood that Jesus was the 'New Passover'.

A meal invested with new and important meaning

The Passover meal helps us to understand who Jesus is. The symbols he used spoke for themselves because they already had a long and rich history; but during the Last Supper their meaning was newly defined. In performing the ritual as he did, such as breaking bread and giving thanks, Jesus was simply carrying out what was already an obligation for every devout Jew. So what was it that helped the disciples to grasp that Jesus was the 'New Passover'? What was so significant about his words? What was it that charged the established ritual actions with new meaning?

Jesus spoke about '**My** body which is given for you, **My** blood poured out for many for the forgiveness of sins, **My** blood which seals the **new and ever-lasting covenant**'. These words were prophetic, their full significance seen much more clearly when considered in the light of:
- the Passover (Exodus 12)
- Moses' words at Sinai, 'This is **the** blood of the covenant . . .' (Exodus 24:8)
- the events which followed the Last Supper.

In memory of me

Jesus also said to the disciples, 'Do this in memory of me.' To command them to 'do this' (ie to break and bless bread and to pour out and bless wine) seems unnecessary when it was something they did already—not only at the Passover celebration, but during **every** meal. The significance, then, must lie in the second part of the command, '**In memory of Me**'. In other words, in future, **whenever** you gather together to share a meal and perform the usual ritual acts, 'Remember me'. The significance of these words is intensified when we recall that when Jewish people 'remember', they are able to do so only because God has first remembered, thus enabling the past redemptive act to become a present reality so that they are able to participate fully in the event. Jesus, therefore, transformed the ritual actions, thus providing his followers with a constant reminder that, through his passion and glorification, he has redeemed them. By instructing them to 'do this in memory of me', Jesus was making his redemptive act an ever-present reality in their lives.

My table . . . My kingdom

Jesus' words during the Last Supper also have a future orientation. He looks forward, beyond death, to future meals which he will share with his disciples at table in the kingdom; he looks forward to the Messianic banquet. Thus, the present moment is seen in the light of the past, and looks forward to the future.

Celebrating the Eucharist

So rich in meaning

When we gather together to celebrate the Eucharist, we re-enact the **Ritual** of a Jewish meal. We remember Jesus who is truly present in and among us. As we remember his life, death and resurrection, through which he redeemed us, we are caught up in that great mystery. **It is a present reality and we are part of it**. Through faith, a gift of God, we are able to remember, and therefore participate in, the event that established us as a Christian people; the event that set us free; the event to which we return when we want to explain the rituals and institutions of our faith; the event which gives meaning to the other events of our lives. In just the same way that the celebration of Passover is essentially a **communal meal** having within it a whole mixture of elements such as remembering, story-telling, blessing of bread and wine, symbols, reality, thanksgiving, joy, sacrifice, redemption, songs of praise and reflection upon God's action, so, too, is our celebration of the Eucharist. After all, Christians and Jews do have a common heritage.

Remembering

We should also bear in mind that Jews who have gathered together to share a meal usually think of others who, for whatever reason, are elsewhere. Thus, in being 'remembered', they are truly present in the hearts and minds of those who are celebrating together. We reflect this attitude in our 'General Intercessions' during the celebration of the Eucharist.

Celebrate together

Passover or Shabbat

At this stage of the project, we suggest that you celebrate either a Passover meal or, more simply, a Sabbath meal, *Shabbat Shalom*.

Texts available

Many excellent texts of the Passover meal are available through your local bookshop or library. Some are strictly according to the Jewish ritual, while others have been adapted for use by Christians. (For example, *Focus on Holy Week*, Kevin Mayhew, pages 91–96; *Haggadah*. Passover packs are available from the Jewish Education Officer at Woburn House, London WC1H OEP; some contain artefacts as well as printed material. A tape and full Jewish text, plus translation, of Shabbat Shalom is available from the same source.)

The Jewish ritual may be of greater help at this stage in helping your group to appreciate the foundation of our celebration of the Eucharist. You may also invite one of your local Jewish neighbours to help you. He or she will probably be very willing to lead the celebration for you.

A Christian version of Shabbat

What we provide here is a very simple Christian version of 'Shabbat Shalom'. This is a relatively easy celebration to arrange, and you will find it an experience that is both enriching and full of meaning.

Depending upon the size and nature of your group, you may decide to have a full meal, in which case proceed as described in the paragraphs above, under the heading 'Shabbat Shalom'. If you decide to 'keep it simple' then just follow or adapt the outline provided here for you.

Challah

Here is a recipe for *Challah*:
To make one very large or two medium plaits:

1 lb/450g white bread flour	½ oz/15g fresh yeast,
2 tsp salt	or 2 tsp dried yeast
3 tsp caster sugar	1 large egg and 1 yolk
2 tbsp oil	8 fl oz/200 ml warm water

Heat water until it is at about bath temperature, put into mixing bowl. Add one-third of the flour, all the sugar and yeast. Mix until smooth, cover with a tea-towel and leave for 20 minutes until it looks frothy. Add the remaining flour, salt, oil, the one egg. Mix with the dough hook of an electric mixer at minimum speed until dough forms, then knead with hook at low for 3 minutes. Tip dough on to a floured surface, knead by hand to shape into a ball. (By hand alone, knead the dough 5–6 minutes until smooth.) Texture should be scone-like. Put into a greased polythene bag, large enough for the dough to double in size. Fasten bag loosely. Put dough at bottom of refrigerator for 12–24 hours, leave to rise. To shape: take the risen dough and leave to lose its chill for around 30 minutes.

To make one large plait: divide dough into three pieces. Knead each piece into a round, then roll into a sausage about 12 inches long. Press the strands firmly together at one end, then plait tightly. Put on a greased tray.

To make two medium plaits: divide dough in two and work on each half in the same way.

Put the loaves into a greased polythene bag and leave until they regain their lightness, around 30 minutes. Brush with the egg yolk (diluted with 1 tsp water and 1 tsp salt). Scatter with poppy seeds.

To bake: put in a hot oven at Gas 7, 425°F, 220°C for 15 minutes.
Then turn down to Gas 5, 375°F, 190°C
    for 30 minutes more for the small loaves;
    for 45 minutes more for the large.
When the loaves are cooked they will be a rich brown and will sound hollow when the base is tapped.

As an alternative to making your own *challah*, many bakers are delighted to be given the opportunity to display their artistic talents and will bake a couple of large braided loaves for you—the size depending upon the number in your group . . . but DO give them plenty of warning so that they can plan their baking schedule in time. If you are not having anything other than the bread and wine, you may like to ask the baker to put a sugar glaze on the bread for you (otherwise some people may find it too dry). It is also wise to provide some grape juice for those who do not take wine.

Materials you may need for Stage Six

table, set with cloth and flowers • large wine cup
candles • wine • wine glasses • fruit juice
two loaves of *challah* or other braided bread •
cheese, olives, crisps, nuts and/or other snacks •
handouts or booklets of Sabbath ceremony • Bible

If you decide to have a full meal have everything in
a low oven, ready to serve at the appropriate time.

Notes about the Celebration

The following is a Christian version of the opening
celebration of the Sabbath.

The Jews open the Sabbath on a Friday evening,
once all the members of the family have assembled.
The closing ceremony is held on the evening of the
following day. You may like to hold your celebration
on a Saturday evening, in preparation for Sunday,
the Lord's Day.

The ceremony is usually led by the host or father
of the house or by the leader of a fellowship group.
Decide who will lead your celebration.

The lady of the house welcomes the Sabbath by
lighting two or more candles and saying a blessing
over them. Decide which one of the ladies present
will fulfil this role.

Remembering

Invite everyone to sit around the table. If you have
a lot of people participating in this celebration you
may prefer to arrange the chairs in small semicircular
groups, with the open end of the semicircle facing
the central table.

Briefly explain what you are about to do and
why, basing your explanation upon the preceding
introductory notes. **Do not go into too much detail
at this stage, as the celebration will speak for itself.**

Shabbat Shalom—a Sabbath Celebration

The lighting of the candles

Opening Song: Select a song or hymn according
to the season.
Reading: One of the following, or some other
suitable reading may be selected:

John 1:1–18

John 1:1–5
Ephesians 1:3–14
Colossians 1:15–20
Reading of the Sunday

The Leader prays:

Lord of the Universe, in honour of your Son,
Light of the World and Author of Life, I am about
to perform the duty of kindling the lights for the
Lord's Day, even as it is written: 'and you shall
call the Sabbath a delight and the holy day of the
Lord honourable.' May the effect of our fulfilling
this command be that the stream of abundant life
and heavenly blessing flow in upon us: that you
may be gracious unto us and cause your Holy
Spirit to dwell more richly among us.

Father of Mercy, continue your loving kindness
towards us. Make us worthy to walk in the way of
your Son, loyal to your teaching and unwavering
in love and service. Keep from us all anxiety,
darkness and gloom. Grant that peace, light and
joy ever abide in our home; for you are the fountain
of life and in your light do we see light.

All: **Amen**

Responsorial prayer

*With hands extended towards the unlit candles the Leader
says:*

Let us welcome the Lord's Day.
All: **May its radiance illuminate our hearts as we
enkindle these candles.**
Leader: Light is the symbol of our Lord Jesus
Christ.
All: **The Lord is my help and my salvation.**
Leader: Light is the symbol of the Lord's presence
with us.
All: **He is the true light that enlightens everyone.**
Leader: Light is the symbol of the Lord's purpose
and ways.
All: **His word is a lamp to guide me and a light
for my path.**
Leader: Light is the symbol of the mission to
which the Lord has called us.
All: **You are the Light of the World. Let your light
so shine before us all that we may see your good
works and give glory to your Father in heaven.**

Blessing of the Sabbath Light

Leader: Therefore, remembering the Lord Jesus, who is the Light and Life of the World, and united with all our brothers and sisters and with all the angels and saints, we light these candles.

The lady now lights the candles. Then, with hands raised over the Sabbath light, she prays the following blessing:
Blessed are you, O Lord our God, King of the Universe, who has hallowed us by your loving word and taught us to kindle the Sabbath light.

A hymn may now be sung: eg The light of Christ.

Leader: Father, you glorified the world by the light of your Risen Son, our Lord Jesus Christ. Through him you sent your Spirit into the world, to enkindle in us the fire of your love. Grant that we who are gathered in his name may so live together in the light of his truth that our love for one another may continue to grow each day.
All: **Amen**.

Blessing of the wine

Leader: Come, let us welcome the Day of the Lord in joy and peace. Like a bride, radiant and joyous, comes the Day of the Lord. It brings blessings to our hearts. Workday thoughts and cares are put aside, that we may honour the Lord and celebrate his resurrection. The brightness of the Sabbath light shines forth to tell that the Holy Spirit of love abides within our home. In that light all our blessings are enriched, all our griefs and trials are softened.

At this hour, God's messenger of peace comes and turns the heart of brother to his brother, sister to her sister, brother to his sister, sister to her brother, parents to their children and the hearts of children to their parents, strengthening the bond of devotion to that pure and lofty ideal of brotherhood and sisterhood that is found in Holy Scripture.

The leader pours wine into the large wine cup, raises the cup, and recites the following prayer:
Lord, through your goodness we have this wine, symbol of joy. As we enter into this Sabbath celebration, we thank you for the blessings of this past week; for life, health and strength; for love and friendship; for the discipline of the trials and temptations through which we have been strengthened; for the fruit that has come out of our labours. You have enabled this, O Lord, by the blessing of work and, in your love and kindness, you have made us holy by the blessing of rest according to your commandment: 'Six days shall you labour and do all your work, but the seventh day is a Sabbath to the Lord your God.'
All: **Amen**.

The Leader now raises the cup and says the traditional blessing:
Blessed are you, O Lord our God, King of the Universe, who has created the fruit of the vine.

He now drinks the wine in the large cup. Meanwhile each person receives a glass of wine (or grape juice) from which he or she drinks.

Blessing of the bread

The Leader holds the bread in his hands and prays:

Lord, through your goodness we have this bread, symbol of our unity, as from many grains of wheat comes this one bread. It is a sign of your daily provident care and love. As we share this one bread, may we also share completely our lives together through the power of your Holy Spirit, the Lord and Giver of Life.

All: **Amen.**

The Leader now raises the bread and says the traditional blessing:

Blessed are you, O Lord our God, King of the Universe, who causes the earth to yield food for all.

The bread is now broken and passed to everyone.
As each person receives a piece of bread, he or she may give thanks for a particular blessing he or she has received during the week.
This may be simply in the form of 'Thank you, Lord, for . . .' or in the form of the 'Berakah', ie 'Blessed are you, O Lord our God, King of the Universe, who . . ..'

The Sabbath greeting

All then eat some of the bread and drink some wine while the Leader pronounces the Sabbath Greeting.

This is the Lord's Day.
Let us be glad and rejoice in it.
Shabbat Shalom! (ie A Peaceful Sabbath!)

All: **Shalom Aleichem!** (ie Peace be with you!)

You may like to sing a song, hymn or psalm . . . preferably one that is well-known: eg Shalom my friends, May the peace of Christ be with you today, Peace, perfect peace, Peace is flowing like a river, Peace is the gift of heaven to earth, or similar.
The cheese, olives etc. are now passed around.

If you are going to have a full meal,
serve the meal at this stage of the celebration.

When everyone has finished eating,
the Leader says the concluding prayer.

May the Lord bless us and keep us.
May the Lord make his face to shine upon us
and be gracious unto us.
May the Lord look on us with favour
and give us his peace.

All: **Amen.**

If there are children present, then the father may bless them in these or similar words:

God has given you . . . (*child's name*) to us as a special gift. He calls you to be a true child of God and to live a life that is truly Christlike. So that you may experience the fullness of life in Christ, I now call upon you the blessing which God commanded Aaron to pray over the chosen people.

. . . . (*Child's name*),
may the Lord bless you and keep you.
May the Lord make his face to shine upon you
and be gracious unto you.
May the Lord look on you with favour
and give you his peace.

All: **Amen.**

(In the same way, those present may pray for one another: eg engaged couples for one another, sponsors for Confirmation candidates and so on.)
Conclude your celebration with a psalm or hymn of thanksgiving.

Celebrating Stage Six with the Parish

Remembering

There are many ways in which you may decide to celebrate this stage of the project with the parish. A few alternatives are suggested here.

1 • Invite members of the parish to your own celebration.

2 • Celebrate a Passover meal with the project group and invite members of the parish to a celebration of Shabbat.

3 • Celebrate Shabbat with the project group and have a parish celebration of Passover.

4 • Highlight the relevant aspects of the parish Mass on Holy Thursday.

Alive!

Introduction

By now the members of the project group will have been together for a considerable amount of time, searching together and sharing the mysteries of the Christian faith. Changes will have taken place for all those involved.

In this stage of the project we ponder over some of those changes, together with others that occur in the Christian life. Christianity is about a living, changing relationship. It is, therefore, important to explore changes in both the Christian story and our own lives.

The general purpose of this stage is:

a • To enable the whole parish to develop and share its faith and belief in:

Jesus, the Risen Lord, as the centre and meaning of all life

the gift of the Holy Spirit, through which Jesus forms us and enables us to understand and relate to others as he does

the power and authority of Jesus, through and with which we are sent to bring about a new and better way of life for all, especially those whom we meet in our everyday lives;

b • to help each participant be open to responding to the gift of the Holy Spirit in his or her life and to have hope in the mission he or she is called upon to pursue;

c • to hand on the faith, sharing with the group a way of life which acknowledges that the story of the Risen Jesus is echoed in each person's own story.

The specific aim is:

1 • to encourage participants to share and explore together stories of Christian life, including:

- their own personal experiences and stories of Christian living
- the foundation stories recorded in Scripture
- Christian stories about people and events they know, have seen or have heard;

2 • to share the following truths with each other, to support each other as we grow in our understanding of these truths and to celebrate them in prayer. The truths are:

The Risen Lord forms us and shapes us, filling us with the same Holy Spirit that filled, empowered, and guided him. Slowly but surely, each one of us is being made like him.

We are being formed by God, in our understanding as well as in our power to act, because we are being drawn into and sent to do **his** work in all the relationships we have with others. In serving others, we manifest to them the new life we have in Christ.

To belong to a parish is to be part of a people who have been chosen and sent by God, both individually and corporately, to bring to others—and themselves—a new life and a better world in which to live.

It is both normal and acceptable that, at some time, we disbelieve in God, give up, do not understand or lose a sense of direction in life. Indeed, it is often a most important part of growing in faith. Whether or not we recognise the fact, the Risen Jesus is **always** with us.

Comments on approach

1 • Because we are drawing close to the end of the project, there may be **a temptation to try to do too much** at this stage. Care is needed to see that we do not succumb to that temptation. The participants have their own level of faith and this, like our own, will mature and change. The most important thing to do at this time is to share with them and encourage them to continue exploring together. It is essential in this stage that each person's contribution is supported and, if necessary, clarified.

2 • **For each one of us, the 'shape' of faith is very variable.** We **all** have much to learn, each one of us having been invited to make an individual journey.

For some people, Christian life centres upon relationships and the goodness of these; for others it centres upon a sense of the presence of God and a relationship with him. The first may have to do with a sense of, 'I am a Christian when I do certain things or behave in certain ways'. The second may be identified with the person of Jesus or with the guidance and protection of the Holy Spirit. The reverse is also true, in that people may identify themselves as being un-Christian because of particular relationships or behaviour.

This diversity will be manifest as people share their own personal stories, as well as those of other people and events. It is important to support all these rich expressions of faith and to help participants connect them with the foundation stories and the truth expressed in the Church. *Remember that the work you do with them is God's work. It is* **he** *who knows their hearts and has been forming them in the faith ever since their conception. Reach out to him, in confident prayer, to guide and strengthen you.*

Many people experience times when they feel either Godless or forsaken. You may find that this is the feeling of some members of the group—even now, here with you. Such an apparently meaningless sense of being lost, abandoned and rejected is at the heart of all human life. The stories that may emerge are Gospel stories. They grasp real life fully, and relate to the foundation stories and the pouring out of the Holy Spirit. They are expressions of Jesus' death in our times. Our own stories express the way he fully takes on our humanity and is submissive to the will of his Father with total trust.

It is normal for all of us to experience brokenness at some time in our lives. It is through such experiences that we grow in faith and come to know God's love; to know that he enters into our pain and never lets go of us. The theme of the cross and the victory has a place here. To be broken, to feel Godless and forsaken is part of the journey in Christian faith. We are moulded and fashioned by God, as was his Son, so that we, too, may bring new life into each other's lives.

It is important that, as brothers and sisters, you show a willingness to accompany people who are in a broken and painful state. In doing so, you are sharing their faith and supporting the work of God in them as he is moulding, forming and leading them. Listen to their faith stories; hear God speaking through them; and reverence them. Allow their stories to resonate with your own. You may feel incompetent to so much as even reply, unable to offer anything or explain. It is sufficient simply to be with them, together growing in understanding of God's presence and knowing acceptance. This is a privileged relationship. It is a prayerful experience and, as such, gives direction to your own prayer, a direction that will become clearer as you discover more fully what it is to be a minister of faith to others.

3 • As you already know, **the prayer together in the session is important and greatly valued** by the members of the project group. It is an active way in which you share your faith with them.

In this stage of the project, the emphasis is upon sharing our lives and the sense that we are together because God has called and chosen us to be here so that we may minister the faith to each other. We are servants of the Lord, whose purpose is to bring about a new and better world for all humankind.

Materials you may need for Stage Seven
Easter candle • table cloth • paper
background music • tape recorder
matches • flowers • hymns/songs/psalms
charcoal • table • slides of bread & wine
stone tile • Blu-Tack • wine or juice
bread • newsprint or similar • pens or pencils
salt • methylated spirits • metal dish
thick table mat • list of project events
Copies of:
- Scripture passages for the Foundations Stories
- 'Needs that are essential . . .' (Worksheet 21)
- 'My personal story' (Worksheet 22)
- Copies of the project evaluation (Worksheet 23)
- Appropriate illustrations for discussion

A Welcoming Atmosphere
At this stage it may be as well to recall the suggestions made at the beginning of Stage One concerning the importance of a welcoming atmosphere. As time moves on there are many things we tend to take for granted – and sometimes even forget! As we share and explore our faith more deeply it becomes even more important to create the right kind of atmosphere within which this may happen. The **focal point** for this stage should be the Easter candle, a symbol of the Risen Lord. You may also decide to have a fire, or bread and wine, depending upon the nature of your closing prayer.

Ideas for your Seventh Session
To be selected and adapted

The Foundation Stories

Stories of the risen Jesus 30–60 mins
Have available copies of the following passages of Scripture:

1 • Luke 5:1–11 Peter meets Jesus for the first time
2 • John 18:15–27 At the house of the High Priest
3 • John 20:19–23 Jesus appears to the disciples
4 • John 21:1–19 The Risen Jesus provides breakfast for the disciples beside Lake Tiberias

• Consider these stories one by one. (You may, of course, decide to select others.) As on previous occasions, have the story read aloud, either by one person reading to the whole group, or by forming small groups and having one person read in each of those groups.
• When the reading is finished, invite people to reflect upon the story for a while, either in silence or by individuals offering to the group (without explanation) the single word or phrase that has particular significance for him or her.
• After sufficient time for reflection, encourage discussion in small groups.

Notes to help you explore the foundation stories
1 • Luke 5:1–11 Peter meets Jesus for the first time
You may have read and shared this story during Stage Four of the project. If you did use it then, simply spend a little less time on it now; but **do** recall the story and the steps that occur at this stage of Peter's spiritual journey. (These are given in detail in the notes for Stage Four of the project.) Refer especially to Peter's fear and lack of comprehension, as well as Jesus' power to remove these.

2 • John 18:15–27 At the house of the High Priest
It is another night. Peter, who had been so bold and courageous during the arrest in the garden, follows Jesus, but stays away from the group surrounding him. He has lost all hope. Feeling very cold, he approaches the warmth of a charcoal fire—but that draws him into a situation he cannot handle comfortably. Full of fear, he lies and denies knowing Jesus.

Meanwhile, Jesus is interrogated. He is open, truthful and, in the real sense of the word, free—yet he is publicly abused.
• Allow the story to be read, reflected upon and discussed.
• Give everyone a blank piece of paper (A4 size or less) and a pencil or biro.
• Suggest that everyone considers what it would be like to dramatise the passage. Invite each one to try to indicate, on the paper, a plan of the stage. Where would the actors stand? What props would be used?
• Allow time to discuss this, encouraging the groups to draw simple sketches—perhaps using matchstick people.
• After they have spent some time discussing and sketching, suggest that each group consider the lighting needed for its stage setting. Invite everyone to discuss this within the small groups.
• When you think sufficient discussion has taken place, ask everyone to stop. Invite different groups to explain how they would dramatise this story. Depending upon how you plan your session, you may invite the groups to read the parts in the stage positions. Allow plenty of discussion to follow this sharing of ideas.
• If it has not already emerged in the discussion, point out that John is telling two stories side by side. There are two scenes, one by the fire and one around Jesus, both going on at the same time. Ask the group what they think is happening in these two places. Encourage them to discuss this.
• After a short period of discussion, invite them to consider that, in fact, there are two trials being described here. In one of them Jesus speaks and acts truthfully, yet he is physically attacked and denied. However, in the real sense, he is truly **free**. Peter, on the other hand, in the other trial, lies and goes unharmed, but, **how does he feel?**

• Invite everyone to consider how they think Peter felt physically. Point out that John tells us Peter was **cold**. He possibly felt his whole commitment to Jesus had been a waste, a sham. Jesus has left him. Feeling desolate and lonely, he is drawn by the warmth of the fire. Huddling close to it, he anguishes over the fact that the person whom he trusted with his life is now simply a plaything in someone's courtyard, and appears to have neither power nor authority. Peter possibly felt he had lost everything of which he ever dreamed. He is frozen cold, as if his very life is draining out of him. The flames and the fire of that night would possibly remain in his mind forever.

• Invite each one to think about his or her own feelings when s/he feels afraid, disillusioned, disloyal and/or angry. How do they tend to behave when they are experiencing such feelings? Allow time for discussion about feelings and behaviour.

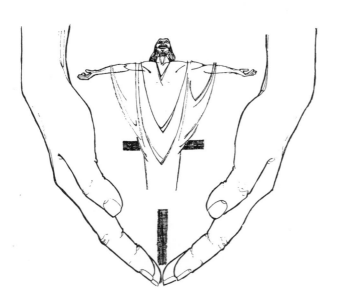

3 • John 20:19–25 Jesus appears to the disciples
Jesus is risen and shows himself to the disciples. He breathes upon them his gift of the Holy Spirit and tells them that his work, and theirs, is to forgive sin.

• In small groups, read, reflect upon and discuss this story. Encourage everyone to consider Jesus' words concerning forgiveness. What do they mean? To whom are they addressed, both then and today? Is the power to forgive sin given to all Christians—or just to a select and chosen few?

• After sufficient time for exploration, together ponder over the fact that the power to forgive sin, to push aside fear, and to liberate people for a new way of life, is the work of the Holy Spirit, in all baptised Christians, for others. It is Jesus' mission. It is the mission of the Church, and it is also the mission of each one of us.

Note. Our experience has been that this story, especially when read in the context of this stage of the project, provokes a lot of discussion. The fact that each one of us is called to proclaim, in an active manner, the healing and reconciling nature of the Church—to which we not only belong, but which we **are**—is understood as this time often in a new and more profound way. Many people find their new concept both exciting and disturbing. Invite them to illustrate their thoughts by sharing stories from their own experience of life, demonstrating forgiveness and healing as it occurs every day within their own family lives. You may use examples (such as Mother Teresa, Jean Vanier, Sue Ryder and Oscar Romero) to illustrate the power of the Holy Spirit to enable one human being to bring the forgiveness and freedom of God to others.

You will probably find that people will touch upon the importance of celebrating forgiveness together, through the priesthood and the ministry of the Church. It is important that everyone be helped to understand that **God always and everywhere forgives sin**. The Sacrament of Reconciliation verifies and makes public what God is already doing. We need such grace to support us and to help us to understand how God loves us, forgives us and never leaves us. He always heals us and leads us to freedom. We require the action of the Holy Spirit in us, however, to enable us to live the new, free kind of life to which we are called. God pours out his Spirit upon us but does not force us to respond. It is the responsibility of each one of us to **receive** his Spirit; to grow and change so that his Spirit may find a home in us.

4 • John 21:1–19 The Risen Jesus provides breakfast for the disciples beside Lake Tiberias
This is the last story of John's Gospel. He tells us there are many more stories, but the ones he has chosen to share with us reveal to us all we need to know. This particular story is one of the great stories about Jesus. It shows us, very clearly, something about the work of God in each person's life. Every word is significant; every phrase carries profound truths. These will resonate with people differently, according to each one's own personal experience of life and of God. We should bear in mind, however, the limitations of both written words and symbols to express the depths of these truths.

John, energetically and with enormous passion, wishes to share with us something of what he, over a period of time, has come to live and understand about Jesus.

• In small groups, read, reflect upon and discuss this story.
• One by one, draw attention to some or all of the following details:
a • Peter has returned to fishing. **He has gone back to his old way of life—even though Jesus has breathed out his Spirit upon him and the others**. The disciples have **seen** the Risen Jesus —but it does not seem to have changed their lives! In some kind of way, they are 'stuck'. A familiar, secure model of life seems, in some way, to bind them. They are still afraid. They do not understand and are not able to act with the power of the Spirit—with which later they will grow accustomed. The new life and new purpose have evaporated.

This state of affairs is familiar to all of us. We hear the truth, but nothing changes.

b • John tells us that **'the sun was rising'**. Symbolically, he is saying that something is about to happen; something is about to change; new light is about to be shed. On Easter Sunday it was Jesus, the Son of God, who rose from the darkness of death and filled life with new meaning—with new light. This time it is Peter and his friends who are about to see things in a different light and to grow and change.

c • The disciples are very slow to recognise Jesus —a fact that is so often true of ourselves! What helps them is the way in which their memories are stirred concerning a similar event some years earlier. In fact, parts of this story are almost like an 'action replay' of the first story considered in this session (cf. Luke 5:1–11)! They have been fishing all night and have caught nothing. Then they meet Jesus and are told to throw out the nets again, and these are filled to breaking point. One of the disciples then realises who the man on the lakeshore is. He tells Peter, who immediately jumps into the water and runs towards Jesus.

d • The charcoal fire and the fish provide a focal point. They probably confront Peter with his anguish and his state of hopelessness. The fire reminds him of the reality of his sin. Just as the nets are weighed down with the fish, so too is Peter 'weighed down' as memories are being brought alive. We are told in verse 11, 'Simon Peter dragged the net ashore.' Was he, by that stage—having got over his initial excitement—also dragging himself as things begin to surface in his mind? Things that are painful, at this moment, to think about, such as that first meeting with Jesus . . . the last meal together . . . and then that fire outside the courtyard.

Sitting and eating together, the disciples are reminded of their last meal with Jesus, of the time they were with the person who longed for that special night; who longed to eat with them and share his life with them. 'Come and eat' is a true **'remembering'**.

Such things as fear, distortion of the truth, and lies all prevent us remembering the reality that has taken hold of us. Part of the process of our conversion, through forgiveness and healing into freedom, is our need to go back and understand events in our life in a new and truthful way. Such conversion is always God's work in us, as he illuminates our darkness and our forgotten areas with his light.

e • The Last Supper was also part of that dreadful night of the arrest, trial and death of Jesus; that night when Peter, in utter desolation, drew near to a fire to keep warm; that night when Jesus had left him; that night when all sense of power and presence had vanished; that dreadful night when he denied being a friend of Jesus.

Here, on the lakeside, Jesus is beside the fire. Peter knows now that what he thought and felt on that dreadful night was not true. Jesus was close to him all the time. He had not left him. Even during the time Jesus was on trial in the courtyard, Peter now realised that he had also been there beside him as he was questioned by servants and surrounded by soldiers. As they sit and eat together near the water, those previous events are brought alive and, in remembering them here, in the presence of the Risen Lord, Peter is changed.

f • The group may notice that it is only **after** the Eucharist event—of being with, sharing with and knowing the Risen Christ—that Jesus opens Peter's wound. First Jesus invites him to 'come and eat', then he is able to speak to Peter about that terrible night. Three times he asks Peter, 'Do you love me?' Peter says, 'Yes'—but not as he would like to be able to do. His love is very fragile.

The three questions of love are very special. In the Greek version of John's Gospel, Jesus uses the word **agapan** in the first two questions, but in the third one he uses the word **philein**. The shift in meaning is lost when we translate these words into English because we use the one word **'love'** for both of the Greek expressions. **Agapan** expresses a total, committed love that is given freely and voluntarily, there being no natural obligation on the part of one person to love the other. **Philein**, on the other hand, expresses the love of friendship or the natural love that exists between members of a family. Jesus, therefore, begins by asking Peter if he freely chooses to love him in an **agapan** way. Peter answers 'yes', but uses the word **philein** for love. In other words, 'I love you as a brother, as a friend.' When Jesus asks the question the third time, he uses the same term as Peter, ie **philein**: 'Do you love me as a brother?' This portrays a great deal of tenderness as Jesus reaches out to meet Peter where he is on his faith journey. Peter is not able to surrender to Jesus in an **agapan** manner at this moment in time. That will come later.

g • Jesus talks to Peter about the journey they have already begun. 'When you are old you will stretch out your hands and someone else will bind you and take you where you do not want to go,' Jesus tells him. In other words, Peter would be bound in the same way that Jesus was bound.

Jesus is telling Peter that they will always be close, that they will journey together. He is also conveying to him that one day the Holy Spirit will have taken

up a home so deeply in his heart that Peter will never be shaken, will never be afraid. He will be free. But that time is not now. At the moment it is all right to be afraid, to worry, to feel as if he is falling apart. Jesus will never let go of him.

The experience of his own gradual conversion, and his subsequent response to the power of the Holy Spirit in his life, later enabled Peter to minister to others who were suffering in a similar way. This is also true for each one of us.

h • Peter is not only reconciled to his Lord, but he is reaffirmed in his ministry (cf. Luke 5:1–11). Peter has failed; he has sinned; but Jesus reconciles him to himself and confirms the mission he had been asked to pursue. No action of ours, no matter what failure or sin diminishes us, prevents the Risen Jesus from continuing to act in us. The restoration and healing of Jesus is total.

John's final story is also our story: it is the story of the Church.

Our Personal Stories

If we are to **grow** in faith **together**, then we must be willing to **share** our faith with one another. This means each one being prepared to **take the risk** of speaking to others about his or her own, personal understanding of God and of life; about the way God is working in and through him or her; and about the way God is working in and through other people whom he or she knows. This type of sharing, as you are already well aware, is central to the project.

Having explored some of the foundation stories related by Luke and John, we now need to help each person see his or her own, personal story in the light of them.

The foundation stories contain essential truths about our own efforts to live Christian lives and therefore give meaning to our struggles as we try to grow and develop in faith. Our capacity to understand these truths and the meaning they have for each one of us, personally, is greatly increased when, in the light of the foundation stories, we explore our personal stories **in the company of others**.

The following ideas may help you enable people to explore their own stories.

Needs that are essential Worksheet 21

Needs that are essential if we are to be fully human, fully alive

15–25 mins

1 • Invite people to discuss, in small groups:
what needs they consider to be essential if a person is to be fully human, fully alive;
why they think these things are essential.

2 • The basic needs of LOVE, FOOD, CARE, HEALING and TRUST probably will be among those discussed. Write these words on a piece of newsprint (or similar) before the session. After sufficient time for discussion, display the words where they may be seen clearly by everyone. Invite comment and ask people if they cover the needs discussed in their groups.

3 • Show the group how John's last story describes the ways in which Peter's needs are met. Do this briefly and fairly quickly, perhaps using worksheet 21 (You may ask the participants how they think love, food, care, healing and trust are illustrated in the story.) Point out that Jesus' actions were not extraordinary. He brought forgiveness and wholeness to Peter—thus enabling him to continue his journey of faith—by preparing a meal and inviting the disciples to come and eat it. Even more important than his actions, however, was the fact of his presence: **he was there**— with them.

4 • Invite everyone to discuss the **feelings** he or she thinks may have been engendered as Peter's needs were met. How would each one feel, for example, having been disloyal to a loved one, when later that person asks, 'Do you love me?'

5 • Invite participants to consider and share among themselves how the **ordinary** actions of our daily life are the ways in which we bring love and forgiveness to others and help them grow in faith. Each one might also consider occasions when he or she was aware that, at that moment in time, his or her presence was all that another person needed.

(As always, be sure to share your own stories of life with the project group.)

My personal story Worksheet 22

My personal story 15–25 mins

• Give each person a copy of worksheet 22, and a pen or pencil.
• Invite each person, alone, to identify—in his or her own life—experiences which are called to mind by the phrases on the hand-out. They may indicate these on the paper.
• Invite each one to share, as freely as he or she wishes, one of these events.

Project evaluation Worksheet 23

Personal stories of the project

20–30 mins

By this stage of the project, we know that central to our growth and development in faith is our ability to link our experience of life with our experience of Jesus and the Church. We have already, on previous occasions, seen ways in which we may help people explore their **personal** experience of God's work in the world. See, for example:

1 • Times When I Felt . . . Times When Jesus Felt . . . (Stage Two)
2 • No One Makes the Journey of Faith Alone (Stages Three and Five)
3 • Giving and Receiving Gifts (Stage Five)

During this session (or perhaps during the vigil), it may be useful to look back, together, over the sessions, the parish celebrations and any other activities in which the project group has been involved. Using our memories in this way, particularly in the light of the foundation stories we have been considering, often enables us to be touched in a new and deeper way by the truths to which we have been exposed.

- List some of the events in which members of the project group have been involved. For example:

The service project

Mass of the Word of God

Taking hold of one's own Baptismal candle

The anointing of ears and mouth with olive oil and perfume of frankincense

Mrs Wright's trial

Shabbat Shalom

Mass of the Healing of the Sick

The story of Peter's first meeting with Jesus

Exploring relationships between parent and child and between ourselves and God

Anointing with myrrh

Burning incense

Holding the oil of chrism

The special group Mass

Remembering of the living and the dead during the group Mass

The stories of the Holy Spirit in Jesus' life

The Mass of Inscription

and so on.

- Invite each person to sit alone.
- Provide everyone with a pen or pencil.
- Give out copies of worksheet 23, and pens or pencils.

1 • Invite everyone to write down in the upper part of each of the **outer** circles (but **not** the central one) five moments in the project that they remember and find meaningful.

2 • Then, in each of the circles, write below the line what was important to him or her about those events.

3 • Now invite each one to look at the central circle.

In the top part write 'The most important thing . . . (*inserting his or her own name into the space*) has learnt is . . .'

and then, below the line, indicate whatever it is s/he has found most important.

4 • Invite everyone to move into small groups and share with one another whatever each one found to be most important for him or herself, and why.

Prayer Celebration

Alternative celebrations are offered, depending on whether you have already celebrated a Passover Meal or Shabat Shalom

Celebration One 15–20 mins

(Suitable if you have not celebrated either a Passover meal or Shabat Shalom)

Invite everyone to sit in groups of three, gathered around the 'focal point' which has been prepared with an Easter candle, flowers and a small charcoal fire. There should also be one bread roll and one glass of wine (or grape juice) for each group of three people. (You may, of course, decide to have one glass per person.)

Leader: Introduce the prayer by briefly reflecting upon:

a • the Easter candle, symbol of the Risen Jesus, present here among us;

b • the charcoal fire, reminding us of both the new fire of Easter and Peter's story;

c • the fact that we have been called to share our lives and our faith with one another, and with others.

Invite everyone to sit in silence for a few moments as we remind ourselves that now, as always, we are in the presence of God.

Music and/or slides on wheat and bread may be used (4–5 mins) either during or immediately after this silent period. You may decide to have music playing quietly in the background throughout the period of prayer. Appropriate slides, used sensitively, can also help create a prayerful atmosphere.

Leader: Let **us** break bread together.

(You may like to sing the first verse of the hymn *Let us break bread together on our knees* or a similar one.)

Leader: God created each one of us in his image. Each person here reveals something of the nature of God. It is his life and power within us that makes us what we are.

- Invite everyone to consider each member of his or her group in turn and to think about one of that person's gifts.
- Invite one member of each group of three to take a bread roll and break it into three. One by one, each person takes a portion and offers it to the person on his or her left, saying:

Name, this is a sign of my life that I share with you now. I thank God and I also thank you for your gift of . . . (*state the person's gift, eg gentleness, joy, or understanding*).

• Each person then eats the bread he or she has been offered.
• Allow a few moments of silent reflection, by which time all the groups should be ready to proceed.

> *Leader*:   Each one of us has a mission, but we often deny it. Like Peter, we prefer not to take risks. Yet the Risen Jesus affirms our mission—just as he did Peter's. He asks us to bring his love and healing to each person we meet.

Slides on wine and grapes (4–5 mins.) may be used.

> *Leader*:   When we share food with one another, we share our friendship with one another; but to drink wine together is to express our love for one another.
> Let us do this now.

• Invite each one to call to mind the people who are loving towards him or her; the people who are really important in his or her life; and then to thank God in his or her heart for each one of those people. (Pause)
• Ask each group to take a glass of wine (or three glasses).
• Invite each person, in turn, to offer the glass of wine to whoever is on his or her right, saying:

> *Name*, I thank the Father for all the encouragement, support and love you have brought me in my life.

• The recipient takes a drink of the wine and replaces the glass on the table.

Close with a suitable blessing and song.

Celebration Two 10–15 mins
(Suitable if you have celebrated either a Passover meal or Shabat Shalom, or are going to do so later, eg at the vigil)

Invite everyone to gather around the 'focal point', which has been prepared with an Easter candle, flowers and the materials for a smokeless fire, as illustrated. Dim the lights.

> *Leader*:   Invite and lead people to reflect upon the importance of **remembering**: events, relationships, people, and places; the importance of going back over our lives, recalling sounds, words, sights and feelings. God speaks to us in and through our lives. It is important, therefore, that we 'listen' to our lives; to what he tells us about the moments we remember; to know the Risen Jesus was there, and is here, present with us, now.

• Invite everyone to think of **one** moment in his or her life; to think about where this was; when? who was there? what was said? what happened? Ask each one to 'stay' with that moment and reflect upon it, and to pay particular attention to his or her feelings as he or she thinks about the event.
• Now invite each one to listen in silence to the Risen Lord, as he speaks to him or her in and through the remembered event.
• Ignite the fire and play some reflective music.
• Sit in silence with the music and the flames of the fire.
• After a suitable period of time:

1 Comment upon the fire: how this reminds us of being with the Risen Jesus . . . the new fire of Easter from which the Paschal candle was kindled . . . the fire on the lakeside of Tiberias where the Risen Jesus prepared breakfast for the disciples and reaffirmed Peter's mission, and our own mission to bring to each person we meet the love, peace and healing of Christ.

2 Invite everyone to sing a song together (eg *Kyrie eleison*).

3 Select a short passage of Scripture.

• Pause for a few moments of silent reflection.
• Close with a simple blessing.

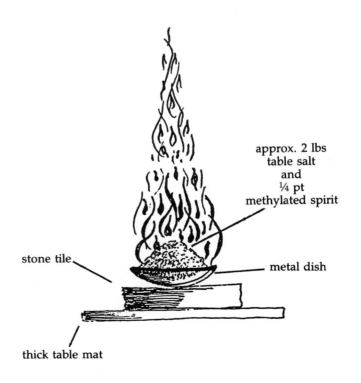

approx. 2 lbs table salt and ¼ pt methylated spirit

stone tile

metal dish

thick table mat

Celebrating Stage Seven with the Parish

The focus of our work at this stage of the project is a deepening understanding of the **New Life** we have in our Risen Lord. It is, therefore, appropriate for the parish to celebrate its own 'new life', through which it has grown and been both blessed and enriched.

Our suggestion is that **everyone** (whether baby, child or adult) who has been baptised during the last twelve months is invited, together with his or her family, Godparents, sponsors and friends, to a special Mass (on one of the Sundays of Eastertide) during which the parish celebrates in a special way, its 'new life'.

The intention is to offer the whole parish an opportunity to realise the life of the Risen Jesus active among them. A number of baptisms still, for whatever reason, take place when only family and friends are present, and many people are unaware of the growth taking place in their parish family. This special Mass enables everyone to realise, more fully, his or her incorporation into the Risen Lord and also provides parishioners with an opportunity to support and congratulate the families of the baptised.

A celebration of this nature conveys much about Christian life to those who participate. Understanding of the Easter mysteries is extented; the primacy of the Christian family is affirmed and faith in the People of God is strengthened.

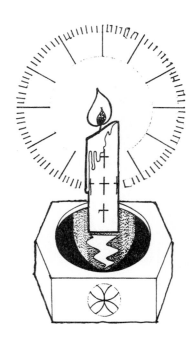

Some ideas to help you plan your celebration

1 • An occasion such as this offers an opportunity for a social event. The whole parish may be invited to celebrate with the baptised and their families in an informal way, perhaps after the Mass or in the evening (eg a parish picnic, barbecue and/or dance). Such events help people to get to know one another, to spend time together and to support one another.

2 • Members of the project group may help to organise the Mass and the social event.

3 • Members of the project group or, possibly, housebound people who are able to do so, may prepare invitations.

4 • Members of the project group may welcome those who have been recently baptised, and their families, and lead them to prearranged seats.

5 • If possible, those who have been baptised are situated (with their families) where they may be seen together.

6 • The assembled community prays with and for the baptised and their families, eg during the Prayer of the Faithful. (*The prayers of the Masses of Eastertide are about our new life.*)

7 • Members of the families of the newly baptised form the procession with the gifts.

8 • There may be a special incensing of the group of baptised and their families.

9 • Flowers may be given to the family of each newly baptised person.

10 • Each family may be given a small plant to indicate that, like the planted seed, the gift of faith must be nurtured if it is to grow and develop.

11 • A group photograph may be taken for the parish photographic record.

12 • Names and addresses of the newly baptised may be given to the housebound, perhaps with a copy of the group photograph.

13 • The group photograph and/or others may be displayed on the parish notice-board.

14 • The homily may be about family and parish life and the responsibility of **every** member of the parish to nurture the faith of each person it receives in Baptism.

15 • Reference may be made to other aspects of parish life that manifest the activity of the Risen Christ in our midst.

Stage Eight

Watching . . . Waiting . . .

This is the final stage of the project. Its general purpose is to provide people with a structured period of time for **prayer, reflection** and **reconciliation**. If the members of the project group are preparing for a particular event (for example, Baptism, Confirmation or Marriage), then this is a time of **waiting** as they prepare to continue their journey with the Holy Spirit. For others, it may be a time of **strengthening** their commitment to Christ and the Christian way of life.

The specific aims are:

• to enable members of the group to celebrate the time they have spent together and to bring the project to a close

• to encourage people to continue their journey of faith and to help them overcome any fear or anxiety that may hinder God's free action in them

• to help participants understand their mission of serving others and bringing the Good News to all they meet

• to offer people an opportunity to celebrate the Sacrament of Reconciliation in a meaningful and appropriate way.

Comments on approach

This final stage is based upon a **Vigil Mass**, parts of which may take place in different locations. The way in which you organise this vigil will depend very much upon the nature of **your** group and the personnel and facilities you have available. Our original concept was that the vigil should last all night and that it should, if possible, take place within the parish community. This works very well for most parishes. Some, however, prefer to take the group away for a weekend, while others find a three-hour vigil more suitable for their particular situation. **Decide what is best for you and your group**, and don't be afraid to try different things with different groups. What works well with people preparing for retirement does not necessarily suit young adults!

Plan the Vigil Mass in sections, for example:

1 • the announcements to the parish (via newsletters, homilies, invitations and notices)
2 • beginning the vigil
3 • the Word of God
4 • the preparation of the altar and the gifts
5 • the Penitential Rite and the Sacrament of Reconciliation.

6 • the Sign of Peace
7 • the Eucharistic Prayer—remembering the living and the dead
8 • Communion
9 • the Dismissal

The Vigil Mass is about **reconciliation** and **the work of the Holy Spirit in our lives**. Readings and prayers on these themes may be found in the Lectionary.

The next few pages contain a variety of ideas, approaches and activities which may be adapted to suit various parts of the Mass. Consider your group, the situation in which you are working, and the length of your vigil; then **select and adapt** the ideas accordingly. Among those that follow, you will find ideas on the themes of:

> Water and Baptism
> Stones
> Watching at the Altar
> Fire
> Flowers, Messages and Blessings
> Anointing
> An Emmaus Walk
> A Guided Meditation
> Reconciliation

Decide what your overall theme is going to be, and then choose appropriate ideas either from those below or from other stages of the project. The vigil is an extended Mass, lasting several hours (perhaps even two or three days). Be sure to apply the S•P•R•I•N•G•S principle! It applies as much to this session as any other. Whatever kind of group you have, be sure to use a variety of approaches, with plenty of movement for some of the time and stillness at others. Remember, the Lord speaks in different ways to different people. Try to provide the right environment for **each** person to be, at some time, where s/he is most receptive to his word.

Remember, as outlined earlier, **the different parts of the Mass** may take place in a variety of locations. It may, for example, begin in a garden with a bonfire or barbecue, proceed from there to one or more houses, then to a local night-refuge or help-line centre, and finally close in a church, community centre or hospital chapel. Explore the possibilities available to you!

Celebrating Stage Eight with the Parish Community

Instead of having a separate parish celebration at this stage of the project, members of the parish may be involved in the Vigil Mass in a variety of ways. It is important, however, that a good part of the vigil is attended by members of the project group alone, so **parishioners may be invited to attend at specific times**. Following are some examples.

a • People may come for the beginning of the vigil, to share the initial celebration, to pray with members of the project group and to assure them of their prayer throughout the night.

b • Night workers may join the group for a short time, either on their way to work or as they return home.

c • People may join the group at the end of the vigil, to greet the members of the group. If the vigil has been celebrated outside the parish, make the church the point to which they return, and encourage parishioners to be there to welcome them back.

Apart from these specific times when parishioners may visit the project group, everyone in the parish may be invited to remember the group in their prayers at home.

In the course of the vigil, there may be opportunities for members of the project group to go out, in groups, to people in the parish. How you use these opportunities will depend very much upon the nature of both your group and your environment.

Materials you may need for Stage Eight

water • container for water • flowers • food
stones • spray lacquer • water-based felt pens
fire materials • paints • Easter candle • paper
• spray paints • chalice(s) • wine • altar breads
altar cloths • table • cloth • paten(s) • stole
Scriptures • pens/pencils • projector • slides
bowls for water • towels • hymns • background music
tape recorder • olive or almond oil • greetings cards
essence of perfumed oil, eg jasmine, orange blossom
candles to provide light

Ideas for your eighth session
To be selected and adapted

Water and Baptism

During Stage One of the project, water was blessed and 'baptismal' candles were placed in it. The whole process of 'remembering' is very important, as we have already seen and, as this is the last time the members of **this** group will be together, it may be helpful for them to remember the earlier stages of the project, especially the beginning.

There are several ways in which water may be used during the Vigil Mass. Following are some suggestions.

1 • The Easter candle may be lit from the fire (cf. 'fire', page 96) and used to bless the water. The priest and/or each person, in turn, may place the candle in the water. This may be used to express sorrow for sin, uniting with Jesus in his death, helping to place him in the tomb and joining him there, and waiting for new life with trust and hope.

2 • During the Mass, the priest washes his hands after offering the gifts. This symbolic gesture could be explored.

Everyone may wash his/her hands, perhaps in water that has been blessed.

Others may take hold of our hands, wash them (using scented soap and warm water), and then dry them for us. This may be seen as an expression of both our trust and our wish to be free of hurt, as well as our desire to serve others.

The washing of hands may be part of the Penitential Rite and/or the Sacrament of Reconciliation. For example, an examination of conscience (or consciousness)—perhaps before the time spent watching the altar, may be followed by the washing of hands and a time for celebrating the Sacrament of Reconciliation (with individual confession).

3 • During the vigil a portion of blessed water may be taken home, along with flowers and a message (cf. 'Flowers, Messages and Blessings', p.nnn, e). It may be left there, with a lighted candle, as a reminder to pray for the project member when s/he returns to the group. It may also serve, later, as a reminder to the project member to continue developing his/her relationship with God.

4 • There are a number of other ways in which water may be used in a significant way during the vigil and/or the celebration of Reconciliation. For example, people may use it:

to drink—as an essential for life;
to water plants—recalling the need to nurture faith;
to wash the altar or the sanctuary area.

Stones

Either ask each person to bring to the vigil a stone s/he has chosen, **or** provide a variety of stones from which people may select one. It is best if the stones are of a size that fits and fills the hand.

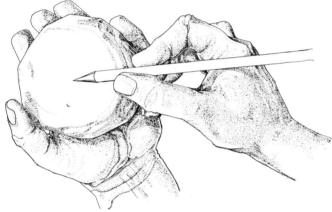

Some general ideas about stones

A variety of meanings may be attached to stones:

1 • Ezekiel refers to 'hearts of stone' and reminds us that God can change our lives, giving us hearts of flesh and warmth.

2 • Stones are often used to mark important places and moments. Our countryside is full, for example, of tombstones, milestones, 'standing' stones and cairns. Jacob set up a stone as a memorial of a time when he was very aware of the presence of God (Gen 28:18).

3 • Stones have been, and still are, used to symbolise the presence of God. Most altars are made of stone and we have a number of ancient monuments such as Avebury and Stonehenge.

4 • Stones are all different, each having its own character. Every one contains an expression of God; it tells a story. The work of sculptors, therefore, is a spiritual expression, as may be seen, for example, in the works of Michelangelo, the African sculptors of Zimbabwe and the Inuit sculptors of Canada. The stonemason tunes into the stone in his hands, feels the nature of life that belongs to it, and works with this to bring about a shape. The graining, texturing, and fracture lines are all part of the life in the stones.

5 • Stones are very old. They have been formed and shaped over a long period of time. They have been in existence long before us, standing before God, declaring his existence. They have been pushed and pulled by all kinds of elements to reach the shapes we see today. Each one has survived its own very long journey!

6 • Stones are durable—and human beings have instinctively left marks, signs and signatures upon them, so that something remains and is seen by others long after the person is dead.

7 • All stones are beautiful—but some are strikingly so. Some are cut and polished to bring out their beauty, colour, graining and ability to capture light. From the earliest times, precious and semi-precious stones have been used to decorate people, articles and places, as well as to celebrate rituals, such as engagements and coronations.

8 • Few stones have tidy lines, symmetry or efficient functions. They contrast, therefore, with the design of human beings in industry and technology. They belong, rather, to a nature that has no straight lines and is always changing in its cycles of birth and dying.

During the vigil stones may be used in a variety of ways, examples of which are given below.

1 • **The reading of the Word of God**

Invite each person to choose a stone and then, in small groups, share what it was about this stone that made him or her select it. This may be because of its attractiveness or because it expresses something of the character, state of relationships or future hopes of that person.

The stones are washed in the vigil water (cf. 'Water, page 94), blessed and left to dry, an action which may be incorporated into the Penitential Rite or celebration of Reconciliation.

When the stones are dry, or later in the vigil, each person is invited to put his/her name on the stone, using a felt pen. (*Note: Water-based felt pens are more successful than spirit-based, should you wish to 'seal' the stone later with lacquer.*)

Each person is invited to sit alone and reflect upon whatever word or phrase of Scripture is very important to him or her. This 'special' piece of Scripture may be written on the stone also, either at this time or later in the Vigil Mass, for example, after Communion.

2 • The Preparation of the Altar and the Gifts

The stones may be placed on the altar or, if this part of the vigil is being celebrated in a house or garden, on a table or in some other prominent place. Use a suitable introduction, enabling each person to express, through the stone, his/her offering of his/her life to God.

3 • The Eucharistic Prayer

Invite each person to take his/her stone from the altar and mark on it the names of two or more persons, living or dead, who are important to him/her in his/her life at the present moment. After this is done the stones are returned to the altar.

4 • The Dismissal

As the vigil draws to a close the stones may be finally sealed. They may be taken from the altar and decorated with quick drying paints and felt pens. Each stone is then sprayed with rapid-setting lacquer. (Our experience has been that, by this time, each person has become very 'involved' with his/her stone and a lot of sharing takes place.)

Once the stones are dry they may be replaced on the altar. They may be blessed by the priest, anointed with oil (cf. Gen 28:18) and returned to each person with a blessing, after which the final blessing of the Mass may be given to the whole group.

(Note: Personal value is often attached to these stones. People tend to take them home and keep them as a reminder of a very special part of their Christian journey. Like Jacob's stone, they mark an important moment in life.)

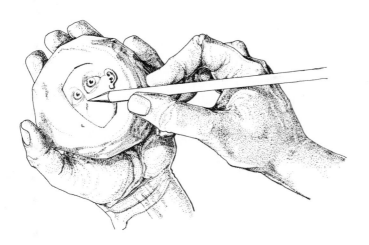

Watching at the Altar

In days of old, when a knight took up his time of vigil his sword, lance, spurs, shield and armour were laid on the altar. The knight then spent the night before the altar, in prayer. He attached much importance to this period of 'watching' and 'waiting' prior to his investiture.

Each baptised person is invested with the Holy Spirit —a Spirit which empowers and leads us ever more deeply into an understanding of life and of Christian service. Like Jesus in the Garden of Gethsemane, there are times when we, too, need to 'wait' and 'watch': to stop and ponder in our hearts, most especially when we are preparing to make an important step in our journey, such as Baptism or Confirmation. Part of the vigil, therefore, may be spent in the church in candlelight (or with the lights dimmed).

• Prior to the vigil, each person is invited to bring an object that is personal to him/her in his/her journey of life and faith.

• During the vigil, each person is invited to place his/her chosen object upon the altar and then spend time in prayer, alone, wherever s/he chooses to be in the church. Each one should be encouraged to assume whatever position is most prayerful for him/her, whether this be kneeling, sitting, lying on the floor, standing, leaning against a pillar or whatever.

• Following this period of silent prayer, the priest may bless each person and return the object to his/her safekeeping.

• People may now gather in small groups (perhaps around the fire, or in a person's house, with refreshments) and share something of the significance of the chosen objects.

Fire

Fire has been seen at the Easter Vigil and pondered upon in the stories of Peter. It is a symbol of the Holy Spirit, but it also has many other symbolic meanings.

If you are conducting this stage of the project in the period around Pentecost, early in the summer, the weather **may** be warm and dry. You may consider having a large fire for the vigil, perhaps in the church grounds, on a beach or in a parishioner's garden.

Young adults, in particular, find a night fire an important experience. It draws people together and may be used in a number of different ways.

For example, it may be used:
1 • to share stories: of the journey of faith . . . of the experiences of this night . . . of the events for which we wait . . . of hopes for the future;
2 • to celebrate and pray, using songs, meditation, dance and/or fireworks;
3 • as a focus for the celebration of Reconciliation. 'Change' may be expressed symbolically. Each person may place into the flames objects symbolising his/her fears, hurts and failure to love;
4 • to burn incense;
5 • to cook food;
6 • to provide a warm place for gathering together.

Flowers, Messages and Blessings

During the vigil you may consider sending people out in groups of three or more, to take flowers and messages to the world about. The message may be written on a card but should also be delivered verbally by the group. The messages may be to express care and concern for people who work through the night; to convey greetings from the parish and a blessing for protection and peace; or to express concern about any aspect of life that is relevant to your particular area.

It is important to be in touch with the world 'out there'. It enables us to verify what we believe. God is everywhere, present to all people, whether those people acknowledge him or not. It also enables us to share with the wider community something of our understanding about God, Jesus Christ and the Christian way of life.

Obviously every city, town and village is different, and arrangements may need to be made in advance with people concerned. The following suggestions of places to visit are given simply to provoke thoughts about your own area. Bear in mind the nature of both your group and your environment before making any decisions! It may be that, during the vigil, it is wiser simply to prepare things for these places and pray for the people concerned, and then make the visits at some other time.

Places you may consider include:
    local radio and/or TV stations
    local newspaper offices
    hospitals: casualty waiting rooms, staff areas
    drug centres
    Salvation Army hostels —old people's homes
    —children's homes where there are night staff on duty
    university and college common rooms or 'drop-in' centres
    airports, railway stations and bus depots
    security firms—night-watchmen
    police stations
    industries where people work at night
    all night cafés and transport cafés – perhaps pausing to buy food and sit with people
    night clubs and discos
    organisations such as Nite-line and Samaritans
    take-away food shops
    all-night garages
    'cardboard cities'
    night-time soup kitchens.

Anointing

In the course of the project we have suggested several 'anointings', including the anointing of the ears and mouth with oil perfumed with frankincense, and the anointing for service with myrrh.

During the vigil we suggest that people anoint each other and pray for each other, thus exercising their right as people baptised to minister to others. To touch and anoint in this way images the way that Christ himself touched people. You may like to develop the significance of this according to the group with whom you are working. With a group of young parents, for example, you may explore the importance and significance of 'touch' in both marriage and parenthood.

The most suitable time for the anointing may be towards the end of the vigil, after Communion, when it may be used as part of the Rite of Dismissal. It is an appropriate expression of saying 'goodbye' to each other and blessing each other as the project draws to an end. It may also be used as a form of the Kiss of Peace.

If there is a large number of people involved, invite them to form small groups and anoint one another on the forehead. The following or similar words may be spoken:

> *Name*, I anoint you and give you my blessing. May you continue, in faith and trust, to share your life with others, as you have done with me. I pray that God, our Father, will strengthen and protect you; that Jesus, our Risen Lord, will fill your heart with trust and courage; and that the Holy Spirit will be with you and lead you in everything you do.

An Emmaus Walk

Precede this activity by gathering the whole group together for a reflective talk. Your presentation may include slides, music and/or hymns, possibly offering insights into the meaning of this vigil.

The following notes may help you:

1 • Talk about the purpose of the project, why this particular group came together initially, the fact that the project is now drawing to a close, and what the future holds —perhaps, for example, Confirmation or Marriage.

2 • Over the last few months we have, together, had experience of God and his presence among us. We have, perhaps, found that our understanding of God and of life has changed.

3 • Jesus tells us that where two or three are gathered together in his name, he is there in the midst of us, walking with us —in just the same way he walked with the two disciples on the road from Jerusalem to Emmaus.

(Slides, music and/or a reading of the Emmaus story would be appropriate here.)

4 • Jesus also sent his disciples out in pairs, to proclaim to others the love of his Father for everyone, and later, to tell them that God had reconciled the whole world to himself, through Christ his Son.

5 • Like the disciples, we are all, now, going to walk in pairs. It will be a special walk because we walk, in faith, with a brother or sister who has faith and who knows God.

6 • During the walk, one person will speak while the other listens and supports what is said. The listener may ask questions, but should not advise or speak about his/her own experiences. His/her turn to speak will come later, during the second part of the walk.

7 • Preferably, you should walk with someone you know well, and begin by deciding which one of you will speak first.

8 • While you are walking:
tell your companion a little about yourself: where you were born; your brothers and sisters; who and what is most important in your life;
say a little about the way you experience life at the present time, and what the future seems to hold for you;
then speak about your experience of the project. How has it affected you? Have you found any parts of it difficult in any way? What has been most important for you over the last few months? Explain why this is so.

9 • After a pre-arranged time (from ten to thirty minutes) the roles are exchanged, the speaker becoming the listener and vice-versa.

10 • Listen to the presence of God in your companion's story and, when it is your turn, speak to your friend with courage—knowing that the Risen Lord is there with you.

Celebrating Reconciliation

The Penitential Rite is celebrated usually at the beginning of Mass, but it may take place later, such as after the Liturgy of the Word or after the Offertory. Because this vigil is an **extended** Mass and you may wish to enable people to celebrate the sacrament of Reconciliation, we recommend that you use either of these two places, perhaps using the fire, the water or the stones to help people express sorrow for sin.

You may decide to invite several priests with whom the members of the group may celebrate Reconciliation. (This, of course, would need to be timetabled.) Alternatively, you may arrange for participants to call on priests who live near by.

To help the people with whom you are working, you may design an examination of consciousness based upon the following notes and your own experience of the group. You may then decide **either** to guide people through it together, in a meditative and reflective way, **or** to duplicate it, so that it may be given to participants to be used at a time appropriate to each individual. Some people may prefer to reflect upon it in pairs (eg married couples) or in small groups (eg older teenagers and young adults).

In touch with my real self before God

'Come to Me'

At every moment of every day, God is calling us into an ever deeper union with himself in and through the Risen Jesus. We know it in the depths of our being. Every part of us is touched by that knowledge: our feelings, our moods, our instincts, our yearnings. It is more through our deep-down feelings and moods that God reveals himself to us than in any other way.

He does speak to us through our minds and our reasoning powers also; but, having thought things over, we then have to descend with our minds into the depths of our being, and stand there in the presence of God. That is where our **true** knowledge lies. It is essential, therefore, to be in touch with what is happening in those areas of ourselves. By listening to God and responding to his word as we **feel** it deep within us, we may become all that he wishes us to be. We can become one with him.

It is not superficial feelings to which we are referring, but rather to what is going on at the very centre of our being: right down, deep in that place where we **know** God, that place where he has sown his word. It is there that we discover our true selves. Our behaviour, our attitudes, our actions are a response to the relationship developing there.

We have a problem, however, in that our sinful nature also touches our total being – our feelings, our moods, our instincts, our yearnings. How, then, do we sort out what is of God and what is not? How do we identify the feelings that are leading us to him and which are not?

Do you remember times when you asked yourself such questions as:
Do I really believe in God?
Is he real? . . . to me?
Does Jesus mean anything at all to me?
Do his life, death and resurrection make any difference to my life?

These are basic questions we all face at sometime in our faith journey! Probably – sooner or later— you managed to pull together (however flimsily) the various threads of your faith experiences, and found welling up within you the feeling that, 'Yes, he is real! I **know** it deep inside me! And not only that, but I have experience to support my deep-down feeling.' At such times your faith matures. You come out of the experience with a better understanding of yourself and of your relationship with God.

Such a moment of conviction may be described as a 'core experience of God'. It provides us with a kind of yardstick against which we can measure our other feelings. When we examine our present inner feelings in the light of that core experience of God and find that they 'fit', that there is a sense of rightness, peace and joy, then we know the feelings are right and good and of God. However, should we find that, no matter how hard we try to make the feelings 'fit', the result is turmoil, upset, or anxiety, that we are disturbed, that 'something is not right', then we can be fairly sure that they are not of God.

Being in touch with our true selves before God is, therefore, one of the most intimate ways in which we may encounter the Risen Jesus. Many of us are most conscious of that encounter in times of quiet prayer, which may be while we are washing the dishes, cutting the grass or whatever, as well as in times of 'formal' prayer. It is in prayer that each one of us experiences God's **personal** call, his personal invitation, his personal challenge. And it is generally through prayer that we sense and recognise the way in which we should respond.

The notes below may help to put you in touch with **your** feelings and examine them against **your** core experience. They offer a way in which you may examine your relationship with God – a process which also may help you prepare to celebrate the sacrament of Reconciliation. The five steps of the process are as follows:

1 • Ask the Spirit to help you and enlighten you.
2 • Thank God.
3 • How is God at work in your life?
4 • 'I give you a new heart and a new Spirit.'
5 • 'I trust him and place my hope in him.'

Remember, God calls each one of us in a unique and intimate way. Only you know the full story of your own faith journey . . . the special ways in which God is calling you . . . how you have responded in the past . . . the way your life has developed because of your response . . . the way you feel about this in the inner-most depths of your being.

Use the notes in whatever way you find best for you. If you feel drawn by a particular movement within you, then stay with that for as long as you wish. God is there, supporting you and holding you throughout every single moment.

Ask the Spirit to help you and enlighten you

Just as Jesus did throughout his life, ask the Holy Spirit to be with you, to guide you, to enlighten you, to help you understand how God is speaking to you in every moment of your life: at work, at home, at play, in and through all your relationships.

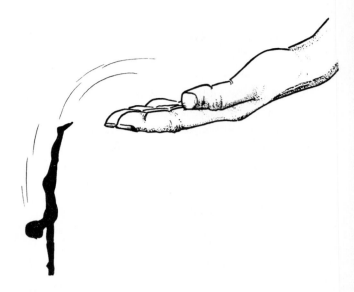

Thank God

Begin by thanking God for all the gifts you have. Think back over the last few hours, days, weeks, years. Tell him how grateful you are – for certain qualities you have, for opportunities, family, friends. Remember that everything and everyone is his gift to you.

Reflect upon what has happened during the last 24 hours. Is there something for which you are particularly grateful? Tell God about it.

Is there anything for which you find it difficult to be thankful? Talk to God about that. Tell him how you feel about it, and listen to him.

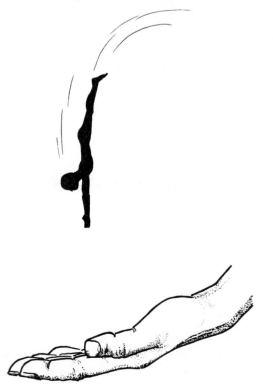

How is God at work in your life?

Consider, now, all that has been happening **to** you and **in** you. Some of the following may help you:

• Is there someone—a friend, member of your family, someone with whom you work – through whom God seems to draw closer to you? Think about that person, what you say and do together. In what way does God speak to you through him/her? To what is he calling you?

• Have you read a book recently or an article, watched a TV programme, been somewhere **special**, noticed something – and felt moved in **a special way**? Think about it. How did you feel then? How do you feel now?

• Is there a place that is 'special', where perhaps you like to be alone? Where is it? Think about it for a while. What do you feel God is saying to you at this moment about your special place?

• Have you felt afraid recently? . . . worried? . . . or anxious? Why? What was happening? Talk to God about your feelings and ask him to help you understand. Be still and, with him, look again at what was happening. How do you feel about it now?

• Have you felt particularly happy recently? When? Where? Who was with you? What happened? Tell God about the way you felt then and now.

• Have you been involved in a misunderstanding? How did the situation arise? What happened? Who was concerned? How do you feel about it now? Tell the Lord, and listen to him.

• Has there recently been pain or suffering in your life? What caused it? Was anyone else involved? Think about it. Look at it now, knowing the Risen Jesus is here with you. What are your feelings about it now?

• Do you always find it easy to pray? Be honest about this! Talk to the Risen Lord about the times that are easy and the times that are really difficult. Tell him how you feel on those occasions. Notice your feelings now.

• Have you reached out recently to someone who was lonely? . . . sad? . . . discouraged? . . . in need? . . . rejected? How do you feel about having been with that person? What is the Lord conveying to you about those moments?

• What are your feelings concerning the Church? Do you experience any 'problems'? What, and why? Share your feelings about this with the Risen Lord.

• What do you feel about such things as injustice? . . . prejudice? . . . racial discrimination? . . . sexual discrimination? Share your feelings with God, and remember that he created each person in his image.

• How do you feel when you are loved? . . . when you love? Think of the people concerned, and stay with the feelings those thoughts cause to well up within you. Share them with the Lord. What are they telling you about your relationship with him?

• Are you aware of having conveyed the love and presence of God to someone recently? . . . at home? . . . at work? . . . a friend? . . . a stranger? In what ways?

• Have you known moments when you have felt mean? . . . Godless? . . . forsaken? . . . bitter? . . . a failure? Remember those moments, and share your feelings about them with God. What is he telling you about those times?

• Are you aware of a part of you that does not yet belong to the Lord? . . . where you keep the door tightly shut? . . . where, perhaps, you are afraid of the consequences should you let him take possession of that part? Share your feelings with him about this. Ask him to help you, to give you the courage you need. Look at him, and notice how he is looking at you. How do you respond?

I give you a new heart and a new spirit

You have probably found that, as you were praying, a whole mixture of feelings flooded over you:

- a mixture of wonder and sorrow
- a sense of joy and gratitude
- feelings of mistrust in self and trust in God
- awareness of areas of weakness
- a sense of failing to respond to love
- feelings of inadequacy
- a sense of being changed, converted
- a sense of hope for the future – knowing it is in his hands.

Remember that God is here with you. Share with him your feelings about those aspects of your life that particularly bother you. He will lead you and set you free.

Be aware of your feelings, and stay with them, especially those of sorrow for the times when you responded in an inadequate way to his love working in and through you. God wants you to love him with every part of your being, as he loves you. Trust him. Reach out to him. Hope in him.

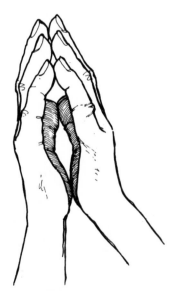

'I trust him and place my hope in him'

How do you feel about the future? Encouraged? . . . discouraged? . . . hopeful? . . . dejected? . . . afraid? . . . excited?

Why? What is causing those feelings? Pray about them. Ask God to help you as he calls you to be fully the person he wishes you to be. Notice the way he is leading you, and pray for the courage you need to follow.

The more you place your trust and hope in him and allow him to lead you on his path for your life, irrespective of your feelings of inadequacy and weakness, the more you will experience his joy and his peace deep within you.

'Leave the past behind and with hands outstretched to whatever lies ahead, go straight for the goal.' (Phil 3:13)

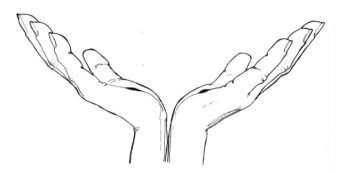

When celebrating the sacrament of Reconciliation some people **may** find it helpful to share with the priest, in so far as each one is able, something of the situation that most hurts, disturbs or hinders them. A little may be said about that part where the door is closed, and the fears they have concerning that area. The important thing is that each person be comfortable with the way in which he or she chooses to celebrate this special moment.

Closing the Vigil

After Communion you may like to draw the vigil to a close using one or more of the following ideas:

1 • Complete the decoration of the stones, which may then be blessed and returned to participants.

2 • Give a solemn blessing as part of the final dismissal.

3 • Invite people to gather around the fire to share breakfast.

4 • Invite parishioners to join the project members in their celebration of the closing moments of the vigil, and perhaps to bring food to be shared by all.

5 • Invite the families of those participating in the vigil to come to greet them, to welcome them back should they have been away, and perhaps to share transport home.

Thinking it over

Pages 15-17 suggest ways in which the team may evaluate its work, both during the project and once it is finished. It would be wise for the team to meet together soon after the completion of the project to consider various aspects of the work, to note those things that were particularly successful and those things that did not work with the group concerned. If possible, the team should try to identify the reasons for the success or failure of particular tasks so that improvements may be made in future projects.

Use pages 16-17 for your initial evaluation, remembering that you also need to consider the following:
• Were the various tasks assigned to the appropriate people, or were some people not happy with some of the things they were asked to do? Would some prefer to do other tasks?

• Are any members of the project group potential team members for future projects? What particular skills do they have? How may these be used to full advantage? Do any of them appear to be natural leaders? Over the past few months have any other people 'surfaced' who may help in future?
• Is the team happy:
with the basic content it selected for this particular project?
with the supplementary material?
with the way materials were used?
• What changes need to be made?
• Was the place used for the project the most suitable one for this group, or do you need to consider another location?
• In what ways would you like to see the project material developed next year? What is your dream?

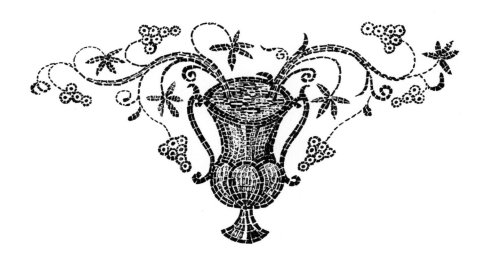

Useful Addresses

If you have difficulty finding such things as
frankincense in your area, the following people may
be able to help you.

Suppliers of incenses, perfumed oils (including
frankincense), icons, etc.:

Eikon
221 Barclay Road, Bearwood, Warley,
West Midlands B67 5LA
Tel 021 429 7023

Suppliers of incenses and perfumed oils (including
frankincense):

Baldwins
173 Walworth Road, London SE 17
Tel 01 703 5550

Suppliers of all kinds of candles:

Thyateira
184a Mare Street, Hackney, London E8
Tel 01 986 6356

Supplier of Jewish religious materials:

Mrs Young
21 Colchester Road, Southend on Sea
Essex
Tel 0702 331218

Appendix 1: Worksheets

Throughout the main text there are clear cross-references to worksheets. This appendix offers master copies for all of these worksheets.

All the worksheets in this appendix may be photocopied or reproduced onto an overhead transparency without fee or prior permission, subject to both of the following conditions:

that the page is reprinted in its entirety, including the copyright acknowledgement;
that the copies are used solely within the faith-development group that purchased the original book.
For copying in all other circumstances prior written permission must be sought from the publishers.

Relationships

1 • Parent with unborn baby or child in arms

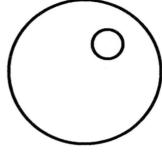

2 • Parent with toddler

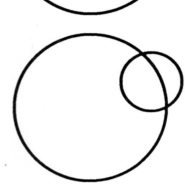

3 • Parent with child of primary school age

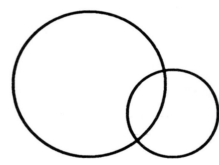

4 • Parent with adolescent child

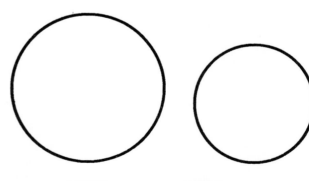

5 • Parent with child who is now an adult

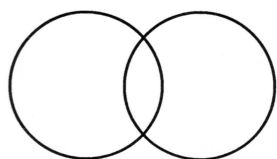

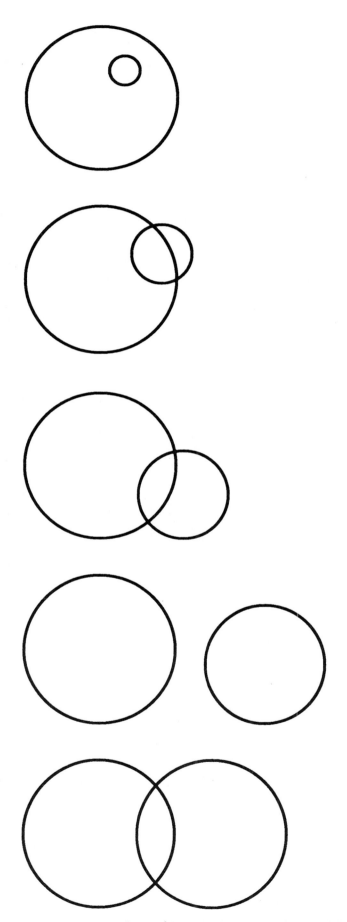

1

a • Child needs love, food, warmth—everything.

b • Parent is experienced as one who protects and cares, provides everything.

c • Child feels safe, content, held.

2

a • Child needs parent to fix things and explain.

b • Parent experienced as one who does things for child, provides security and knowledge.

c • Child feels curious, dependent on the parent, trusting—but may at times feel rejected.

3

a • Child needs guidance, reassurance, to belong, rules.

b • Parent experienced as one who instructs, advises, encourages.

c • Child feels adventurous but uncertain, unsure.

4

a • Child needs to belong, to be free, to leave, to be independent.

b • Parent is experienced as a controlling lawgiver, interfering, difficult, the enemy.

c • Child feels confused, rejected, misunderstood.

5

a • Child needs to be equal, to be friend, companion.

b • Parent experienced as equal, loving, respecting—proud!

c • Child feels protective, loving, trusting, caring.

Parent–child relationship

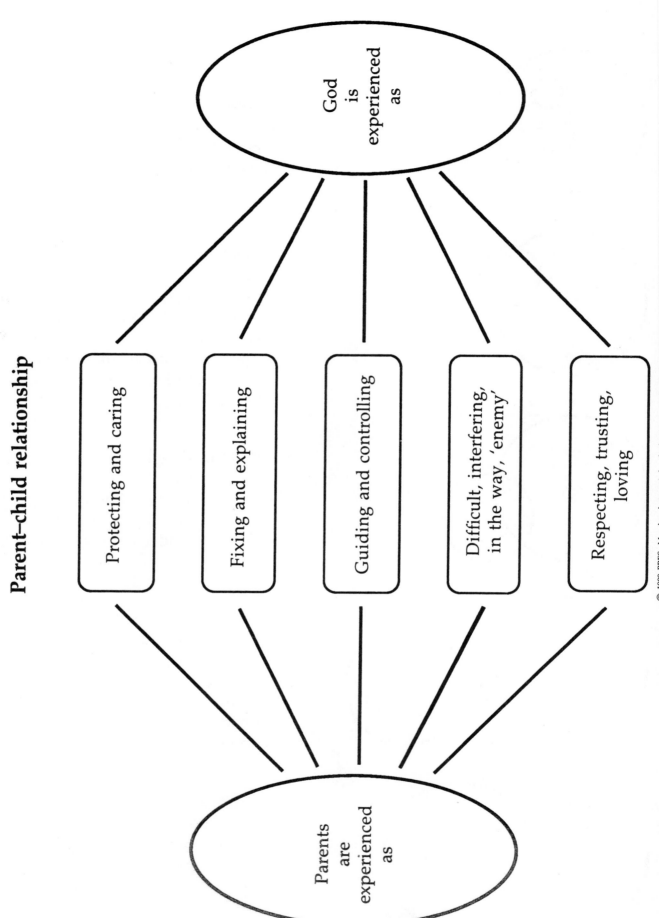

God
is
experienced
as

Protecting and caring

Fixing and explaining

Guiding and controlling

Difficult, interfering, in the way, 'enemy'

Respecting, trusting, loving

Parents
are
experienced
as

On Prayer

It is in prayer that Jesus leads us to his Father. It is in prayer that the Holy Spirit transforms our lives. It is in prayer that we come to know God: to detect his presence . . . to hear his voice . . . and to treasure his gift to us of personal responsibility for our lives and for our lives and for our world . . . We begin to see things his way. Prayer transforms our individual lives and the life of the world. Young men and women, when you meet Christ in prayer, when you get to know his Gospel and reflect on it in relation to your hopes and your plans for the future, then *everything is new*. Everything is different when you begin to examine in prayer the circumstances of everyday, according to the set values that Jesus taught. . . . In prayer, united with Jesus, you begin to breathe a new atmosphere. You form new goals, new ideals. Yes, in Christ you begin to understand yourselves more fully. This is what the Second Vatican Council wanted to emphasise when it stated, 'The truth is that only in the mystery of the Incarnate Word does the mystery of man take on light' (*Gaudium et Spes*, 22). In other words, Christ not only reveals God to man, but he reveals man to himself. In Christ we grasp the secret of our own humanity.

Pope John Paul II to the Young British Church in Cardiff

Times when I felt . . .
Times when Jesus felt . . .

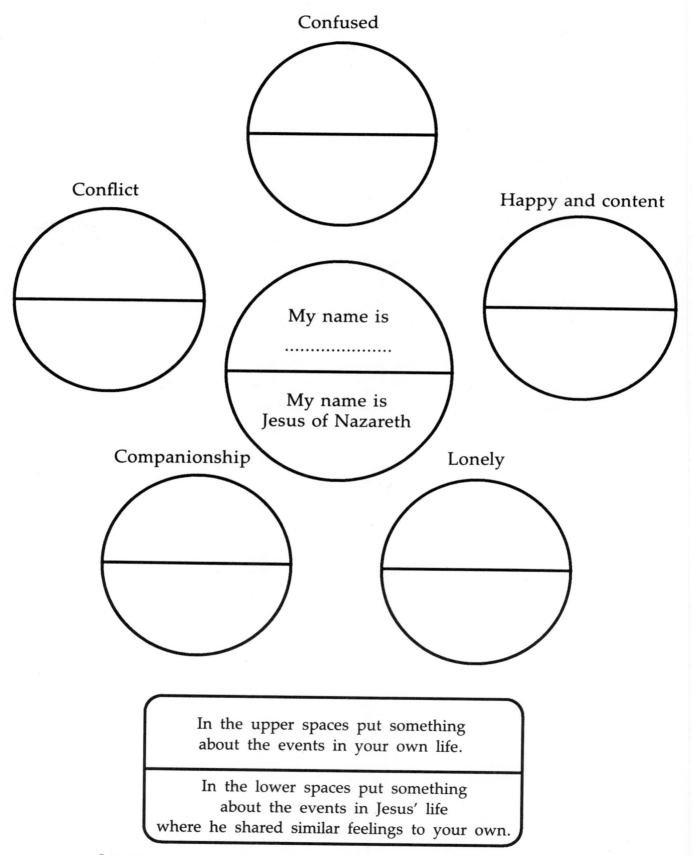

Confused

Conflict

Happy and content

My name is

....

My name is
Jesus of Nazareth

Companionship

Lonely

In the upper spaces put something
about the events in your own life.

In the lower spaces put something
about the events in Jesus' life
where he shared similar feelings to your own.

Images of the Risen Lord

Reflect upon the following list, and place a mark beside the
phrases that most accurately describe your images or ideas of
the Risen Lord. If you wish, you may add other words, or even
pictures, of your own.

He is strong and powerful man.
He understands me.
He is from a more advanced planet.
He is my brother.
He is my brother, but older and wiser.
He is a powerful leader.
He is a kind of spirit.
He cares for me and looks after me.
He is invisible and always there.
He is a Superstar.
He is in control.
He is powerful and demands things of me I cannot do.
He leaves me to go and look after others.
He is everywhere and knows everything.
He is inside me.
He is up there.
Wherever I am, he is there with me.
He is a spirit from another world.

Then, in your small groups:
   find out what images each of you has;
   discuss why you hold your particular
   ideas of the Risen Jesus.

A survey of prayer

Positive	1	2	3	4	5	6	7	8	9	10	Negative
I believe, beyond a shadow of doubt, that God answers prayer.											I believe there is a God but I question that he is personally interested in each human being.
I do not know how God answers prayer, but always have faith that he will.											If I do not see an obvious answer, I begin to wonder if God answers prayer at all.
I often praise and thank God, as well as ask him for what I need.											I treat God like Santa Claus: I want this . . . Give me that.
When God says 'No' I feel it is for my own good.											I find it very hard to accept a 'No' answer.
When God answers my prayer my faith is strengthened.											It is pure coincidence if prayer is answered.
If God seems to be saying, 'Wait a while,' I accept that without reservation.											I prayed once and God didn't answer, so I don't pray any more.
I find myself praying almost all day.											Days go by without my praying at all.
I make a real effort to pray when I don't feel like praying.											If I don't feel like praying, then I don't.
I am comfortable praying in public.											I do not like praying in public.
I feel my prayer life is really growing.											I feel my prayer life is almost dead and buried.
Positive	1	2	3	4	5	6	7	8	9	10	**Negative**

I called out your name and you answered me.
I called upon you to help—and you stepped
forward.

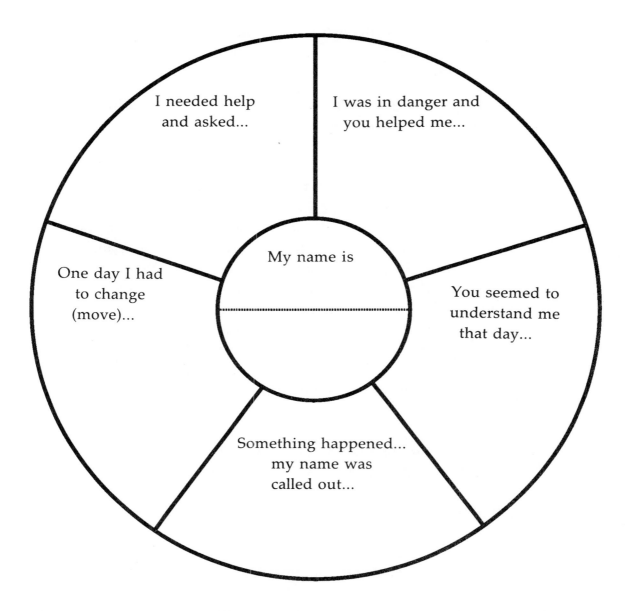

In one half of the centre circle write your own name; in
one half of each segment put something about your own life.

In the other half of the centre write Jesus' name; in the other
half of each segment put something about the events in Jesus'
life where he shared similar feelings to your own.

Alternatively the whole group may choose to focus entirely
on events in the lives of the group members.

The Thankful Leper
(Luke 17:11–19)

Read the following Gospel extract. As you read, try to identify with the various characters involved, and notice your feelings as the story develops.

> On the way to Jerusalem Jesus travelled along the border between Samaria and Galilee. As he entered one of the villages, ten lepers came to meet him. They stood some way off and called to him, 'Jesus! Master! Take pity on us.' When he saw them he said 'Go and show yourselves to the priests.' Now as they were going away they were cleansed. Finding himself cured, one of them turned back praising God at the top of his voice and threw himself at the feet of Jesus and thanked him. The man was a Samaritan. This made Jesus say, 'Were not all ten made clean? The other nine, where are they? It seems that no one has come back to give praise to God, except this foreigner.' And he said to the man, 'Stand up and go on your way. Your faith has saved you.'

How do you think Jesus felt when only one of the lepers returned to thank him?

What do you think the thankful leper thought, and how do you think he felt during his encounter with Jesus?

Can you think of any excuses for the nine lepers who were healed but did not return to express their gratitude?

With whom in this story do you most identify?

What excuses do **you** usually make for not thanking Jesus for all he has done for you?

What has Jesus done for you or provided for you recently, for which you would like to thank him now?

Make a colourful 'Thank You' card for Jesus, using the paper and colours provided. You may like to put symbols or splashes of colour on the front of the card, to express something about the thing or event for which you are thankful. Inside the card write a short letter, poem or prayer expressing your gratitude.

1 Corinthians 13

If I have all the ability to talk about . . . .

but have no love, then I am nothing but a big mouth.

If I had all the power to . . . .,

but have no love, then my life is a waste of time.

If I understand everything about . . . .

but have no love, then I might as well sit in a gutter.

If I give away everything that I have,

but have no love, then I . . . .

Love is patient and kind.

Love is . . . .

Love is never jealous or . . . .

Fill in the blank spaces with whatever words or phrases you feel
are most appropriate. This will help you to enter more deeply
into the passage and make it your own. You may then share your
completed versions with one another and compare these with
the texts in your Bibles.

The Road to Emmaus
(Luke 24:13–35)

Find Luke 24:13–35 in your Bible. Slowly and prayerfully take time with this reading. Reach out to the Risen Lord who is with you.

After you have had enough time to enter into the story, move into groups of four or five and discuss your thoughts on the following points:

1 What was the disciples' problem?
2 Did the disciples see their problem in a different light? How?
3 Why were they not able to recognise the Risen Jesus?
4 How did they come to recognise him?
5 In what ways had appearances changed?
6 In what ways had their understanding changed?
7 How did they feel?
8 After they recognised the presence of the Risen Lord in their lives that day, what course of action did they take?
9 What does this story say to you, personally?

To be a Christian is to know that the Lord is the centre of my life. It is he who guides me, protects me, enlightens my mind and changes my whole life.

Guidelines for reading the Bible

Try to set aside a specific time each day.

If you can, find a quiet, comfortable place.

Relax and be at peace. Try closing your eyes for a few moments and taking three or four good, deep breaths, breathing in the love of God and breathing out all your fears, frustrations and tensions.

Recall that you are now, as always, in the presence of God, and be reconciled with him, with yourself and with others.

Ask the Lord to enlighten your mind and to inflame you with his love. You may like to use the words of a prayer such as:

> Come, Holy Spirit, fill the hearts of your faithful and light up in them the fire of your love. Send forth your Spirit and they shall be created, and you will renew the face of the earth.

Now, slowly and prayerfully, read the passage of Scripture you have chosen.

Try to picture the scene about which you are reading. In your imagination, look at the people who are there; listen to them; hear what is being said; notice how people react to what is said or what is happening; observe where you are and/or who you are on this occasion; notice how you react and how you feel.

Have a heart-to-heart conversation with God/Jesus about your reactions and the way you feel.

Listen to what the Lord is saying to you, praise him and thank him. Sometimes the words you read may evoke a song or hymn. If they do, then sing it to the Lord softly and prayerfully.

Write a brief summary of your meditation in your notebook.

Praise and thank God for his love for you.

The Trial Continues

Judge

Ladies and gentlemen of the Jury, Mrs Wright stands before us, accused of being a Christian. Yesterday we listened to the case presented by the Counsel for the Prosecution. We also listened to those witnesses called to the stand by the Prosecuting Counsel in support of their case. I now call on the clerk to read the summary of yesterday's proceedings.

Clerk

The Counsel for the Prosecution presented the following evidence in support of their case against the accused. Mrs Wright has regularly been seen attending church services on Sundays. She has also been seen going into the church on some weekdays. She has, on many occasions, been observed receiving Communion. Four witnesses gave evidence concerning these facts. Two others stated that she has often been heard proclaiming her belief in the teachings of the Christian Church, especially when they are contrary to the law of this country. She sends her children to a school originally opened by members of her church, even though there is an excellent school almost on her doorstep. On several occasions she has been overheard expressing her anger concerning the inadequate teaching of religious beliefs in the school, in spite of the fact that she knows such teaching is against the law. She is known to have had all of her children baptised and has recently requested that the older ones be confirmed.

The case for the prosecution rested there.

Judge

Thank you.

I now call on the Counsel for the Defence to present his/her case.

Defence

My client, Mrs Wright, stands accused of being a Christian. She does, in fact, admit the charge. I propose, however, that she is not a Christian and intend to defend her against the charge.

(*He turns towards Mrs Wright.*)

Would Mrs Wright please come to the stand?

Clerk

Mrs Wright to the stand, please.

Raise your right arm.

Do you swear to tell the truth, the whole truth, and nothing but the truth.

Mrs Wright

I do.

Judge (*nodding towards the counsel for the Defence*):

You may proceed.

Defence

Mrs Wright, are you aware that, should you be convicted for being a Christian, you will be sent either to prison or into exile?

Mrs Wright

I am.

Defence

Do you still insist that you are a Christian?

Mrs Wright (*emphatically*)

I most certainly do—no matter what the consequences may be!

Defence

Do you acknowledge the evidence put before the court by the Counsel for the Prosecution?

Mrs Wright

I do. Every bit of it is true. I am a Christian.

Defence

Mrs Wright, would you please tell the court if you know any of the following people: Mrs Julie Taylor, Mr John Cooper, Mr Peter Woods and Miss Diana Miller?

Mrs Wright

I know all of them. I used to work with Mr Woods. Mr Cooper is related to me and the other two are neighbours.

Defence

So—let us begin with one of your neighbours, Mrs Taylor. Are you aware that her husband died some months ago, leaving her to bring up four young children on her own?

Mrs Wright (*contemptuously*)

Of course I am. The whole street knows about it—the filth and the noise of them! She has no control over them whatsoever—leaving them running and screeching around the street in their filthy rags. Something should be done about it!

Judge

Mrs Wright, please just answer the question.

Defence

Mrs Wright, may I ask what you have done about it?

Mrs Wright

What do you mean, what have I done? Isn't that what people in Welfare and Social Security are paid for? It's got nothing to do with me!

Defence

But isn't it true that you are fairly well off?

Mrs Wright

I have a good bit put by, just in case. But what has that got to do with Mrs Taylor?

Defence

May I quote you, Mrs Wright? A few moments ago you said that her children were 'running around in filthy rags'. You are aware that Mrs Taylor has to wash by hand or else drag a heavy load along to the launderette. Indeed, you have often driven past her as she has been struggling home with her bundle. Have you ever even **thought** to invite her to use your washing machine occasionally, even though it stands idle six days out of seven? And what about the piles of good clothes you have stored away, that your own children have outgrown? Have you ever considered how welcome they would be in your neighbour's house?

Isn't it also true that when your eldest daughter offered to help Mrs Taylor look after her children while they were playing, you called her away and said you did not want to see her with the likes of them again?

Mrs Wright (*shaking her head*)
But you don't understand. You don't know the kind of a woman she is.

Defence
And yet—you still say you are a Christian?

Mrs Wright (*emphatically*)
I am. I go to church every Sunday.

Defence
Let's have look, then, at Mr Cooper. You say he is related to you?

Mrs Wright
That's right.

Defence
Yet, since he was diagnosed a victim of AIDS eighteen months ago you have not visited him once. You have not so much as bothered to contact him—even though you knew his wife walked out on him as soon as the diagnosis was confirmed.

Mrs Wright (*in an exasperated tone*)
But he's in a hospital on the other side of town! Anyway, we were never that close. In fact, we haven't spoken to each other since he got himself attached to that good-for-nothing woman of his. We fell out because of her. Queer sort of female, she is! You should have heard the insults he hurled at me when I told him what I thought of her! He's no gentleman, that's for sure!

Defence
And you've never forgiven him? You've allowed bitterness from something that happened years ago to keep you from visiting him when he's been most in need of your friendship?

Mrs Wright
(*shrugs and frowns*)

Defence
You said earlier, Mrs Wright, that you used to work with Mr Woods?

Mrs Wright
Yes. That was years ago—just after I got married.

Defence
Isn't it true, Mrs Wright, that you were very friendly with him in those days? That, in fact, you nurtured the friendship in the hopes that it would increase your chance of promotion?

Mrs Wright

We were friendly, yes. But that had nothing to do with my promotion; I was good at my job.

Defence

Yet, now, you don't even greet him when you pass him in the street?

Mrs Wright (*indignantly*)

I refuse to associate with drunks.

Defence

You do know that he is now a confirmed alcoholic?—And that he is now unemployed?

Mrs Wright

Yes, I do. You can't have a drunk doing the kind of work he did.

Defence

Have you any idea what made him drink in the first place?

Mrs Wright

How should I know? He only used to have the occasional pint. Then he started going to the pub whenever it was open. You're bound to end up an alcoholic if you do that.

Defence

Do you remember that both Mr Wood's wife and ten-month-old baby were killed in an aeroplane disaster?

Mrs Wright

I do. But that was years ago. What's that got to do with the mess he's in now?

Defence

I think it has a lot to do with it. I think it was the very reason Mr Woods began to seek the company and comfort of the pub every night. In the early days, just after he lost both his wife and child, did you ever call in to see him?

Mrs Wright (*indignantly*)

I was too busy for social visiting. I had my hands full looking after my own young children.

Defence

Did you ever invite him into your own home?

Mrs Wright (*shaking her head*)

He'd already started drinking. I wasn't going to have that in my house! I don't touch the stuff!

Judge

Mrs Wright, please—just answer the question. A simple 'yes' or 'no'.

Mrs Wright

No.

Defence

Finally, let us consider Miss Miller, a young neighbour of yours. How well do you know her?

Mrs Wright

Not that well. She went to my daughter's school, but she's a few years older than my girl.

Defence

Are you aware that she was pregnant a few months ago?

Mrs Wright (*scornfully*)

I would say so! Everyone was talking about it. And it's no wonder, the way she dresses! Indecent, that's what it is! She might just as well be naked as wear some of the stuff she goes about in! Then she went and had an abortion. And what's she doing now? Earning money on the streets and getting high on drugs, that's what.

Defence

Isn't it true that you, Mrs Wright, were one of the neighbours who made life impossible for Miss Miller when she became pregnant? Isn't it true that it was gossip that drove her to have an abortion in the first place? And then, when she came home in a state of depression, didn't you make it even more difficult for her by continually, and loudly, airing your views about abortion being murder? You, Mrs Wright, have driven that young woman to the life she leads today.

Mrs Wright (*turning to Judge*)

This is absolutely crazy!

Judge

Would the Counsel for the Defence please say just what, exactly, he is getting at?

Defence

Your Honour, my client, Mrs Wright, is accused of being a Christian. I propose that she is not. One of Christ's followers, a man by the name of Matthew, quoted some of Christ's own words. May I read them to you?

(*He looks at the Judge, who nods his/her agreement.*)

Defence

'I was hungry and you fed me, thirsty and you gave me a drink;
I was a stranger and you received me in your home, naked and you clothed me;
I was sick and you took care of me,
in prison and you visited me. . . .
I tell you that whenever you did this for one of the least important of these brothers and sisters of mine,
you did it for me!'

In this same document—known to Christians as the *New Testament*—another follower, called James, interprets Christ's words in several ways. I quote some of them: 'What God the Father considers to be pure and genuine religion is this: To care for orphans and widows and to keep oneself from being corrupted by the world . . . to not look down on poor people' . . . to 'love and help your neighbours just as much as you love and take care of yourself.' 'Faith that doesn't show itself by good works is no faith at all.' 'Don't be too eager to tell others their faults, for we all make many mistakes.' 'The tongue is a small thing, but what enormous damage it can do.'

Your Honour, this document is full of such statements, but these are more than enough to support my case.

Mrs Taylor, Mr Cooper, Mr Woods and Miss Miller are all the very kind of people Christ himself went out of his way to help. They are the kind of people followers of Christ **should** be helping if they really are worthy of the name 'Christian'. In fact, Christ said his followers would be judged on the way they respond to the needs of such people.

(*Turns to Jury*)

Ladies and gentlemen of the Jury, I put it to you that my client is simply deceiving herself. She considers herself to be a Christian because of her faithfulness to the external observances of her religion, but she does not put the teachings of Christ into practice. Can any of us seriously accuse her of showing any genuine concern for the rejected, the sick, the poor or the needy?

Mrs Wright (*indignantly*)
But this is ridiculous! I am a Christian. How dare you suggest that I am not?

Defence
Christ himself was quite clear about whom he considered his real followers to be. I put it to you, ladies and gentlemen, that there is insufficient evidence in her life, in her behaviour, or in her dealings with other people to support the case that Mrs Wright is a true Christian. In fact, I consider the lack of evidence to be such that the case should be dropped entirely.

Mrs Wright
(*shakes her head and looks bewildered*)

Judge (*stands and speaks to the large group*)
Ladies and gentlemen of the Jury, you have heard the evidence placed before you. May I ask you to consider all the details carefully before you reach your verdict: is Mrs Wright a Christian—or is she not?

No one makes the journey of faith alone:
We are helped by others

When I was
a small child
I was helped by
....

In my teens
I was helped by
....

..............'s
journey of
faith would
have been very
lonely without
....

When I was
a baby
I was helped by
....

At the present
time I am
helped by
....

As a young
adult I was
helped by
....

1 • What did s/he do?

2 • How did that help me?

Name ....

FRIEND

PARENT

BOSS

MYSELF

GOD

Through our Baptism
We are called to be Christians

In BAPTISM we celebrate the fact that we are members of God's family and, therefore, belong to one another. In the spaces provided, try to give three reasons for each of the following:

A . I belong to a religion because:

1...

2...

3...

B . I belong to a CHRISTIAN church because:

1...

2...

3...

C . I belong to the CATHOLIC (or ANGLICAN, METHODIST etc.)
Church because:

1...

2...

3...

I am gifted!

a • **Put a tick beside any of the following gifts you have received:**

...sight ...taste ...hearing ...touch ...friendship
...ability to smell ...ability to walk

b • **We receive many material gifts from others—but they wear out. Most of the gifts we receive from God, however, develop as we grow. Put a tick beside those gifts he has given to you.**

...cooking ...talking ...writing ...acting ...art
...music ...singing ...packing ...sports ...comforting
...baby-sitting ...cleaning ...organising ...praying
...sewing ...helping others ...reading ...selling
...nursing ...driving ...smiling ...gardening ...listening
...teaching ...mechanics ...enjoying life ...other gifts.

c • **St Paul talks about the spiritual gifts that God gives to us. Different people are given different gifts. Put a tick beside the ones you think God has given to you.**

...wisdom ...sincerity ...knowledge ...counsel ...love
...perseverance ...hope ...willingness to share belongings
...ability to work hard ...humility ...helping others
...authority ...respect ...prayer ...understanding others
...peacefulness ...faith ...feeding others ...miracles
...preaching ...interpreting ...patience ...kindness
...healing ...generosity ...tongues ...truthfulness
...prophecy ...encouragement ...teaching ...listening
...serving ...joy ...welcoming newcomers ...forgiveness
...doing good ...caring ...wonder ...other gifts.

d • **St Paul also tells us about the FRUITS of the Spirit – gifts and qualities that are the result of a habit of listening to the inspirations and invitations we receive from God. Put a tick beside those you have felt at any time in your life.**

...love ...joy ...peace ...patient endurance ...kindness
...faith ...mildness ...goodness ...modesty
...generosity ...chastity ...temperance ...gentleness
...trustfulness ...self-control ...justice

e • **Write down other—perhaps special—gifts and talents you have been given by God.**

1

In this space indicate
whatever word, phrase
or action meant the
most to you in our
celebration of the
presence of the Risen
Lord in our lives.

2

In this space put a
name or symbol to
indicate one person
you would like to
bring before the Risen
Lord at this
particular moment.

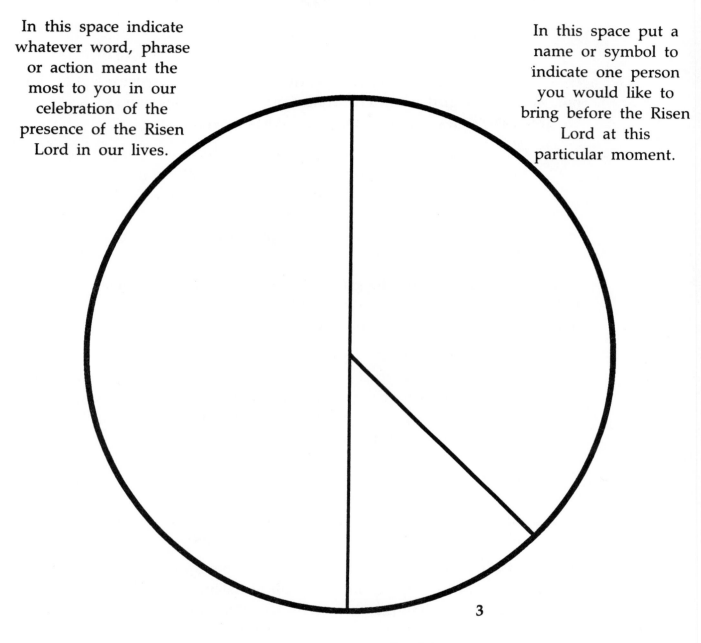

3

In this space put some
symbol or word to
indicate the thing (or
person) for which you
most wish to thank the
Risen Lord.

No one makes the journey of faith alone:

**We are always part of the way other people grow in faith.
We have helped others**

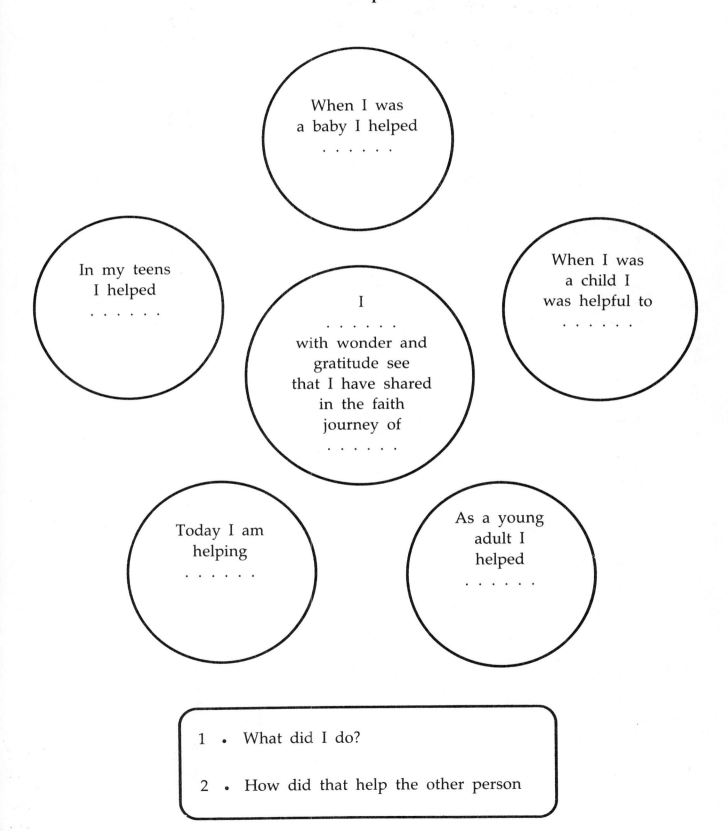

When I was
a baby I helped
· · · · · ·

In my teens
I helped
· · · · · ·

I
· · · · · ·
with wonder and
gratitude see
that I have shared
in the faith
journey of
· · · · · ·

When I was
a child I
was helpful to
· · · · · ·

Today I am
helping
· · · · · ·

As a young
adult I
helped
· · · · · ·

1 . What did I do?

2 . How did that help the other person

A letter to God

6 I am frightened to grow up. All around me people are growing up and seem to like it but I don't. I try to put on an outer shell and make it seem as if I am enjoying it. I'm used to my parents deciding everything for me but now I have to decide for myself. Help me to understand myself better and stay with me. 9

6 I definitely believe in you but there are some points I need to get straight. Why do such horrible tragedies occur over the world and many people lose lives or livelihoods? I can sense you exist and love us all, but when I ask these questions I meet a blank wall. We find out about the Third World and how they are starving and I feel that I should do something but what good could I do against such a big problem? 9

6 I have been told I am brainy but I am too lazy to use it. If I try to study it goes in one ear and out the other. I try to work in class but then start messing around and get told off and never learn anything. Please help. 9

6 At the moment I am very muddled up with life. Half the time I would like to feel that I am growing up and I like to wear fashionable clothes and everything. Other times I feel that I would still like to be a child. I am very churned up inside and although I love my family very much I sometimes feel that I am not cared for at all. I believe in you Lord, but sometimes I want to do what I want and not what you want. 9

6 Sometimes I think that no one likes me or listens to me when I try to be friendly by talking to them. Please help me to speak out more because I am very shy and quiet and I get teased about that. 9

6 How can I believe in you when you have taken so much away from me? My Dad died about three or four years ago, followed by my Gran and Grandad. Now my Mum has got cancer so you tell me how can I believe in you? I've given up. I feel suddenly violent and want to smash everybody up. 9

The extracts from teenagers' 'letters to God' were first published, with their permission, in the catechetical magazine *New Review*. Reprinted here by arrangement.

The Fruits of the Spirit

1 • What conditions are needed to produce fruit?
Consider the care we need to give plants during their growth: the condition of the soil—is the same needed for every plant? . . . water . . . gentle handling . . . pruning . . . space to grow . . . light . . . etc.

2 • What happens when a plant is NOT cared for after it has produced its first fruits?

3 • Do we ever experience anything similar to this in our parish: eg after Baptism . . . First Communion . . . Confirmation . . . Marriage?

4 • What must we do if we want a tree to continue bearing fruit?

5 • What can we learn from our response to 4 that we perhaps need to apply to our response to 3?

6 • There is really only **One** fruit of the Spirit—and that is **Love**. All the others are simply highlighting different aspects of love, as may be seen in the illustrations. Discuss this.

(Cf. Galatians 5:22)

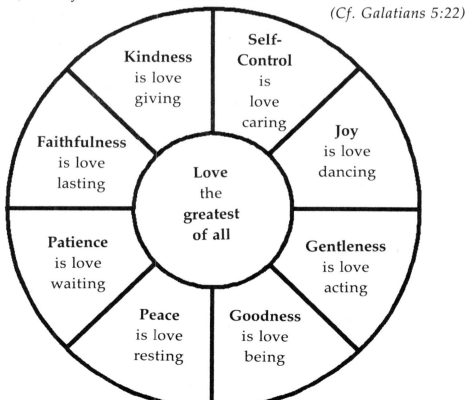

Needs that are essential
if we are to be
fully human, fully alive

BASIC NEEDS	KEY WORDS OR PHRASES
LOVE	'Do you love me?'
FOOD	'Come and eat.'
CARE	A fire to warm and cook. Breakfast prepared. Food Provided: the catch of fish. Gentle recalling of memories
HEALING	Peter's statement of love. Affirmation of call and ministry.
TRUST	Peter learns to trust again, to be led by the spirit, and finally to allow himself to be bound.

Needs that are essential
if we are to be
fully human, fully alive

BASIC NEEDS   KEY WORDS OR PHRASES

LOVE

FOOD

CARE

HEALING

TRUST

My personal story

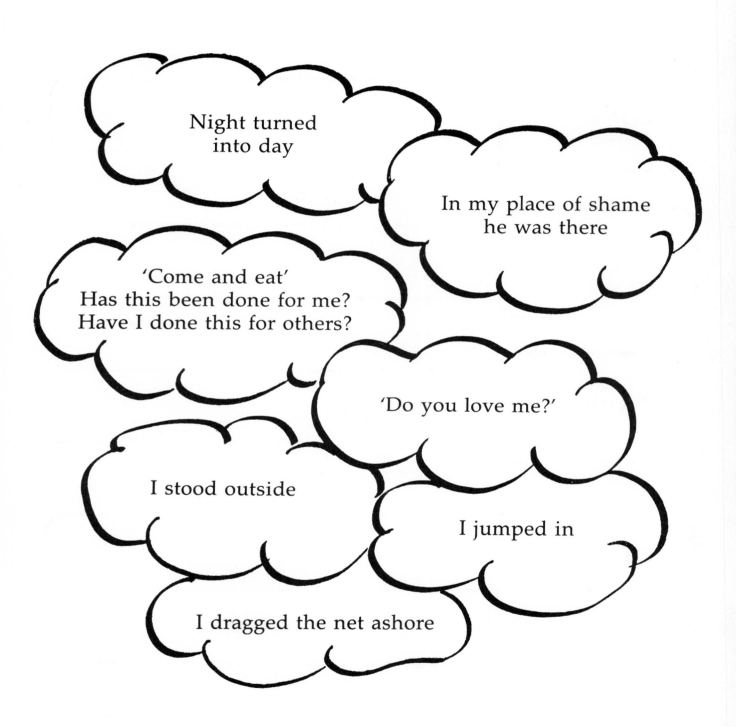

My personal story of the project

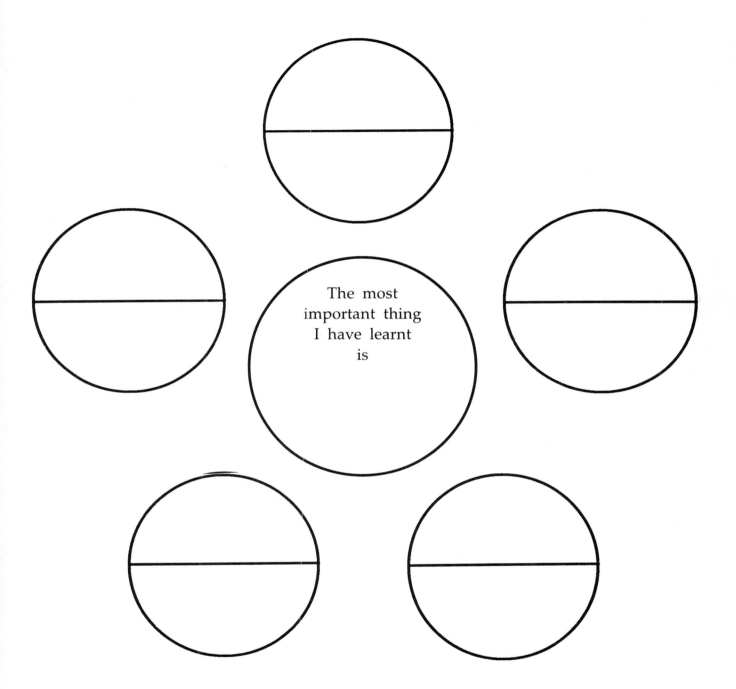

The most
important thing
I have learnt
is

1. In the upper half of the five *outer* circles write down five moments from the project that you remember and find meaningful.
In the lower half of the *outer* circles write down what it was that made that moment or event important to you.

2. When (1.) is complete, decide which of these five you found most important, and write this in the *centre* circle.

3. Move into small groups and share with one another what each found to be most important, and why.

Appendix 2: Illustrations

The illustrations in this book are an essential part of the project and may be used in a number of different ways. Many groups have found them very good as discussion starters or as focal points for story-telling, reflection or prayer.

In the earlier stages, suggestions are made as to which illustrations might be used in connection with the particular themes. There are many more than you need, so choose one or two that are appropriate for your particular group, or disperse a number of them through the session. It is unlikely to happen, but should you find there is little or no response, simply move on to another illustration.

By the time you reach the later stages of the project, you will have discovered the most appropriate way for you to use the illustrations, so the choice of illustrations has been left to you; and we have not allocated a specific amount of time for their use.

All the worksheets in this appendix may be photocopied or reproduced onto an overhead transparency without fee or prior permission, subject to both of the following conditions: that the page is reprinted in its entirety, including the copyright acknowledgement; that the copies are used solely within the faith-development group that purchased the original book.
For copying in all other circumstances prior written permission must be sought from the publishers.

We would like to re-echo our gratitude to Jim Bray, the artist who provided these illustrations for the project. Throughout the development of the programme he was a constant source of fresh and stimulating insights, which we hope you will now share.

Illustration 1

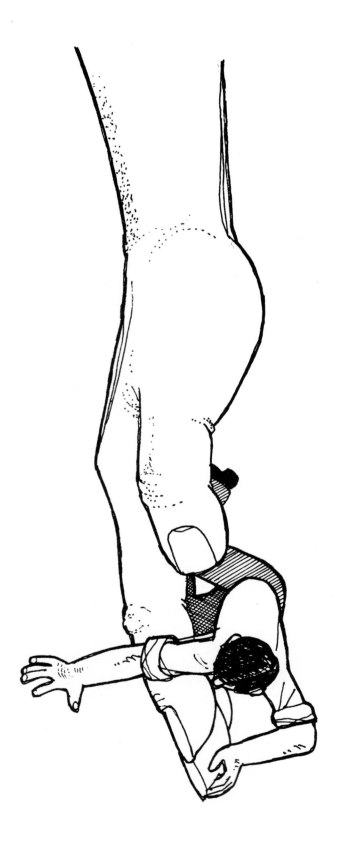

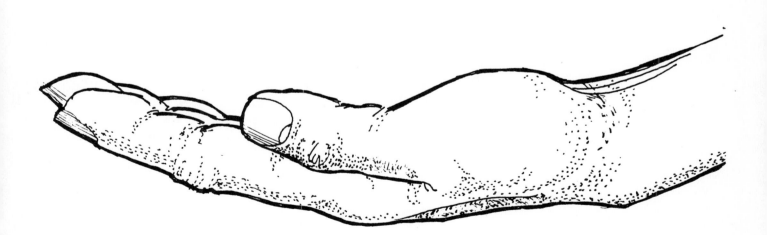

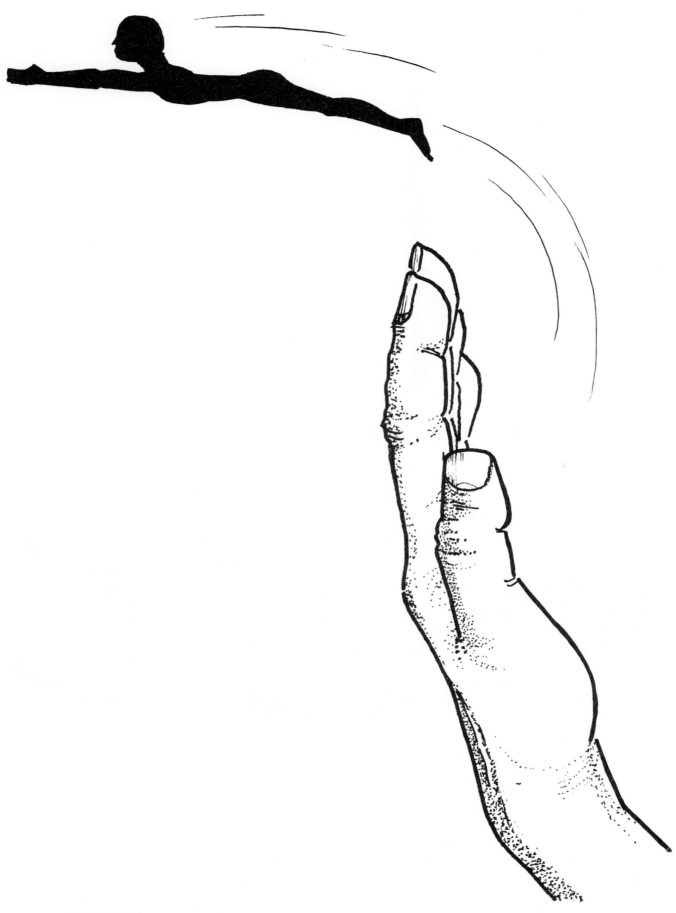

Illustration 3

Illustration 4

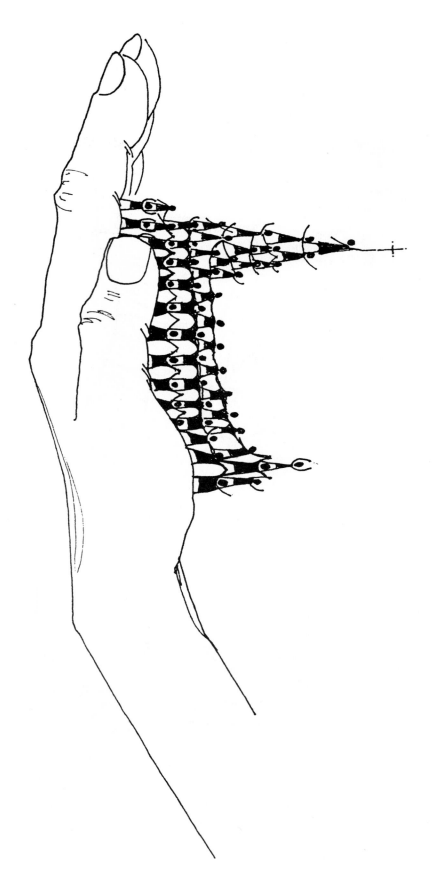

Illustration 5

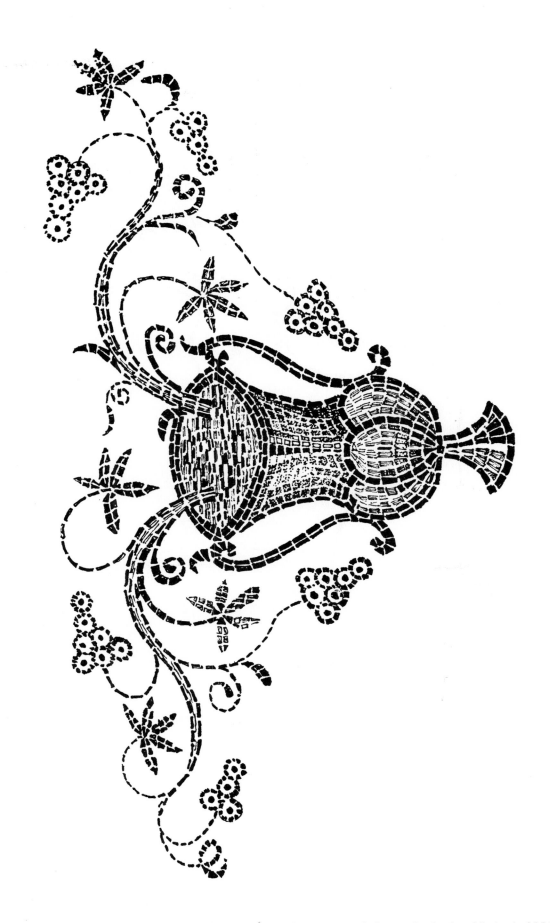

Illustration 6

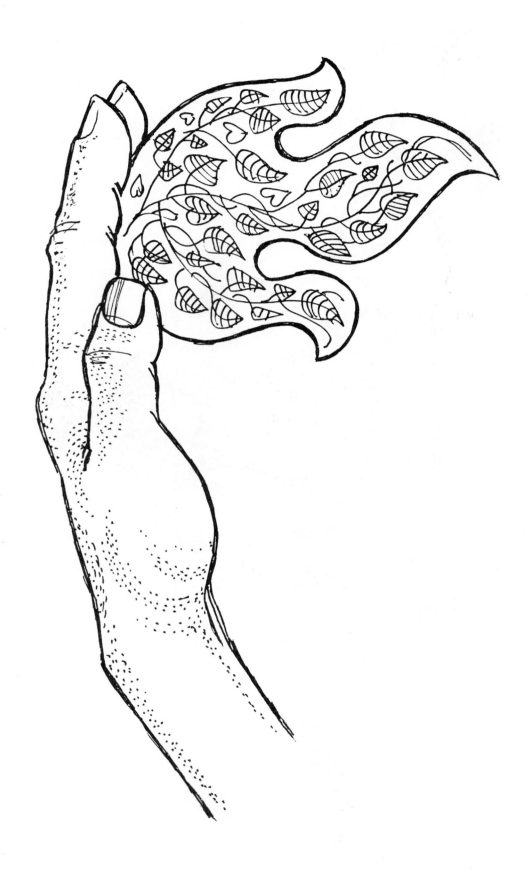

Illustration 7

Illustration 8

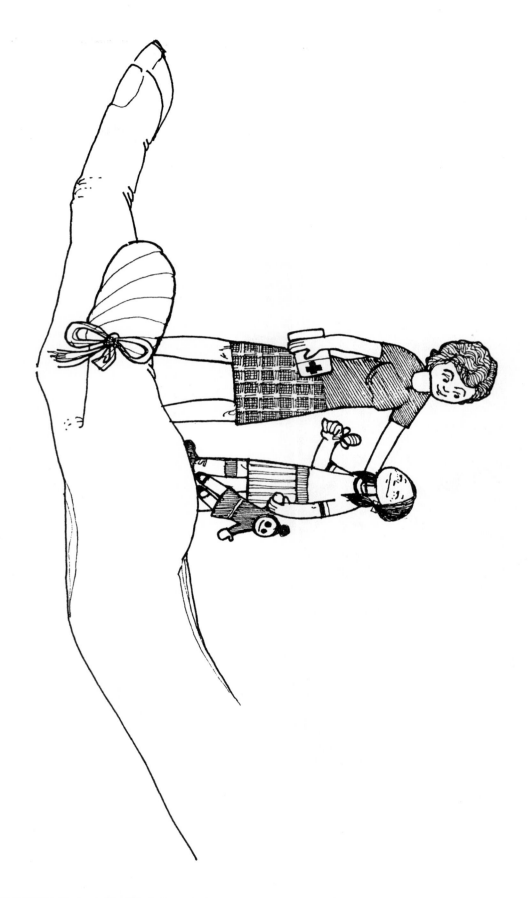

Illustration 9

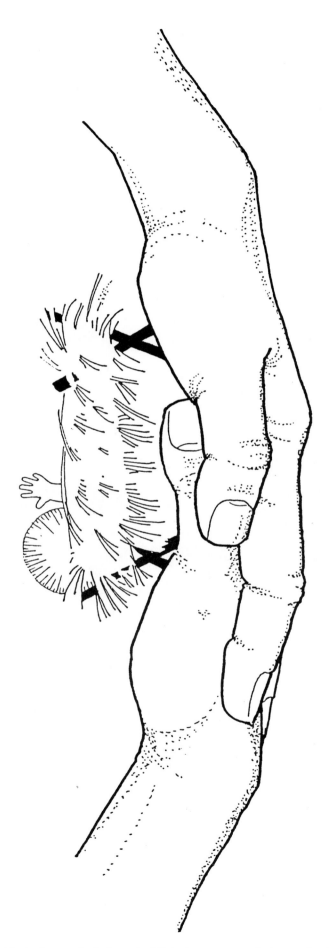

Illustration 10

Illustration 11

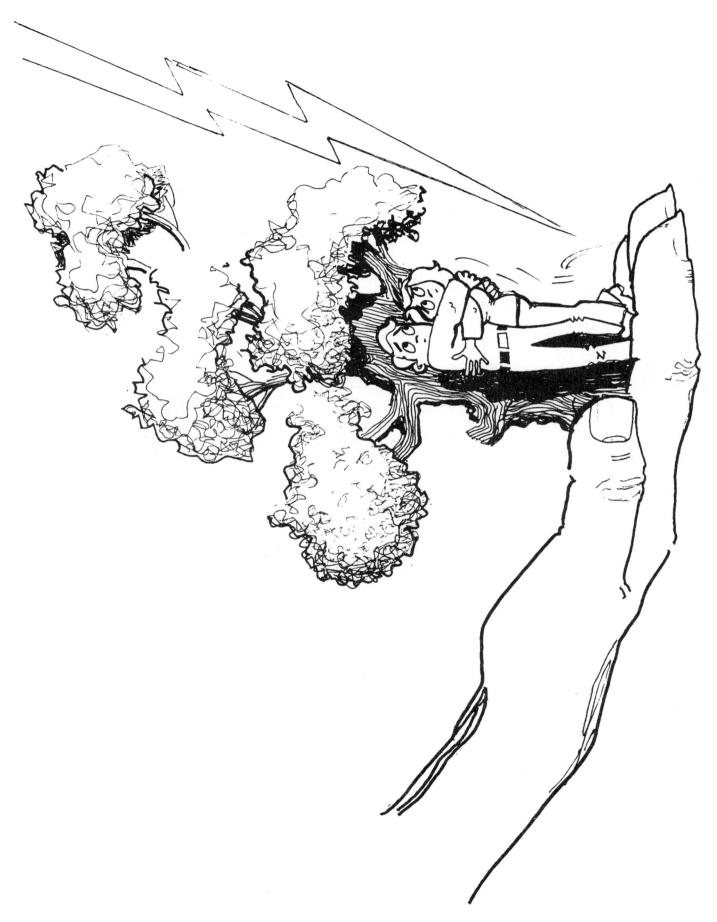

Illustration 12

Illustration 13

Illustration 14

Illustration 15

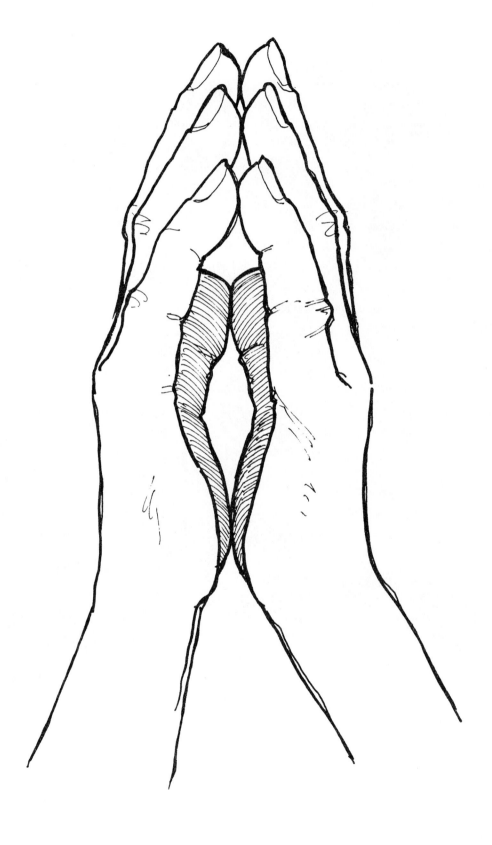

Illustration 16

Illustration 17

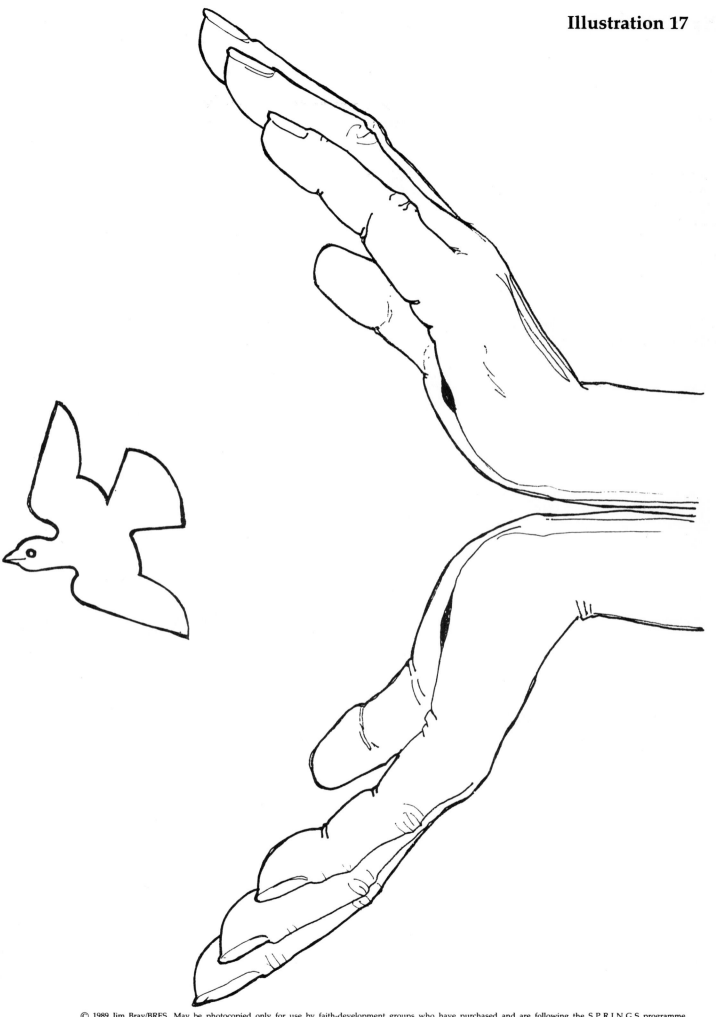

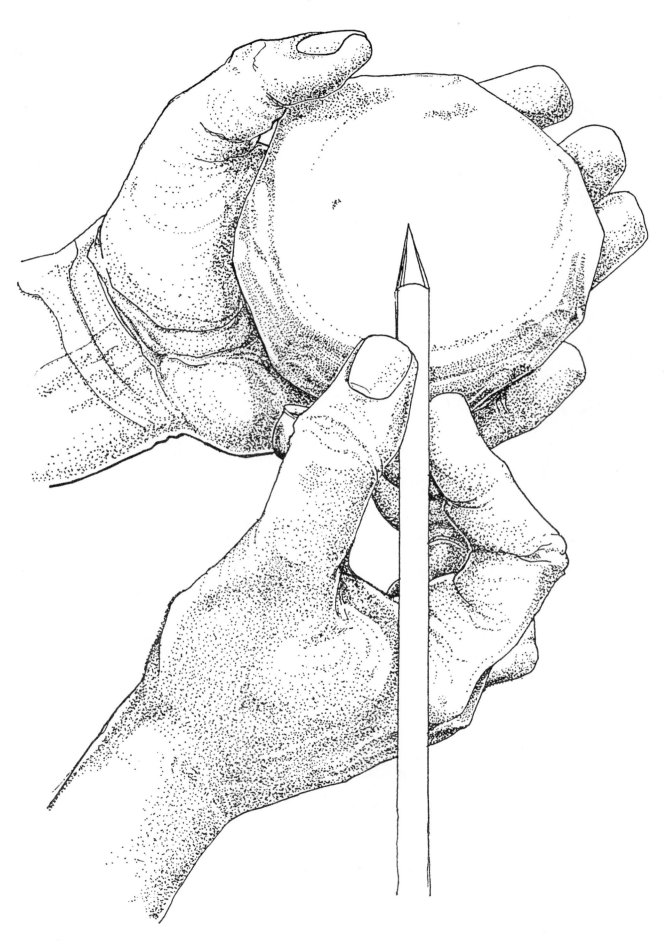

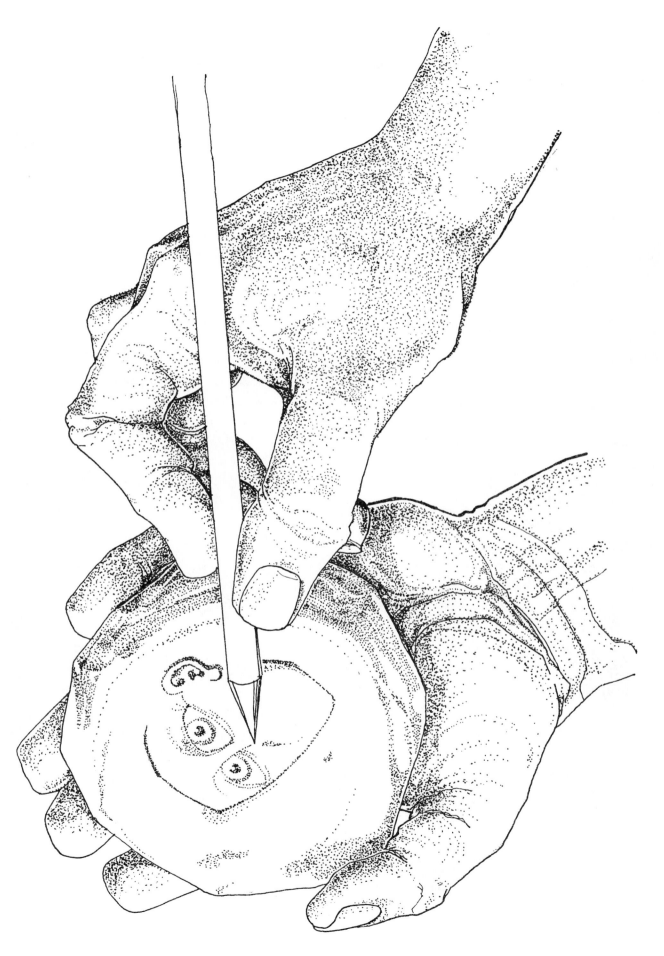

Illustration 19

Illustration 20

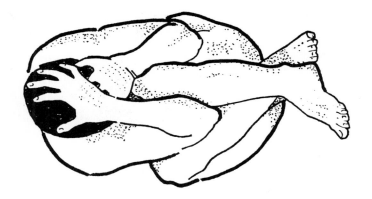

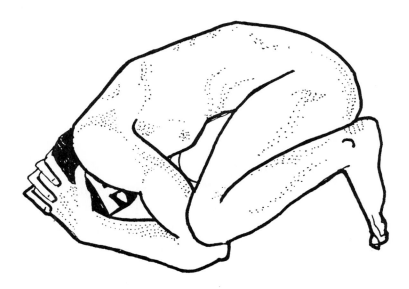

Illustration 21

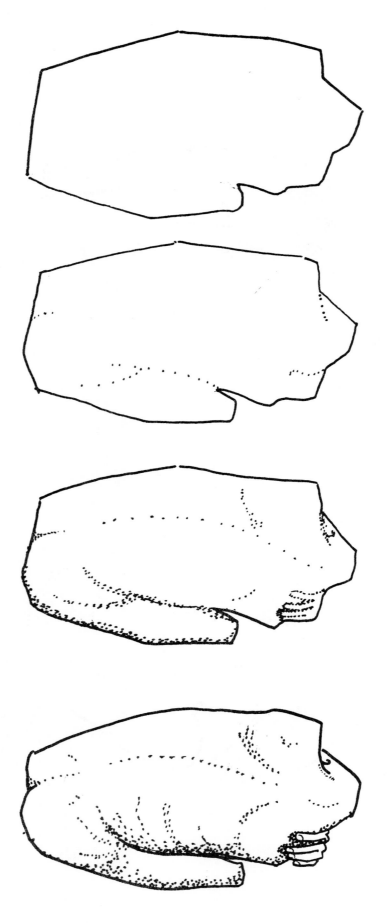

Illustration 22

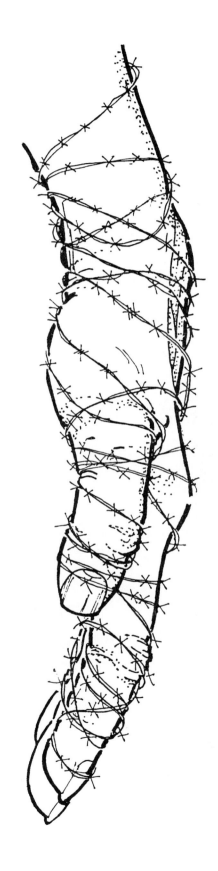

Illustration 23

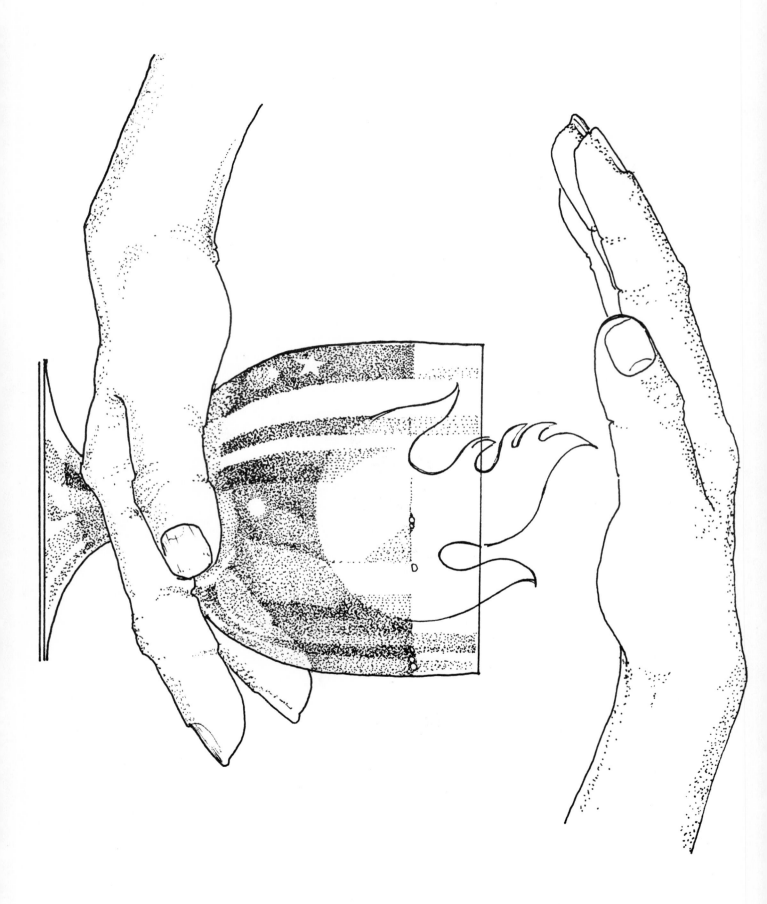

Illustration 24

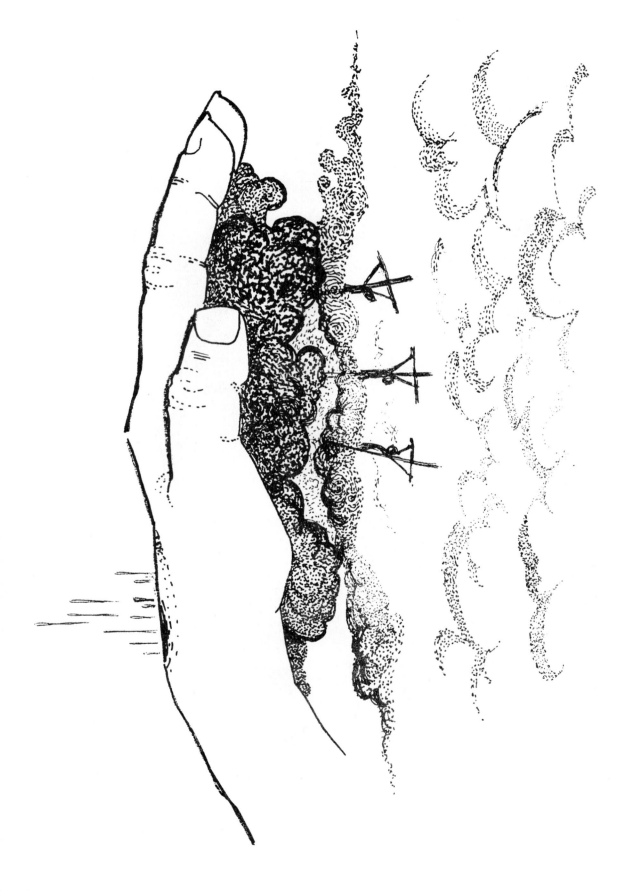

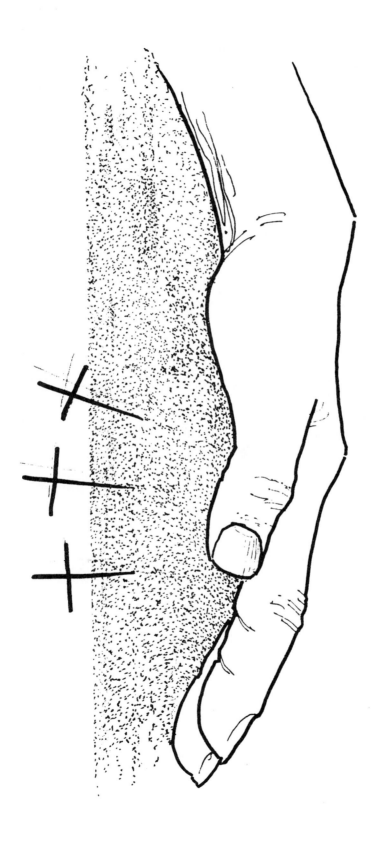

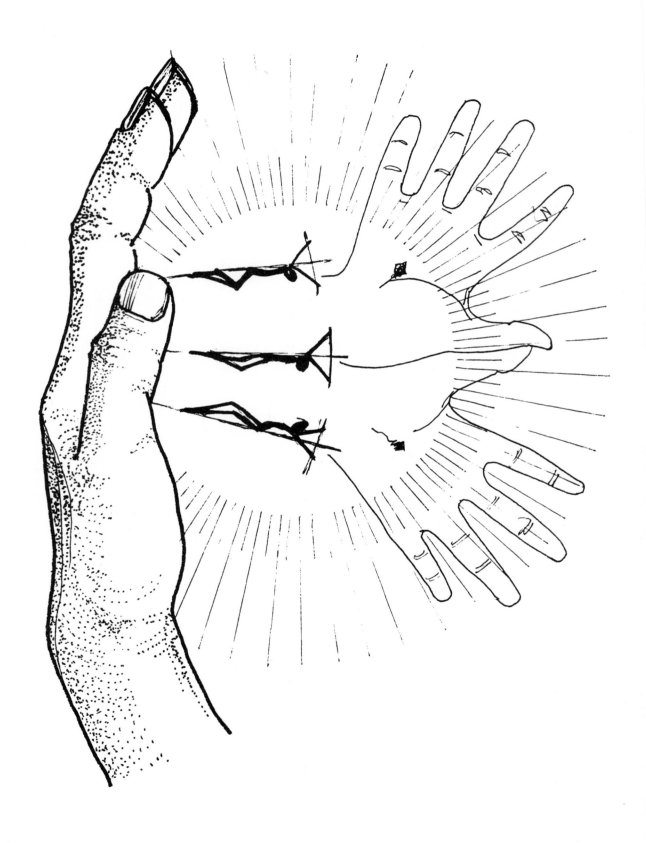

Illustration 26

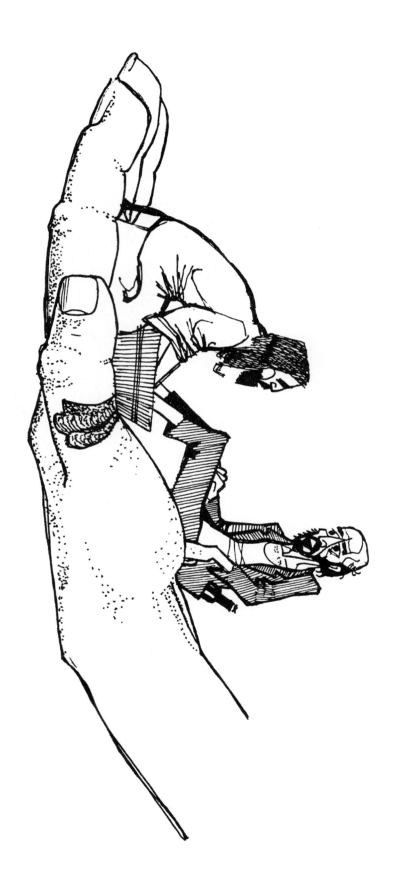

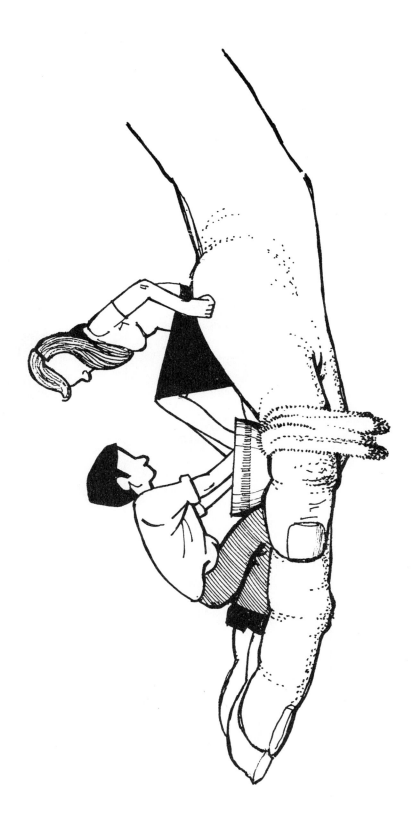

Illustration 28

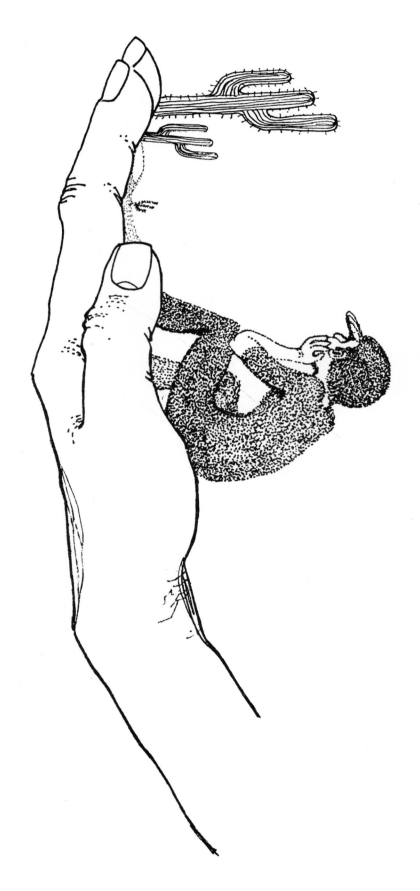

Illustration 29

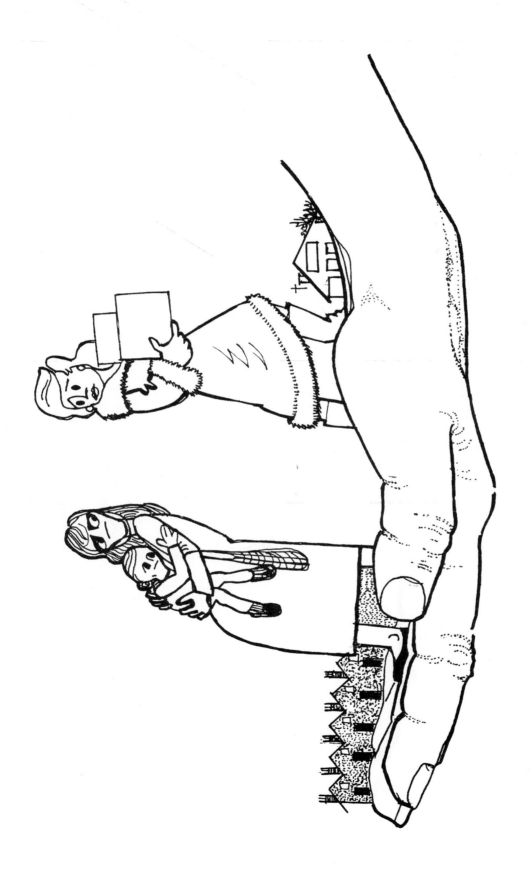

Illustration 30

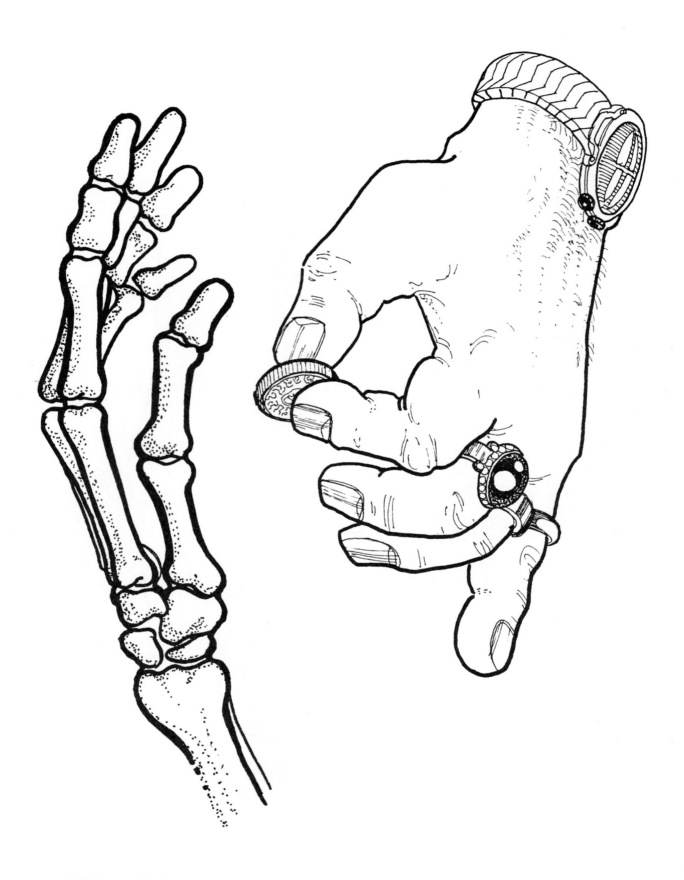

Illustration 31

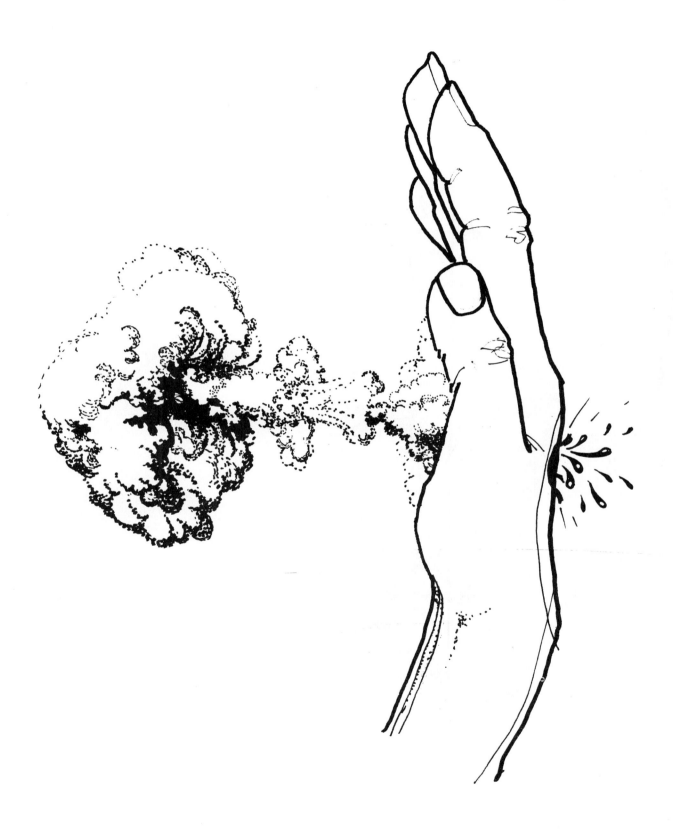

Illustration 32

Illustration 33

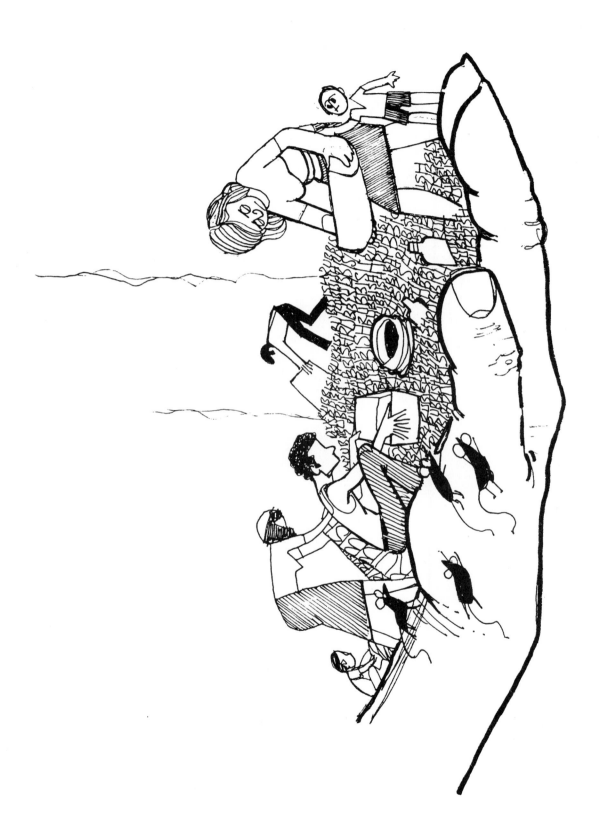

Illustration 34

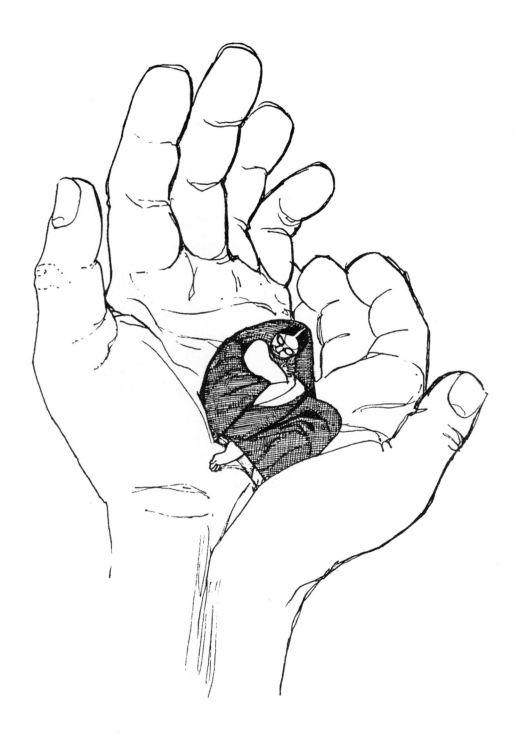

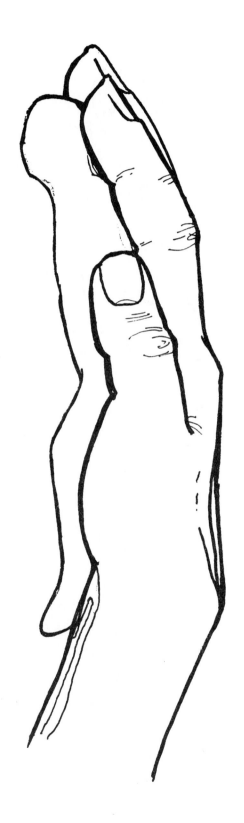

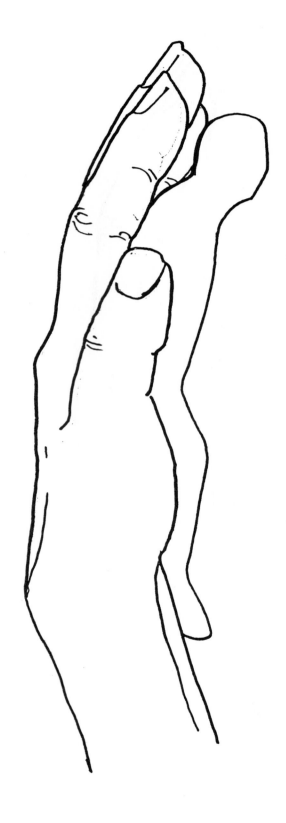

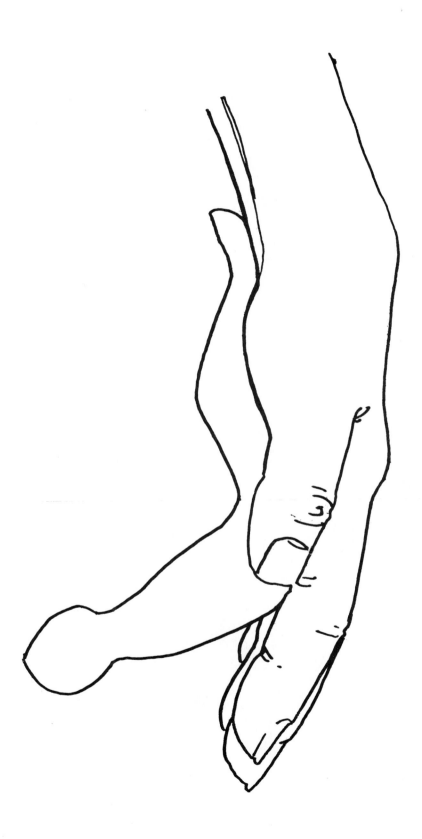

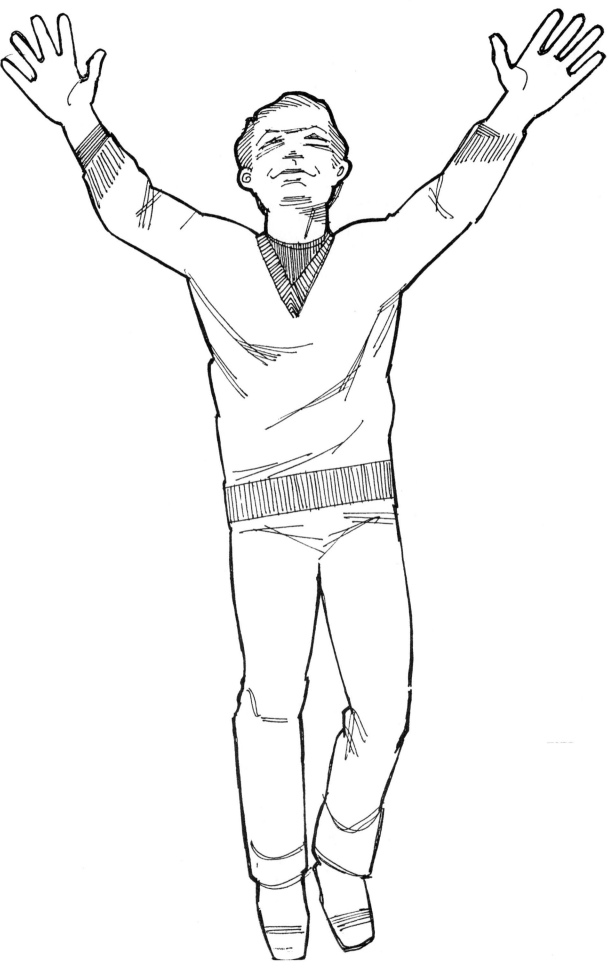

Illustration 37

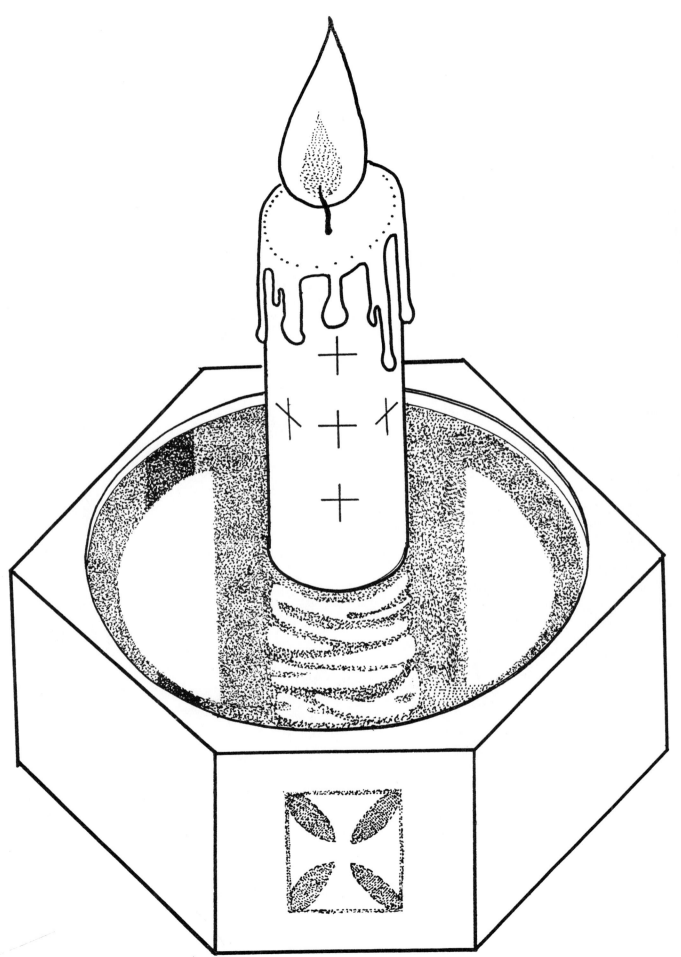

Illustration 38

THE NEW JEROME BIBLICAL COMMENTARY

Edited by Raymond E Brown ss
Joseph A. Fitzmyer sj and
Roland E. Murphy ocarm
Foreword by Cardinal Martini

THE NEW JEROME BIBLICAL COMMENTARY

Edited by
Raymond E. Brown, S.S.
Joseph A. Fitzmyer, S.J.
Roland E. Murphy, O.Carm.

This highly thought-of and best-selling (over 200,000 copies) Commentary reappears now in a form about two-thirds new.

The two decades since the first edition (1968) demanded a new Commentary:

– the past twenty years have seen great advances in virtually all fields of biblical scholarship, for example, in relevant archaeological discoveries, manuscript discoveries, new perspectives in hermeneutics . . .

– the bibliographies have been extensively updated

– whereas the original contributors were almost all clergy, in the New edition there is a significant number of lay contributors, men and women

The New edition should be easier to use because the page heads now give chapter and verse references.

Despite this, the goal and level of the New edition remain the same as for the original: to offer a *commentary* for those who wish to *study* the Scriptures. The prospective audience, too, remains the same: all who are interested in religion and theology on all levels and feel the need for an adequate and comprehensive background to the Bible.

Just as the original edition met the needs of the 1960s and beyond, so the New edition has been designed to meet the more demanding standards of the 1990s – more demanding in the sense that Catholic biblical scholarship has had time to mature, and more is expected of it by Catholic and non-Catholic alike.

As in the original edition, the articles offered are of two types: topical and commentary. The topical articles present the necessary background information before the verse by verse commentary begins. In the New edition the topical section has been enlarged, for example by articles on Jesus and on the early Church.

Hardback c.1500 pages 0 225 66588 3
£65.00
Publication: Summer 1989.

Also available:
JEROME BIBLICAL COMMENTARY
Original 1968 edition
Hardback 1564 pages 0 225 48812 4 £50.00

Other books by Raymond Brown,
see pages 33-34.
Other books by Joseph Fitzmyer,
see pages 7, 28 & 33.

EARTHING THE GOSPEL:
AN INCULTURATION HANDBOOK FOR PASTORAL WORKERS
Gerald A. Arbuckle SM

The title of this book deliberately evokes Jesus' own imagery of seed, earth and sower. Together these symbols dramatically convey precisely what is meant by the dynamic of inculturation: seed, earth and sower are all changed by their interaction; and out of this team effort comes growth.

In the same way as his *Out of Chaos* offered the insights of the social sciences in the task of rebuilding religious communities, so now *Earthing the Gospel* offers the same insights for anyone involved in parish pastoral work.

The book highlights:
the need to take culture seriously, to understand what it is, to grasp its power in people's lives and to use it to help the Gospel permeate their lives;
the urgency of seeking out people who have apostolic creative imagination, people to translate the Gospel into today's language, both spoken and unspoken.

The book has three main parts:
- theoretical considerations, where key concepts are introduced, defined and explained;
- anthropology is applied to particular contemporary pastoral issues;
- finally the book addresses pastoral agents, offering guidelines on how the imaginatively creative evangelizer can relate personally to culture and culture change.

Large format paperback 192 pages 0 225 66584 0 £11.95
Publication: Spring 1990

By the same author:
OUT OF CHAOS

MAKING SCRIPTURE WORK
Christine Dodd

Practical, down-to-earth, help on how scripture can be used throughout the range of local Church activities, including:
- in small groups
- in worship, formal and informal
- in pastoral care
- in sacramental preparation
- with children and young adults
- in private prayer
- in evangelisation
- organising biblical events

The author, a prominent member of national and international biblical associations, has been Adult Education Adviser for Hallam diocese since 1983.

Paperback 168 pages 0 225 66524 7 £8.95

OUTSTANDING CHRISTIAN THINKERS

Series Editor: Brian Davies OP

The Series offers a range of authoritative studies on people who have made an outstanding contribution to Christian thought and understanding. The Series will range across the full spectrum of Christian thought to include Catholic and Protestant thinkers, to cover East and West, historical and contemporary figures. By and large, each volume will focus on a single 'thinker', but occasionally the subject may be a movement or a school of thought.

Spring 1989
YVES CONGAR

Aidan Nichols OP

The book first examines Congar's life and his work as a whole, then considers in turn his fundamental theology; his doctrine of the Church; Congar as an ecumenist; Congar as a theologian of the Holy Spirit; Congar as Church reformer; Congar as a historian of theology. Finally, the book offers an assessment of his overall significance, especially as a model for theologians today.

Paperback 224 pages 0 225 66537 9 £7.95
Hardback 224 pages 0 225 66569 7 £16.95

Brian Davies OP, the Series Editor, is Vice-Regent of Studies at Blackfriars, Oxford, where he also teaches philosophy. He is a member of the Theology Faculty of the University of Oxford and tutor in theology at St Benet's Hall, Oxford. He has lectured regularly at the University of Bristol, Fordham University, New York, and the Beda College, Rome. He is Reviews Editor of *New Blackfriars*. His previous publications include: *An Introduction to the Philosophy of Religion* (OUP, 1982); *Thinking about God* (Geoffrey Chapman, 1982); and he was editor of *Language, Meaning and God* (Geoffrey Chapman, 1987).

ANSELM

G R Evans

This book provides an authoritative introduction to Anselm, and to the full range of his writings.

Perhaps best known as the inventor of the famous 'Ontological Argument' for God's existence, in fact Anselm's writings go much further to cover all major aspects of Christian doctrine, and had a major influence in the development of western theology.

This book also shows Anselm the monk, notable for his prayers, which are a profound and reflective contribution to the literature of Christian spirituality.

Paperback 128 pages 0 225 66536 0 £4.95
Hardback 128 pages 0 225 66568 9 £12.95

DENYS THE AREOPAGITE
Andrew Louth

A key feature of this book is the attention given to all the traditions on which Denys draws: the 4th century Greek theologians; pagan philosophy; and Syrian Christian thought. His world is Christian, monastic, but above all liturgical – the heart of his theology is the vision of the Church as a reflection of the eternal and heavenly liturgy.

Though the author of these writings ascribed to Denys remains an insoluble mystery, they have, ever since their appearance in the 6th century, had a bewilderingly diverse influence on Christian thought – both East and West – and they are an eloquent testimony to the immense fecundity of Denys' vision.

Paperback 144 pages 0 225 66538 7 £5.95
Hardback 144 pages 0 225 66570 0 £14.95

Autumn 1989

THE APOSTOLIC FATHERS
Simon Tugwell OP

In this book, the reader can make the acquaintance of a brilliant and passionate martyr (Ignatius of Antioch); a stolid down-to-earth primitive canon lawyer (the unknown author of the *Didaché*; a spokesman for the Church of Rome, interpreted in retrospect as the third pope (Clement of Rome); and several other interesting figures from the early Church.

The problems they had to confront are surprisingly like those which Christians of today have to face, and so their message is often highly pertinent in our contemporary age of anxiety and uncertainty.

Paperback 160 pages 0 225 66539 5 £5.95
Hardback 160 pages 0 225 66571 9 £14.95

REINHOLD NIEBUHR
Kenneth Durkin

Hailed as the greatest of American theologians, Neibuhr's views and projects varied considerably over time. This book traces the continuity, change and progression in his thinking.

In particular Durkin examines what Niebuhr called the 'mythical method': using biblical mythology as a sociological paradigm, that is, as a tool for interpreting events and devising strategies.

The book also examines the hitherto neglected area of the direct relationship between Niebuhr's developing theology and his varying political stances. This has enormous contemporary relevance, since the issues Niebuhr confronted are still shaping the modern world.

Paperback 204 pages 0 225 66540 5 £6.95
Hardback 204 pages 0 225 66572 7 £14.95

In Preparation

BEDE
Benedicta Ward
Paperback 0 225 66542 5
Hardback 0 225 66574 3

JOHN CALVIN
John Platt
Paperback 0 225 66543 3
Hardback 0 225 66575 1

JONATHAN EDWARDS
John E Smith
Paperback 0 225 66544 1
Hardback 0 225 66576 X

AQUINAS
Brian Davies OP
Paperback 0 225 66545 X
Hardback 0 225 66577 8

KARL RAHNER
William Dych SJ
Paperback 0 225 66541 7
Hardback 0 225 66573 5

TERESA OF AVILA
Rowan Williams
Paperback 0 225 66547 6
Hardback 0 225 66579 4

GATHER
– THE HYMNAL FOR THE 1990s

Co-published by GIA Inc and NALR, distributed throughout Europe and Africa by Geoffrey Chapman.

GATHER features:
Order of Mass with appropriate music in place ● plus three additional Mass settings ● plus a Psalter section ● a broad selection of liturgically appropriate songs ● Morning and Evening Prayer with complete music settings ● the hymnal is organised around the liturgical year ● scriptural, liturgical, thematic and first line indexes ● carefully edited, elegant, easy-to-read design ● practical editions for choir, for guitar and for keyboard ● idiomatic keyboard accompaniments.

'GATHER is one of the most welcome collections of liturgical music to be published for a long time. Tapping sources in Africa, America and Europe, it presents us with a wide-ranging choice of inspired, prayerful music which I feel sure can expand the liturgical repertoire of any parish anxious to improve the standard of its celebration. Quite apart from settings of the Mass and Morning and Evening Prayer, the texts have a heavy scriptural bias, which for me makes this collection doubly welcome.
Fr Edward Matthews

GATHER includes the best of:
David Haas ● Marty Haugen ● Michael Joncas ● The Saint Louis Jesuits ● Tom Conry ● The Dameans ● Bob Hurd ● Christopher Walker ● Paul Inwood ● Bernadette Farrell ● Taizé ● and dozens more, including songs from Africa.

GATHER is published in four editions:

● **MELODY LINE EDITION**
Plastic-coated paperback, section sewn for durability
0 225 66580 0 Per single copy £4.50
Special prices for bulk purchase; see below

● **KEYBOARD EDITION**
Hardback, twin spiral bound spine to ensure pages lie flat, and to eliminate awkward page turns
0 225 66581 6 Per single copy £25.00
Special prices for bulk purchase; see below

● **GUITAR EDITION**
Hardback, spiral bound
0 225 66582 4 Per single copy £14.95
Special prices for bulk purchases; see below

● **CHORAL EDITION**
Hardback
0 225 66589 1 Per single copy £12.95
Special prices for bulk purchase; see below

Please note that if you buy a single copy of **GATHER melody line edition**, you can deduct its cost against subsequent bulk purchases. Remember to keep your invoice!

- ● 20 – 49 melody edition copies @ £4.25 per copy
- ● 50 – 99 melody edition copies @ £3.95 per copy   } & 5% discount on accompaniment books
- ● 100 – 149 melody edition copies @ £3.90 per copy

- ● 150 – 199 melody edition copies @ £3.85 per copy   } & 10% discount on accompaniment books
- ● 200 plus melody edition copies @ £3.75 per copy

Many of the songs in the new **GATHER** hymnal are available on record and cassette, produced by the original publishers of the relevant songs (for example, NALR; OCP; etc.).

Music produced by GIA Inc of Chicago is now available from Geoffrey Chapman: this includes the music of **David Haas, Marty Haugen** and **Michael Joncas.**

Six cassettes are available, with their corresponding song-books. The song-books offer not just keyboard accompaniments but many of the vocal descants and harmonies, and the arrangements for other instruments.

TO BE YOUR BREAD
David Haas

Be light for our eyes ● Send us your Spirit ● Jesus, wine of peace ● The harvest of justice ● Remember your mercies ● Song of the stable ● The mountain I see ● Alleluia sing! ● To be your bread ● My soul is still (Psalm 131) ● Nations and heavens ● Blest are they ● At evening

Cassette 0 225 66552 2 £5.95
(£5.17 + 78p VAT)

Music Book 0 225 66553 0 £5.50

SHEPHERD ME, O GOD
Marty Haugen

Song over the waters ● Shepherd me, O God ● Awake, O sleeper ● Healer of our every ill ● Spirit of God ● Your love is never ending (Psalm 136) ● MASS OF REMEMBRANCE: Kyrie eleison; Gloria; Speak, Lord; Acclamations for Eucharistic Prayer for Reconciliation II; Agnus Dei

Cassette 0 225 66554 9 £5.95
(£5.17 + 78p VAT)

Music Book 0 225 66555 7 £5.50

COME AND JOURNEY
David Haas, Marty Haugen, Michael Joncas *Live in Concert*

Gather us in ● Spirit of God within me ● Child of wonder ● Blest are they ● Psalm 23 ● The Lord is my shepherd ● Sing out, earth and skies ● Come and journey ● World Peace Prayer ● God of day and God of darkness ● Canticle of the Sun

Cassette 0 225 66556 5 £5.95
(£5.17 + 78p VAT)

Music Book 0 225 66557 3 £5.15

SONG OF GOD AMONG US
Marty Haugen

Song of God among us ● Lord, make us turn to you (Psalm 80) ● Child of our dreams ● Today is born our Saviour ● Wind upon the waters ● Sing out, earth and skies! ● I offer thee ● Song of God among us (instrumental) ● Bring forth the Kingdom ● Now in this banquet ● Easter alleluia ● God of day and God of darkness

Cassette 0 225 66562 X £5.95
(£5.17 + 78p VAT)

Music Book 0 225 66563 8 £5.95

NIGHT OF SILENCE

Marty Haugen

Creator of the stars of night • Each winter as the year grows older • People, look East • Cherry tree carol • Child of our dreams • Joy to the world • Night of silence • Silent night • It came upon the midnight clear • Carol at the manger • What child is this? • Coventry carol • Arise, shine!

Cassette 0 225 66558 1 £5.95
(£5.17 + 78p VAT)

Music Book 0 225 66559 X £5.95

WINTER NAME OF GOD

Michael Joncas

Advent alleluia • My soul is thirsting • Winter Name of God (Table-prayer) • I sing a maid • PSALLITE MASS: Lord, have mercy; Glory to God; Holy, holy; Memorial acclamation; Doxology and Great Amen; Jesus, Lamb of God • Not for tongues of heaven's angels.

Cassette 0 225 66560 3 £5.95
(£5.17 + 78p VAT)

Music Book 0 225 66561 1 £5.95

PSALMS FOR THE CHURCH YEAR
VOLUME 1

Marty Haugen and David Haas

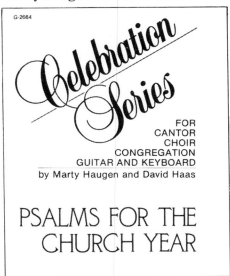

A resource collection of twenty-two psalms to cover all the major feasts and Sundays of the Church year (taken from the common psalms section of the Lectionary).

The Psalm settings are offered with keyboard accompaniment, guitar chords, and vocal arrangements.

The book includes permission to duplicate the people's responses, complete with melody line, and these are printed to make photocopying easy – and legal!

Available as single copies; or in a set of two (one copy each for the cantor and the keyboard accompanist).

Spiral bound large-format paperback 96 pages
Single copies   £7.95 each
Pack of two copies   £14.00 per pack
Available: June 1989
XNA/AUS

MUSIC FOR THE MASS

Edited by Geoffrey Boulton Smith

Over 150 of the most rewarding and singable music settings written for the prayerful celebration of the Mass, collected together for the first time and offering a major opportunity for parishes and other communities to use music positively.

"The book is a mine of good material . . . there is no community, parish or otherwise, which could not find music here to enhance its celebration . . . This is a resource book which for many years will be providing riches within easy reach of us all."
Bishop Francis Thomas

"The music reflects an impressive effort by contemporary composers to fill an urgent need . . . Sunday Mass may soon be a more tuneful and more joyous occasion."
THE TABLET

" . . . a landmark in the progress of liturgical music in this country."   MUSIC AND LITURGY

CHOIR EDITION

Full keyboard arrangements, instrumental and vocal descants, choral parts and guitar chords.

Well-indexed under grades of difficulty, uses, first lines and titles, scriptural references, and authors and composers.

Paperback 336 pages 0 225 66467 4 £8.95

PARISH PACK

Eight copies of the full music edition plus 50 copies of the melody edition for only £160.00 (full value £176.10).

0 225 66506 9 £160.00

ADVENT AND CHRISTMAS CASSETTE

A selection of appropriate pieces, presented in a variety of styles, using a wide range of instruments. As well as being a teaching aid, this illustrates that the songs can be imaginatively interpreted using whatever resources are available.

0 225 66498 4 £7.95 (includes VAT)

CONGREGATION EDITION

Full texts and melody line for all the people's parts.

Paperback 238 pages 0 225 66466 6 £2.25